The Unfilmable
Confederacy of Dunc

C000217318

The Unfilmable
Confederacy of Dunces

*How Ignatius J. Reilly
Defeated Hollywood*

STEPHAN EICKE

McFarland & Company, Inc., Publishers
Jefferson, North Carolina

LIBRARY OF CONGRESS CATALOGUING-IN-PUBLICATION DATA

Names: Eicke, Stephan, 1990– author.
Title: The unfilmable Confederacy of dunces :
how Ignatius J. Reilly defeated Hollywood / Stephan Eicke.
Description: Jefferson, North Carolina : McFarland & Company, Inc.,
Publishers, 2023. | Includes bibliographical references and index.
Identifiers: LCCN 2022048324 |
ISBN 9781476689319 (paperback : acid free paper) ∞
ISBN 9781476647715 (ebook)
Subjects: LCSH: Toole, John Kennedy, 1937-1969. Confederacy
of dunces. | Toole, John Kennedy, 1937-1969.—Film adaptations. |
Unfinished films—United States—History and criticism. |
BISAC: LITERARY CRITICISM / American / General |
PERFORMING ARTS / Film / History & Criticism
Classification: LCC PS3570.O54 C663 2023 | DDC 813/.54—dc23/eng/20221107
LC record available at https://lccn.loc.gov/2022048324

BRITISH LIBRARY CATALOGUING DATA ARE AVAILABLE

ISBN (print) 978-1-4766-8931-9
ISBN (ebook) 978-1-4766-4771-5

© 2023 Stephan Eicke. All rights reserved

*No part of this book may be reproduced or transmitted in any form
or by any means, electronic or mechanical, including photocopying
or recording, or by any information storage and retrieval system,
without permission in writing from the publisher.*

On the cover: drawing by Helmut "Dino" Breneis

Printed in the United States of America

*McFarland & Company, Inc., Publishers
Box 611, Jefferson, North Carolina 28640
www.mcfarlandpub.com*

To all those who refuse to give up.

Acknowledgments

For three-and-a-half years—the time it took me to research and write this book—I fretted over the fact that it can never be complete. Let's be honest: There will always be aspects to this story that remain hidden from the public eye, points of view that will not be shared, details that have escaped my attention, and pieces of information that people will never be comfortable revealing. In a way, it is only fitting that a book about an unproduced movie is itself, in a way, unfinished.

However, this manuscript would be even less complete had several people not assisted me with their gracious support and kindness. I quickly noticed that Ignatius J. Reilly means something to so many people, and those with a strong reaction towards Toole's work were eager to share their opinions and experiences.

I wish to thank especially John Langdon's friends, family and colleagues. Unfortunately, John passed away before I started researching my book, but by all accounts he must have been a delightful and kind soul: Susan O'Connell, Carolyn Pfeiffer, Roderick Taylor, Maidee Walker and Anne Livet were always available to answer my questions and share documents, even when I expected them to be annoyed by my constant pestering and follow-up questions like an especially intrusive Lieutenant Columbo. A huge Thank You goes to the former Bumbershoot crowd.

I also wish to mention Michael Arata, Barbara Boyle, David Esbjornson, Joel Fletcher, Stephen Fry, Frank Galati, Deborah Sue George, Mark Gill, Jeffrey Hatcher, Alexander Ignon, Mike Medavoy, Marcia Nasatir, John Holt Smith, John Schulte and Penelope Spheeris for providing valuable insights and for being always approachable.

Thank you to all the celebrity agent's assistants who agreed to help me and put me in touch with their star clients simply because they love Ignatius J. Reilly so much.

I am grateful to James Long of LSU Press, who rejected my proposal but suggested several structural changes which made my book better, though without Gary Dalkin, it would still be a mess. As my independent proofreader and editor, Gary has assisted me for several years, and I can't imagine working without him. Please never retire.

My thanks also go to all my friends who had to listen to my progress reports, and who cheered me on—especially Gary Yershon and Isabel Grand. You gave me a push when I needed one.

Helmut Breneis drew the most gorgeous cover I could have wished for, and I hope Ignatius would agree.

I had published my previous book with McFarland, and am grateful that they enthusiastically accepted my new work for publication as well. Susan, Beth and Lori are wonderful and never tire of accommodating me.

There it is. It is done now.

The End.

Table of Contents

The Consolation of a Preface

How countless entities tried for over 40 years to set up a screen adaptation of *A Confederacy of Dunces* is the saddest story ever told about the film business. It figures. *A Confederacy of Dunces* is, after all, the saddest novel ever written—and written under the saddest circumstances. Its author, John Kennedy Toole, fine-tuned it tirelessly for years while working in the army and as a teacher, gradually slipping into paranoia. He tried to get it published without success, becoming obsessed and eventually disillusioned before finally giving up and committing suicide at the age of 31. He had lost faith in what he had always considered his mastery, the one thing he was good at: writing. Tragically, he would never see his work receive the praise it eventually did. John Kennedy Toole would never accept the Pulitzer Prize, be showered with fan mail or offered money and fame by the film industry that quickly came knocking at his mother Thelma's door following the book's publication over ten years after his death. For John, it was too late.

Much has been made of autobiographical traits in *A Confederacy of Dunces*, and the novel displays the gloom and doom Toole was beset by in the last

How countless entities tried for over 40 years to set up a screen adaptation of *A Confederacy of Dunces* is the funniest story ever told about the film business. It figures. *A Confederacy of Dunces* is, after all, the funniest novel ever written—and one which provides one of the most uplifting lessons about life. Its author, John Kennedy Toole, worked on his novel tirelessly for years. Although he insisted on submitting his manuscript to only one publishing company, he garnered encouraging feedback and was never given up on. It was he who finally gave up, committing suicide at the age of 31. Had he only endured! It was his mother who finally got the book published. It took her more than ten years, a period during which she tirelessly submitted the manuscript to as many publishing companies as she could. *A Confederacy of Dunces* would go on to win the Pulitzer Prize, inspire countless other creative works, influence pop culture and secure its author a place among the giants of American literature. John Kennedy Toole finally made it. Never give up is the lesson. If you persevere you will eventually succeed. As Boethius said, although not verbatim, look on the bright side.

Much has been made of autobiographical traits in *A Confederacy of Dunces*, but the novel transcends Toole's life with sardonic wit and drollery:

years of his life: Ignatius J. Reilly is a frustrated, lonely, flatulent, overweight and unemployed hobby-philosopher who takes pleasure in berating other people and insulting his poor mother. He is perpetually rude, and for this and various other reasons can't bond with anybody he encounters. Anything he touches ends in disaster. Eventually, he has to flee from the carers who have come to take him away and put him in an asylum—heading into an uncertain future.

Ignatius J. Reilly is a frustrated, lonely, flatulent, overweight and unemployed hobby-philosopher who takes pleasure in berating other people and insulting his poor mother. He will find his redemption eventually, though, without even noticing it. Through his various, hilarious screwball adventures he brings people from all walks of life together, enriches their lives and wakes them from their stupor. It is Ignatius himself who finally, although involuntarily, steps away from home, into a new world.

People thought John Kennedy Toole's *A Confederacy of Dunces* would make a good movie. They were proven wrong. But I'm getting ahead of myself.

Despite its phenomenal success in both hardcover and paperback, the adventures of Ignatius J. Reilly have managed to stupefy some of Hollywood's best directors, producers and writers. That alone is no small feat.

The decision-makers in the film industry often waste no time optioning successful books or even newspaper articles.

It comes as no surprise, then, that *A Confederacy of Dunces* was optioned right away, and over the decades has had the studio suits scrambling for their phones trying to ascertain who owned the rights, willing to shell out millions of dollars to purchase them. In hindsight, betting at the races on a one-legged horse with asthma would have been a better investment.

A film of *A Confederacy of Dunces* has never been made, despite a 40-year attempt to get a screen adaptation off the ground. By way of comparison, the Civil War, which led to the abolition of an actual Confederacy, was won by the Union in only 10 percent of that time.

The story behind the attempts to turn the novel into a movie has fascinated both fans of film and of the novel for many years. Today, almost every book, homepage, blog and magazine article devoted to unmade movies mentions *A Confederacy of Dunces* in the first paragraph, like an ugly, cursed, evil sister to a far more short-lived doomed project like David Lean's *Nostromo*, which was shut down by Columbia after only five years.

The passionate, idealistic struggle of the individual against the system intrigues me, and for many years I have been fascinated with projects that never came to pass.

While looking up films which ended up in development hell, as opposed to becoming big successes on the screen, I found that *A Confederacy of Dunces* was frequently mentioned. Much like Kyle MacLachlan's character who finds a severed ear on the grass in *Blue Velvet*, I sensed there was a story here waiting to be told, and while looking into John Kennedy Toole's work I stumbled across a post on Reddit (which is always how great investigations uncovering international conspiracies start) in which someone claimed to be Maidee Walker's neighbor. Walker was the first author who had tried her hand at adapting Toole's novel.

Without having read *A Confederacy of Dunces*, I got in touch with said neighbor and was swiftly given Maidee Walker's number. When she picked up and started talking I instantly knew I had my story. I picked up a copy of Toole's novel, devoured it in a few sittings, and started my research in earnest.

The reasons for the fascination with Ignatius's attempts to scramble up on the screen are manifold. As mentioned previously, the book was a phenomenal success, so why wouldn't studio heads try anything in their power to produce a film version, and subsequently many bank notes and happy faces in the audience? If *Naked Lunch* can be turned into a film, complete with a notorious liquefactionist and a violent orgy, why can't *A Confederacy of Dunces*? Why did so many key players in this story die a premature, often gruesome death? Was indeed a curse inflicted upon the project, as Steven Soderbergh mused after he had failed to make his vision for a film a reality?

Answering these questions leads down a multitude of rabbit holes. If the Sphinx had asked, "Why has *A Confederacy of Dunces* never been made into a movie," Oedipus would still be standing in front of it and would have never married his mother. Greek mythology would be poorer.

In this book, I attempt to answer this question. By recounting the project's history, the various missteps and strokes of bad luck, an impression is given of everything that went wrong along the way, though it may be stated outright: there is no easy answer to a question which for many years has led to countless investigations in the form of newspaper articles, blog entries and fan videos.

Surely, if offered the choice of writing a book about the many attempts to turn *A Confederacy of Dunces* into a film, or to roll a stone up a hill until the end of time, Sisyphus would have chosen the stone and celebrated an eternity of happiness. Researching this book has equally constituted an up and down adventure, albeit not so literally.

> Now, I have come to accept Fortune spins the wheel,
> and one or another
> number comes up lucky, while the only constant
> is change,
> the ebb and flow of a tide like that of Euripus'
> strait.[1]

As it turned out, many valuable documents related to the project were destroyed either by floods, the studios themselves or by disinterested heirs. (Such is life. As Helen Keller famously said: "Defeat is simply a signal to press onward.") Several people refused to speak with me, preferring to focus on new projects, not being keen to remember their failures, and many key players in this story had passed away even before I started contemplating writing anything even remotely related to *A Confederacy of Dunces*. The memory of survivors is often hazy, tattered like Ignatius' clothes.

Oftentimes, accounts of what transpired between two people conflict. Without any malicious intent, we prefer to remember what we like, to choose to cast ourselves in the best possible light. Memories are diluted over the years: according to a popular theory, whenever we remember something we remember our last memory of that event, not the event itself. Or, as Oliver Sacks put it, much more eloquently than I ever could:

"This notion of memory as a record or store is so familiar, so congenial, to us that we take it for granted and do not realize at first how problematic it is. And yet all of us have had the opposite experience, of 'normal' memories, everyday memories, being anything but fixed—slipping and changing, becoming modified, whenever we think of them. No two witnesses ever tell the same story, and no story, no memory, ever remains the same. A story is repeated, gets changed with every repetition. It was experiments with such serial storytelling, and with the remembering of pictures, that convinced Frederic Bartlett in the 1920s and 1930s, that there is no such entity as 'memory,' but only the dynamic process of 'remembering' (he is always at pains, in his great book *Remembering*, to avoid the noun and use the verb)."

What we are left with is "the best possible version of the truth," as Bob Woodward calls it.

Nevertheless, without the generous support and trust of many wonderfully kind people who entrusted me with their knowledge, this account wouldn't exist at all. Without my having a pedigree, these generous people agreed to speak with me and share documents they had stored away in their dusty basements. Although they are named in the acknowledgments, their names should be on the cover: this book solely exists because of their kindness. I have always relied on the kindness of strangers.

A Note About the Text

For a story beset with tragedy and hardship, it only seemed natural throughout my retelling of what happened during those 40 years to include some wisdom by none other than Ignatius' favorite philosopher, Boethius—as a comment from the Greek chorus, if you will. None of these quotes—taken from the translation by David R. Slavitt—have been altered. Boethius' wisdom certainly seems applicable to all situations in life.

Passages which consist of a dialogue between two or more people (e.g., between Stephen Geller and Harold Ramis), and which I included in the form of a screenplay excerpt, were taken verbatim from my source. Nothing has been added or changed.

Part I
Ken and Thelma and Ignatius

People in New Orleans have a pretty high standard for storytelling. What comes out of their mouths is more interesting than what comes out of the average American mouth. And there's a humor that ripples through everything there

—*Michael Lewis*

It began oddly. But could it have begun otherwise, however it began? It has been said, of course, that everything under the sun begins oddly and ends oddly, and is odd. A perfect rose is "odd," so is an imperfect rose, so is the rose of ordinary rosy good looks growing in your neighbor's garden. I know about the perspective from which all that exists appears awesome and mysterious. Reflect upon eternity, consider, if you are up to it, oblivion, and everything becomes a wonder. Still, I would submit to you, in all humility, that some things are more wondrous than others, and that I am one such thing.

—*Philip Roth*, The Breast

1

A Posthumous Life

How an aspiring writer goes out into the world and tries to make it, but,
alas, fails to do so during his lifetime

On 26 March 1969, John Kennedy Toole was found dead in his car outside Biloxi, Mississippi. The 31-year-old had inserted one end of a garden hose into the exhaust pipe and the other end in the window crevice. It was the end of a journey through the U.S. which had lasted two months. In January, he had had an argument with his mother, Thelma Ducoing Toole, and decided to leave everything behind. It was to be the beginning of the end of John Kennedy Toole's life, but it was only the beginning of his life as an internationally celebrated artist: both of his novels, *A Confederacy of Dunces* and *The Neon Bible*, were published posthumously. In 1981, he was awarded the Pulitzer Prize for the former, a sprawling epic about New Orleans and its inhabitants, primarily Ignatius J. Reilly, a lazy but highly intelligent 30-something-year-old who still lives with his mother, Irene.

Much has been made of John Kennedy Toole's brief life. Here is a young man who grows up with a domineering mother and a mentally ill father, a young genius who shows his talents as a writer but who fails to get the recognition he feels he deserves. As much as he was held back by his environment—his stint in the army in Puerto Rico, a controlling mother who groomed her son for success from the earliest age but who was also his fiercest critic—he was also his own worst enemy, in that he would never seriously consider submitting his manuscript for *A Confederacy of Dunces* to any publisher other than Simon & Schuster. This eventually led him to abandon his plans for the publication of his literary masterpiece. His is a tragic story with a bitter-sweet ending, a dark tale which has nevertheless given people comfort in the realization that any talent might be discovered eventually.

II

John Kennedy Toole was born in New Orleans, December 17th, 1937. At birth he had the beauty and awareness of a six-month-old baby. Every nurse in the maternity ward visited my room and told me he was the first new-born that they had ever seen because of his facial expressions (By the way, I am a retired speech and dramatic art teacher and director.)

He attended nursery school when he was three years old and the teachers said they would hold up his drawings to show the other children how to draw. Entered kindergarten when he was four, and first grade when he was five.

One morning when I was getting ready to take him to school, he fell on the living room floor and began to sob. I asked him what was the matter and he said he wasn't learning anything.[1]

So begins Thelma Toole's biography of her son John Kennedy Toole, a biography she started sketching after his passing and never finished. From the first page, though, it is obvious that Thelma expected great things from her only child, putting those high hopes in him that she had had for her own life and that had never been fulfilled.

Thelma Toole's great-grandfather was Jean-François Ducoing, an associate of the pirate Jean Lafitte. Ducoing served under Andrew Jackson at the Battle of New Orleans, while Lafitte smuggled slaves from Spanish ships to the markets of New Orleans before he was wounded in a battle in 1823 and subsequently died in Mexico.[2]

Thelma Ducoing, who was born in 1901, had a difficult relationship with members of her family throughout her life and sought to escape her household to make it as an actress. Instead, she would teach elocution and piano most of her life, until she found the stage she had always craved when her son's novel *A Confederacy of Dunces* was published and she started giving interviews and going on promotional tours. She relished these engagements since they brought her the fame and respect she had previously been unable to achieve.

Her marriage had turned out to be a disaster. Although her husband, John Toole, Jr.—born in 1899—had been offered a scholarship at Louisiana State University and served in the army, he began managing a parts department at a car dealership before becoming a car salesman and slipping into paranoia, a circumstance which brought shame rather than wealth to Thelma.[3] Her last hope was that at least her son would make her proud.

The first years of John Kennedy Toole's life were promising enough for his mother. Indeed, he entered the second grade when he was just six years old and skipped the fourth grade. At an early age, "Ken" developed a love for opera and Shakespeare and showed a gift for impersonations that landed him roles in school productions. He then joined the Traveling Theatre Troupers and even appeared in a television show called *TeleKids*. Thelma Toole had given birth to a natural actor who could give rapturous speeches.

John Kennedy Toole was devoted to his mother who supported and encouraged him to take to the stage. She even got heavily involved in her son's blossoming career by calling up theater producers and directors to demand bigger and better roles for her talented offspring. Although Ken had a close ally in his mother, their relationship started to change, eventually resulting in the heated argument which preceded his suicide in 1969.

When Ken decided to pursue a career in writing it didn't mark the end of Thelma's interference in her son's life. In fact, it was an interference that knew no bounds, as became evident when Thelma started evaluating a young woman her son had brought home one evening.[4] She needed to judge whether the woman opposite her would be good enough for her underappreciated genius, who deserved only the cream of the crop.

Ken's gift for satire showed itself early, when he joined the staff of the school newspaper at Alcée E. Fortier High School and began writing short essays. He then went on to draw cartoons at Tulane University, one of which featured the great love of his life, Marilyn Monroe, the seductive screen legend he never got to meet.

In 1954, after a trip to Mississippi, he started to write what would eventually become his first novel, *The Neon Bible*. Frustrated by its failure to be awarded the top prize in a competition, he stored the manuscript in his room and left it for Thelma to discover after his passing.[5] It was published 20 years after his death and eventually, in 1995, made into a (financially and commercially unsuccessful) movie starring Gena Rowlands by British director Terence Davies.

III

While *The Neon Bible* was never submitted for publication by Ken, a bright future seemed to be ahead of him. His studies were going well. In 1954, he started studying engineering at Tulane University with a scholarship that allowed him to move to Uptown, away from his parents and into his own apartment. However, he quickly became bored with his chosen subject and enrolled in the English department at Tulane to be trained as a scholar in a PhD program.

He took English, Spanish, history and biology classes, and became infatuated with a city that would change his life: New York. Although Ken was never a socialite, neither was he a pariah, and the Big Apple was—at that time—a haven for aspiring artists, a melting pot that attracted and celebrated Beatnik writers such as Jack Kerouac. It was the place where Ken wanted to go.

However, New York City was also expensive and the cost of living there put additional pressure on him: he could not rely on financial aid from his family. It was soon clear to him that by enrolling at Columbia University to study English, he would have to graduate in only two semesters, something he duly accomplished.[6]

IV

While everything was going swell with his studies, a storm was brewing at home in New Orleans: his father's peculiar tics had developed into full-blown paranoia. John Toole, Jr. was becoming convinced that burglars were going to break into his and Thelma's house at any moment and brutally murder him and his wife.

He had retired from his job as a car salesman after it had become clear that his interest lay in convincing potential customers that no car could possibly be safe enough for them.[7] Since he was unable to work, the financial strain on his family became unbearable; after all, the income from Thelma's lessons in elocution and piano could only cover the barest essentials. It became clear to everybody in the family that John Kennedy Toole could not possibly continue with his PhD program.

In 1959, he graduated with High Honors from Columbia and started looking for a job that could not only support him, but also Thelma and John. Ken therefore accepted a job offer from the Southwestern Louisiana Institute to teach writing courses in Lafayette.[8] It was at SLI that he met Joel L. Fletcher and Patricia Rickels, who would become his close friends. Fletcher would later write *Ken & Thelma: The Story of* A Confederacy of Dunces, his memoir of his time with Ken and Thelma.

Ken's gift for satire partly sprang from the fact that he seemed to have been born in the wrong century. He was old-fashioned in every sense and couldn't hide his bewilderment at the societal changes of the late '50s and early '60s, changes such as the growing Civil Rights Movement.

Elmore Morgan, an artist living in the flat above Ken's in New Orleans, would later describe him with the following words: "He had a sort of detached view, in a sense; he was an observer. Rather than get terribly upset by some situation, he would be more likely to deal with it in a sort of humorous way, to see the absurdity and irony and humor in it…. Humor was a way of dealing with things that he couldn't do anything about."[9]

V

Ken still hadn't given up on his PhD. To sustain his living while studying, in 1960 he started teaching at Hunter College, and then he got drafted. His fate lay in Puerto Rico: after he had joined the army, he was ordered in 1961 to teach English at Fort Buchanan.[10] There Ken quickly became bored of a job that was clearly below his talents and he found an occupation in writing a novel that would eventually become *A Confederacy of Dunces*.

The absurdity of military service as well as the odd behavioral patterns of his sergeant (who acted as if he had come straight out of Joseph Heller's *Catch-22*) inspired Ken to focus on character development and situational humor in his book, while he dutifully continued teaching phonetic English to islanders he neither liked nor understood.[11] While his military service had disrupted his studies—he still hadn't earned his PhD—it provided an income, part of which he regularly sent to his mother in New Orleans, who needed every penny her son could part with.

In letters, he informed his parents about his progress with the novel and his surroundings in Puerto Rico. On April 4, 1963, he wrote:

> In spite of these distractions [regarding military service], I am writing with great regularity. It seems to be the only thing that keeps my mind occupied; I have never found writing to be so relaxing or so tranquilizing, and I still like what I am working on. Quite a bit has been completed already. Some of it, I think, is very funny.[12]

Six days later, he sent another letter, saying:

> Writing feverishly, I have completed three chapters and am deep into the fourth. I only hope that my inspiration and dedication last long enough to preclude abandonment of the project. I want to come out of this experience with something to show for my time. What I am doing will require a great amount of revision, editing, and rewriting, I imagine, but I should have a basis at least. In my private room with the fan, easy chair, book case, and plant, I settle down with a borrowed typewriter (this one) and grind out my deathless prose.[13]

VI

John Kennedy Toole finally returned to his hometown in 1963. He accepted a teaching position at St. Mary's Dominican College, a Catholic School in Uptown. (Coincidentally, Lee Harvey Oswald was living only two miles away from the Toole home before John F. Kennedy was shot.)[14]

It was a busy time for Ken, as he both taught his students and worked tirelessly on revisions of *A Confederacy of Dunces* until he felt ready to submit it to Simon & Schuster. To Ken, the New York–based publishing company was *the* best in the world, and no other company would do. Any other house simply wasn't good enough.

So began his correspondence with Robert Gottlieb, senior editor at Simon & Schuster. Said correspondence would last for years. Gottlieb liked at least certain aspects of the novel, which he didn't dismiss outright. In fact, he encouraged the young writer to revise it throughout the next months. The biggest problem with *A Confederacy of Dunces* was, from his point of view, that it didn't amount to much—it was, after all, strangely episodic.

Ken at first didn't see grounds to abandon his pursuit of getting his work published. He obliged and continued sending Gottlieb his revisions. The senior editor remained encouraging, but refused to make any promises concerning the novel's publication.[15]

Since Robert Gottlieb was one of the most respected editors at the time, he was often difficult to get hold of, and meanwhile Ken grew more and more desperate to finally see his novel on the bookshelves of U.S. stores.

In 1965, Ken traveled to New York City in order to meet with Gottlieb in person. Alas, the editor was out of town. As a result, the desperate writer started giving a rambling speech in front of the secretary and eventually left in humiliation.[16] His correspondence with Gottlieb continued, however. While the senior editor remained supportive, he made it clear to Ken that he would not publish the novel without further revisions.

VII

The author, though, was tired of revisions, and also declined Gottlieb's invitation to start work on another novel. Instead, he put his manuscript in a box—much like he had done with *The Neon Bible*—and gave up. His revisions were later destroyed by his mother, who gave her son's original manuscript to Walker Percy. The revered author, whose novel *The Moviegoer* had been published to wide acclaim, helped in getting *The Confederacy of Dunces* published.

Following his failure to sign a contract with Simon & Schuster, Ken became sloppy, depressed and paranoid. His students started to notice changes in their teacher. He ranted and raved in his classes, giving incoherent speeches about church, state and "mother."[17]

Ken had failed. He had failed Thelma, who had expected great things from and for her son. Soon, Ken's friends also started noticing changes in him. He became convinced that he was being pursued, that Simon & Schuster had stolen his book, that his students from Dominican were chasing him.

Disillusioned with himself and scolded by his mother for his failures, John Kennedy Toole withdrew money from his bank account to finance a trip through the U.S., a journey which ended with his suicide.[18]

He left a note which was later destroyed by his mother. Ken's friend Patricia Rickels mused: "He told me that his father had always behaved so eccentrically when he was a kid that he would never like to bring anybody home from school because his father would embarrass him with his weird ways and his strange eccentricities. But that's nothing compared to Thelma. Oh my God!

"When people used to ask me, 'Why did he commit suicide,' I say, 'Well, you should have met his mother and you wouldn't have to ask.'"[19]

Joel L. Fletcher put it this way: "He had been so groomed for success by Thelma that he could not deal with this setback in his life. He must have begun to feel that he would be a failure like his father. Thelma, in her pain and anger, must have lashed out at him, as I had seen her, when she was in a foul mood, lash out at me and others for no good reason."[20]

When Ken Toole's car was found near Biloxi, several papers were discovered stacked on the front seat. According to several reports, the various papers consisted of handwritten and typed notes.[21] The papers were brought to the basement of the Biloxi Police Department from where they washed away during Hurricane Camille six months later.

Thelma was devastated by her son's death. She stopped playing her piano, ceased teaching and declined to further participate in the world. She stayed at home and nursed her mentally ill husband for the rest of his life, and she tried to make sense of her son's suicide.

She used Ken's life insurance to invest in bonds which provided her with a modest income. Meanwhile, John Toole died in 1972.[22] And then Thelma made a discovery that changed her life again.

VIII

In Ken's room, the manuscripts for *The Neon Bible* and *A Confederacy of Dunces* were still waiting to be published. Following her husband's death, Thelma finally decided to submit *A Confederacy of Dunces*—the book about whose conception she had been regularly updated by her son—to several publishing companies. Aware that Simon & Schuster hadn't been too eager to put it out, she approached eight different houses, all of which turned it down.[23] One reason given was that comedies simply didn't sell. While this claim is disputable—Joseph Heller's *Catch-22* again serves as an example, as do works by Kurt Vonnegut—comic literature has always had a hard time receiving attention, respect and recognition. In his foreword to Umberto Eco's *The Name of the Rose*, David Lodge highlights the importance of Aristotle's *Poetics* as the basis for literary theory. But while Aristotle's musings on tragedy and the epic survived, his study of comedy did not. This is, perhaps, the reason comedy has long been deemed inferior as a genre. As Lodge writes: "The consequences of this loss were immense, because it biased literary criticism in favor of 'serious' literature, and narrative forms that obeyed generic rules and observed stylistic decorum: tragedy and epic."[24]

Despite the rejections from publishing houses, Thelma never lost hope. She maintained the tenacity to see the book through its publication, and when, in 1976, she read that Walker Percy would be teaching at Loyola University in New Orleans, she saw her chance and ordered her brother Arthur (who she was living with at Elysian Fields) to drive her to Loyola.[25] With her was the tattered, filthy manuscript for *A Confederacy of Dunces* which by then had passed through countless hands.

IX

Walker Percy was slightly intimidated by the elderly lady who wouldn't accept his reluctance to read her son's novel. Years later she remembered: "He appeared and

I took about ten minutes of his time. I knew he was a busy man. He said, 'You are a mother. You are prejudiced.' I said, 'Yeah, I would go before the most prestigious publishers of the world and tell them this is a masterpiece because I am a mild critic of literature. I love literature. [...] It's great. It's great, Dr. Percy. Please!' Well, he did plan to read it, take it home with him. Within a week, he sent a card saying it's the most flavorful rendition of New Orleans he had ever read."[26]

But even Walker Percy struggled to get Ken's novel published. Percy's usual publisher, Farrar, Straus and Giroux, declined.[27] This led him to submit the manuscript to Marcia Smith, editor of the *New Orleans Review*, where the first two chapters of Ignatius' adventures were eventually printed in 1978.

An even bigger breakthrough was to follow when the manuscript was sent to the Louisiana State University Press. Although it took editor Les Phillabaum and his colleagues six months to review the work, they decided to put it out in a first edition of 2,500 copies.[28] However, this could only be done after the Toole family (everybody except Thelma) signed over their share in the rights to *A Confederacy of Dunces*, since, according to Louisiana law, they were co-owners of the deceased family member's work.

The reviews that eventually started to come in were glorious, though indubitably part of the reason why this particular work raised so much interest was its complicated publishing history and the tragic fate of its author. Writes Toole biographer Cory MacLauchlin: "This silencing [on the part of various publishing companies who rejected the manuscript] is part of why the story of its publication held such interest to readers. It suggests that the presumed cultural role of publishers to deliver quality literature may be compromised by motives of profit and marketability. Ironically, as this story validates a critique of the commercialism of the publishing industry, it simultaneously made the novel more marketable. Toole didn't have this story to reference in 1963. A solitary writer complaining about publishers, convinced no one appreciates his genius, has few sympathizers."[29]

In his book, MacLauchlin argues that Ken's story enables both writers and readers alike to see their anger at the publishing world as justified.

X

In April 1981, *A Confederacy of Dunces* was awarded the prestigious Pulitzer Prize. Thelma became a star, the celebrity she had always craved to be. She basked in the limelight, blossomed in front of TV cameras and the press when she gave interviews and welcomed fans to her home.

It became clear to everybody around her that she was a force to be reckoned with; as Joel L. Fletcher remembers in *Ken & Thelma* when he recounts the minutes before Thelma was to appear on the *Tomorrow Show* in New York City: "In the green room we found Anthony Quinn, who was to precede Thelma on the *Tomorrow Show*. Thelma, far from being intimidated by his fame, treated him as an equal and told him about her genius son. A photograph I took of them shows Thelma leaning forward toward a rather alarmed looking Quinn. In introducing me, she said, 'Mr. Quinn, I am sure that you have an appreciation of the finer things, including art. I would like to introduce you to my escort, Mr. Fletcher, who deals in the finer things. I think you might be very interested in seeing some of the beautiful and extremely rare works he deals in. You must tell him how he can get in touch with you!' I gave Mr. Quinn an embarrassed smile, but to my amazement he obeyed. [...] He must have been very relieved when he was summoned to the cameras."[30]

On the *Tomorrow Show*, Thelma—as always—wasn't shy to flaunt the genius of her son. When host Tom Snyder asked about her reaction to the Pulitzer Prize, she replied: "I was in a transcendent mood of such triumph for someone who suffered so much during his life. You see, he was so brilliant that, when he was in grammar school, I had to fight twice to have him transferred to another grade, and they fought me, and I was out in the hall with the principal, and his first grade teacher and I said, 'He's a different child. You can't stifle that mind. You have to give him a chance,' so when he was six, he entered second grade, and then when he was in fourth grade, he skipped fourth grade and went into the fifth."[31]

Thelma was all-domineering. Her presence on the small screen rivaled that of the biggest movie and theater stars of the day. And she provided great amusement for viewers and hosts alike. Her appearance on the *Tomorrow Show* concluded with the following exchange:

INT. Tomorrow Show Studio. Early evening.

THELMA
I walk in the world of my son. I'm humble, because I was a vessel
to bring a scholarly genius—he was a scholarly genius
and a literary genius.

TOM
Well, I'll tell you something. His mom ain't too shabby, either.
Now, Mrs. Toole, I want to thank you for coming up here tonight.

THELMA
I ain't something that cat dragged in, am I?

TOM
You sure ain't.

And so Thelma passed her last few years—she started having serious health problems in the spring of 1982, and shortly thereafter she was diagnosed with a cancerous growth in her one of her kidneys.[32]

The Neon Bible was never published during her lifetime, since this time the Toole family didn't want to sign over their rights to the novel, and Thelma, who had loathed every member of her family for decades, didn't want to share the profits from Ken's work with them.[33] After an arduous legal battle, the book was eventually published by Grove Press in 1989.

XI

Critics were tempted to draw parallels between Ken and Ignatius. Was the author, in fact, just a version of Ignatius, an unhappy, overweight, aggressive intellectual? While he was overweight toward the end of his life, intellectual, aggressive and

unhappy at times, describing *A Confederacy of Dunces* as autobiographical is dangerous, misleading and, ultimately, pointless. His mother always outright rejected comparisons between Ignatius and her son, although mostly because of their appearance
rather than their characters: "How could Ignatius, the slob, be my elegant gentleman?
My elegant gentleman with his [...] pride and magnificent sense of good taste and the
nice things of life? There is absolutely no correlation of Iggy Piggy—Ignatius—and my
son. Several people have asked. Why, how could that have been my son?"[34] She felt
outright insulted when she was asked whether Irene Reilly might have been modeled
after her, and snapped back: "A highly cultivated woman, three years old, introduced
to speech and dramatic art? Ten years of piano study, five of violin? Sixteen years of
dramatic art, a public school teacher? Could you honestly ask me ... and my sense of
good taste and dress? Irene Reilly with the pink hat and a yellow topper and a purple
dress and old run-down wedges? No, never!"

Thelma Toole's public appearances have inspired several hobby psychologists to
give their verdict on her motives. Sure enough, Thelma was finally where she always
wanted to be—on stage. But the people who worked with her on various *A Confederacy of Dunces* projects had a less than kind view of the woman who, as Joel L. Fletcher
put it, "never relinquished an iota of control."[35]

Maidee Walker, who wrote a script for a feature film based on Ken's novel and
met with Thelma once to discuss the project, was soon overwhelmed by Thelma's
forcefulness. Walker said: "I wouldn't have wanted her as somebody telling me what
to do because I think that's what she did with [her son]. Probably she told him how
disappointed she was in him all the time because he hadn't lived up to what she
thought, I guess. She was very, very critical. She would have been a terribly domineering mother. And I think his suicide had more to do with her than it did with him.
Thelma Toole was one of the worst things that ever happened to John Kennedy Toole,
and then she got the book published and the Pulitzer. Still, that's posthumously. I
don't know what would have happened had it happened earlier. Maybe she did it out
of guilt."[36]

Joel Fletcher admits this might very well have been the case: "Yes, that may be
part of it. Thelma wanted to control everything."[37] But Thelma was, after all, the person who, along with Walker Percy, got *A Confederacy of Dunces* published. She was
also, as it would later turn out, one of the forces that prevented various projects about
her son and his work from reaching fruition while she was still alive.

2

Knocking on Thelma's Door

How an aspiring writer-for-hire makes his way to New Orleans and finds something he didn't expect

Michael J. Nathanson is not an avid reader, but that didn't matter when it came to John Kennedy Toole's novel *A Confederacy of Dunces*—everybody can enjoy the story of the obese, flatulent intellectual who can't be bothered to waste his time earning money by working odd jobs.

An aspiring author, Nathanson found employment as a staff writer at Twentieth Century–Fox through Julia Phillips, the legendary producer who was responsible for financing projects such as *The Sting* and *Taxi Driver*. As her protégé, he worked on treatments, being paid to find material that the television department at Fox might be interested in pursuing. Along with his creative partner Seth Winston (who won an Academy Award for *Session Man* as Best Short Film in 1992), he would find stories, develop treatments and pitch them to Fox.

One such personal passion project was a proposed television drama about the life and death of John Kennedy Toole. Nathanson had read *A Confederacy of Dunces* and was fascinated by its main character and the book's quick-witted comedic elements. Wouldn't that make a great movie? Yet equally fascinating to Nathanson was the story of Ken's life itself. By the time of the novel's debut various newspaper articles had appeared profiling John Kennedy Toole and his mother's subsequent endeavor to get the book published. In the second half of 1981, Nathanson decided he wanted to write both a theatrical feature based on the novel and a television film about Ken and Thelma. Producers, so he thought, would be lining up to finance both projects. After all, Ken's work was all over the news—on 13 April 1981, *A Confederacy of Dunces* had been awarded the Pulitzer Prize for fiction, an honor which resulted in a staggering increase in book sales. Its deceased author was much talked and written about. Surely, an adaptation and TV film would be hot property.

To Nathanson's disappointment, the film rights had already been sold, but that still left the possibility of a television film about Ken and Thelma. His goal was to tell the story of how John Kennedy Toole gave up his efforts to sell his book to a publishing company and how his mother took up the reigns. That concept included, of course, the tragic story of a talented author's suicide: "I wanted to tell the story of this whole struggle to get something going, of his relationship with her,"[1] remembers Nathanson. "He passed away and she took on the cause and got the school press to publish it. From there it got going. It became a world-wide known piece. I went there at a time to make it a movie for television, not theatrical. It was the kind of story that was marketable at the time because it was female-driven. It could have been a woman in her 50s at that time. There were markets out there and it could have sold, especially with the twist."

The main angle of the television film was supposed to be Ken's relationship with his mother, which Nathanson found especially touching, not least because he had a close and loving relationship with his own mother and in that regard sensed a connection with Ken. Naturally, though, there were differences between the two. Describing his inspiration for the project, Nathanson says, "It's a mother-son-relationship that is the coolest relationship in the world. A crazy mother, a loving son, an educator, an idealist! And she really believed in this book of his."[2]

The death of a young, frustrated writer wouldn't have been enough for a movie. It was Thelma's attempts to get the novel published that made the story work for Nathanson. He had no doubt that Thelma's mission to see *A Confederacy of Dunces* on bookshelves all over the world would put a big, wide smile on people's faces—and, bang, he would have a hit!

Apart from that, though, Nathanson didn't know much about Ken's life. This became evident in his glorification of Thelma, "picking up the flame"[3] and publishing the novel. Was she really the great heroine Nathanson wanted to portray?

II

Based on the little he knew about Ken's life, Nathanson put together a treatment and drafted a contract that he sent to Thelma Toole in the hope of acquiring the rights to her life story. Thelma was, of course, flattered and excited by the prospect of becoming the heroine of her own movie.

She was initially charmed by the young producer and delighted by the prospect of receiving $15,000 if the film actually got made. Before Nathanson boarded a plane from Los Angeles to New Orleans, though, Thelma demanded a few changes to the contract—and because it was "not a big kadoodle,"[4] as the writer remembers, he was happy to oblige.

In September 1981, he arrived at Elysian Fields with an updated contract in his hands. Thelma was even more charmed when she saw him waiting outside her tiny house. He was fifteen minutes early, and so she was able to get a good look at him: "I was still eating a cheese sandwich and I was very annoyed at first. Then I saw how good-looking he was, and I said to myself, 'Could that be him? Could I really get this lucky?'"[5]

Michael Nathanson was also charmed, although in a different way. As he remembers: "She was very gracious. I felt it was Blanche from *A Streetcar Named Desire*. The house was very quaint, it was Southern architecture. It wasn't all that large. I went into the single-story house and it felt like *House of Wax*. She had put on her white gloves and proceeded to have me sit and listen to her play the piano. The place was … not extreme, but it had a Vincent Price feel to it. Not that it was haunted, but it was very dark. I am a Philadelphia guy and lived most of my adult life in California. A ghost could have been there. It was very crowded with furniture and all sorts of things everywhere. It was a different feel."[6]

III

The initial meeting was pleasant enough. Thelma brought in some tea on a silver tray, and discussed the project further with Nathanson, who couldn't hide his disappointment that Thelma still hadn't signed the revised contract. But Thelma wanted to find out more about the proposed production and its potential creator before committing to anything. Keen to get her friend Joel L. Fletcher's opinion on this whole venture, she suggested the three of them meet the next day. By then, though, Thelma had already grown quite weary of her guest, as was plainly evident to Fletcher, who remarked: "She didn't like Michael very much."[7]

"Thelma was very excited. She believed in me," insists Nathanson.[8] But Thelma's reluctance to engage further with the writer endured, especially after Nathanson presented her with the "hook" for the television film: he proposed to start the film with Ken stationed in Puerto Rico, unable to fly home for Thelma's birthday due to lack of funds. His mother would sit at home, depressed and disappointed, when suddenly a knock on the door would change everything. And there he would be, John Kennedy Toole saying: "I knew you really wanted me to be here so I took a part-time job, so I could make enough money to be here to celebrate with you."[9]

Thelma looked at Nathanson in disbelief, but said nothing. Instead, she excused herself and rested for a few hours, before driving that evening to a dinner party at a friend's place. After the dinner—which, unsurprisingly, Thelma dominated—Nathanson, who stayed in a hotel, suggested Joel Fletcher join him for a quick drink. It didn't take long for Nathanson to bring up a topic he had been mulling over for the past few hours. It was a topic he considered discussing in his film. Without any warning, he asked Fletcher whether Ken had been gay.

IV

Since his first visit to Elysian Fields, Nathanson had made what he thought of as a startling advance: after he had mentioned to Thelma that he needed to undertake more research in order to put together a convincing script for the proposed television movie, Ken's mother kindly provided him with a list of three to four people to contact. She suggested the young writer call them to get some background information on her deceased son. He was grateful for the contacts, but his hopes of Thelma signing the contract immediately were dashed, as he remembers: "When we had our wonderful time together and she recommended some people, I said, 'This is wonderful, can I execute the agreement?' 'No, no, I want to take another look at it. We will get together in a couple of days.' I felt a little worried because there was no logical reason, based on all the communication, that she wouldn't have executed the agreement. I remember walking out there without the piece of paper signed. She had been ready to sign it before I walked in."[10]

Instead, he spoke to the people Thelma had recommended, hoping that she would sign the contract before he left for Los Angeles. An even bigger surprise than Thelma's reluctance to execute the agreement came in the form of statements from two of Ken's friends. Although Nathanson doesn't remember their names, he still vividly recalls what they shared with him: "At least a couple of people got into 'the gay thing.' One person I was speaking with used to go to the bars with John and they used to party together. It was explained to me by this fellow. From what I can recall it didn't bother [Ken] that he was gay. What bothered him was the stigma that comes with it. He couldn't deal with the guilt, with being gay and not being able to be the gay person he wanted to be. It's complex. That's the way he explained it to me."[11]

Joel Fletcher muses one of these people might have been Nick Polites, who was gay himself and a friend of his and Ken's. In fact, Polites had taken Ken to a gay party in the French Quarter of New Orleans, which might very well refer to the party Nathanson's contact mentioned over the phone.[12]

For Nathanson, all this was new. Had Ken been gay? He didn't have much time to think about this possibility and what it might mean for his television film, since his train of thought was soon to be disrupted by a call from one of Ken's friends who he had spoken to earlier. This friend felt obliged to warn Nathanson that Thelma was not pleased with his conduct: "I got this call from one of the people I had interviewed. [Thelma] had called them and wanted to know what kind of stuff I was asking about John. 'What is Michael asking everybody?' I would be asking the simple stuff. 'Did he like sports? Did he stay in shape? What made him laugh?' Things like that. 'What would upset him most? Have you seen him angry? What was the situation?' This stuff, to give you a feel for a character that you are creating for television. How I felt for him and what he went through. And the next thing you know everybody is talking about the gay John Kennedy Toole!"[13]

By this time, Nathanson had become aware of Thelma's controlling nature and the fact that she was investigating his conduct shouldn't have come as a huge surprise. For the writer, it explains why Ken's mother decided not to sign the contract: "When I got back to Los Angeles I figured it out: Thelma in her own mind was thinking the gay son that she knew would not be part of this. Now I know about it, the secret is going to be coming out. 'I don't want that, therefore I can't get involved with Michael's movie because he discovered all of this on his own'—from the people she had sent me to!"

Nathanson called Thelma, desperately trying to save the project, but to no avail: "The insanity of this is I just went out and did what she told me to do. We are trying to make this as something for television. 'Please tell me what's wrong and I will try to fix it!' I was trying to salvage this relationship, but it failed. She was very sharp and very to the point and I knew that after that one phone call there was no way of being able to call her back and resuscitate anything. She wasn't rude, but very final."[14]

Thelma never signed the contract. Instead, while Nathanson was still in town, she said to her friend Joel Fletcher: "I am a little leery of a few things, honey," to which Fletcher replied: "As well I think you might be."[15] Fletcher didn't like Nathanson much either and did not try to encourage Thelma to sign the contract. It had become clear to Fletcher that the young writer/producer had no clear grasp of Ken's life and kept mixing up the facts.

V

To this day, there is no clear consensus about whether John Kennedy Toole was gay. Nick Polites said to Joel Fletcher that there had been some sexual tension between Ken and his friend Doonie Guibet.[16] Guibet had been close to the writer of

A Confederacy of Dunces and lived an openly gay life. (In 1981 he was arrested in New Orleans for the murder of his roommate.)[17] However, Fletcher always thought of Ken as asexual, since the topic of sexuality had never come up once during their friendship: "I certainly never picked up on Ken being gay. I was very much in the closet myself at the time. The clincher was talking about Patricia Rickels when he said he would really like to fuck her. That doesn't sound like something a gay person would say. Maybe Ken was bisexual."[18]

Patricia Rickels and her husband Milton were close friends of Ken's, and Polites mentioned to Fletcher that Patricia had been an object of attraction for Ken. The married woman had picked up on that: "A lot of people say he was homosexual, [...] but I never thought that. He liked women ... he liked me, very much. He took a fancy to me."[19]

There also exists a mysterious love letter from a woman called Ellen, addressed to Ken and sent from New York.[20] Unfortunately, the identity of this woman has never been determined. Furthermore, there had been a few love interests in Ken's life, one of whom was Ruth Lafrantz. Although their infatuation with each other would not blossom into a relationship, they remained close friends.[21]

But would Ken's sexuality really have mattered to Nathanson when it came to his proposed television film? Not really, the writer ponders: "I don't think I needed that element to make a movie. I think there was enough of a story there. You have that story of a loving son and his mother, this guy trying to live his life. A lot of this I really can't figure out myself with the guy, but I could have made it work without him being gay because I went there not even knowing that."[22]

Nathanson does concede that it might have been an interesting subplot. After all, Ken's alleged concealed homosexuality could partly explain his suicide—and there was no question that the suicide would be part of the film.

The young TV writer had never believed the story of a talented artist killing himself simply because he couldn't sell his book. Nathanson was sure there must have been more to it. If Ken had been ashamed of being gay, perhaps, he thought, he had found the missing piece of the puzzle. With it came a new challenge, though, since Nathanson didn't feel particularly comfortable writing about a homosexual man—as a heterosexual writer he hadn't enough "knowledge of the gay consciousness," as he puts it.[23]

For the main plot, he considered a "soft TV" approach, a film which begins with Ken's suicide. Nathanson wanted to structure the story in a way that would create an element of suspense that would carry the film: "Is it a homicide? What is it? It turns out to be a suicide, but why?"[24] The rest of the film would have dealt with Thelma trying to figure out why her son had decided to end his life, while at the same time trying to sell her son's book to publishers.

VI

Julia Phillips and Fox TV would have been Michael Nathanson's first port of call to produce his project. He remains convinced that even if they had passed on the property, in the early 80s other studios would have lined up to finance the film. It was not to be.

After Thelma had made it clear that she was not interested in collaborating on the project, Nathanson relented and did not pursue the idea. He was afraid that even if he tried to acquire the rights to a newspaper article on Ken's life, Thelma might sue for defamation. His view of the grand dame of Elysian Fields had changed drastically since he had first read about her shortly after the novel's publication. He knew he had to be careful. Thelma was controlling, as he had found out in the course of his stay in New Orleans.

Joel L. Fletcher concedes that Nathanson might very well have been right in his suspicion that Thelma didn't want him to find out anything about her son—other than the glorifying stories that she had told friends and acquaintances for years about Ken whenever she had the opportunity.[25] *She* was the woman who controlled her son's image—or, rather, the image she had created for her deceased son.

"She was very refined. It felt like a razor blade. She didn't miss a beat," remembers Nathanson.[26] "She was very multi-layered." The writer was left to wonder whether Thelma was indeed her son's best friend or his worst enemy.

Nathanson stayed in the film business in various ways: in 1989, he and Seth Winston released *She's Out of Control*, a comedy starring Tony Danza and Wallace Shawn. It was their only theatrical feature. Seven years earlier Nathanson founded Upstart Productions, with which he created All Kids Count, a film and television production company based in Los Angeles. With this non-profit endeavor, Nathanson and his colleagues remain committed to producing family and children's programs.[27]

3

Queen Mother Is Angry

How Thelma learns about a planned stage adaptation of her son's work
and flies into a rage because she hadn't been consulted

Joel L. Fletcher met news about a musical version of *A Confederacy of Dunces* with delight and trepidation—when he read an article about it in the *Baton Rouge Morning Advocate* in January of 1983, he instinctively knew that Thelma had no idea such a thing was in production. And he knew that his friend's mother would not react kindly to news concerning Ken's work that she hadn't been consulted about.[1]

Thelma's relationship with Les Phillabaum, the director of LSU Press, was already strained since she was convinced that he wasn't paying her royalties from Ken's book on time. She had written him several scathing letters demanding immediate payment.[2] Nevertheless, Fletcher sent her the article that informed its readers about LSU's planned stage adaptation of *A Confederacy of Dunces*, aware that her volcanic anger might erupt as soon as she saw it. Indeed, that was exactly what happened.

Thelma had no idea about the planned musical, and if there was one thing she didn't like, it was not being kept in the loop. She contacted Les Phillabaum immediately, who took his time to reply. Eventually, his letter arrived at Elysian Fields, informing Thelma that yes, indeed, the LSU drama department was working on a musical version of *A Confederacy of Dunces* under the guidance of Dr. Gresdna Doty (professor in the Department of Theatre), who had brought in Frank Galati to direct. But not to worry, he assured her, both Dr. Doty and Dr. Galati would be in touch with her and keep her informed about every step of the development process. She could be sure, since Galati was a renowned director, that her son's work was in very good hands.[3] He had adapted James Joyce and Vladimir Nabokov for the stage and received Chicago's Joseph Jefferson Award for best actor in a production of Tom Stoppard's *Travesties*. At that time, Galati was a professor of interpretation at Northwestern University in Evanston, Illinois. In order to get the new musical off the ground, he would spend several months in Baton Rouge.

II

Thelma did worry, though. She worried mainly because Dr. Doty and Dr. Galati did not get in touch with her as promised. This gave her enough reason for another scathing letter, this time directed jointly at Doty and Galati. While the production was already underway, she wrote on January 6, 1984:

23

Dr. Doty and Dr. Gallati [sic]

Your gross negligence, in not consulting me about the forthcoming musical stage play, astounded me!

Even though LSU Press has control of the movie, stage, and television rights (my contract states so), you should have inherently, legally, logically and righteously acknowledged that "I Am Owner, in Staunch Alliance with the eminent writer, Dr. Walker Percy."

As members of the Groves of Academe, you should maintain high ideals: respect for authority, and a keen evaluation of worth.

Several months ago, L.E. Phillabaum sent a letter telling me of the stage musical. He mentioned that Dr. Doty would soon contact me. That assertion was never realized.

The many people who are basking in the glory, the wonder, and the phenomenal success of *Confederacy*, were not around when I was rearing the literary, scholarly genius with my teaching earnings. His father, highly gifted, made an enviable record at Warren Easton High School: mathematical wizard, serious scholar, and Champion State Debater at a Baton Rouge Rally. He chose the wrong occupation and did not adequately and regularly support his talented wife and genius son.

You were not around when numerous and increasing hardships lashed at my son and me. After ten years of trying to get the book published, I appealed to Dr. Walker Percy, and the result is literary history! [...] I shall expect a letter of apology from the three of you.

Thelma Ducoing Toole[4]

It was a missive that could have been written by Ignatius J. Reilly, full of anger about other people's perceived ignorance; a letter which has its equivalent in the infamous note sent to Abelman's Dry Goods in Toole's novel:

Mr. I Abelman, Mongoloid, Esq.:

We have received via post your absurd comments about our trousers, the comments revealing, as they did, your total lack of contact with reality. Were you more aware, you would know or realize by now that the offending trousers were dispatched to you with our full knowledge that they were inadequate so far as length was concerned. "Why? Why?" you are in your incomprehensible babble, unable to assimilate stimulating concepts of commerce into your retarded and blighted worldview. [...] We do not wish to be bothered in the future by such tedious complaints. Please confine your correspondence to orders only. We are a busy and dynamic organization whose mission needless effrontery and harassment can only hinder.

If you molest us again, sir, you may feel the sting of the lash across your pitiful shoulders.[5]

It took a while for Dr. Doty and Dr. Galati to get back to Thelma. The reason was simple: they were busy with the stage adaptation of *A Confederacy of Dunces*. It was by no means a small feat. Purchasing the option was difficult enough in the first place. When International Creative Management Properties had optioned the movie rights to the book on behalf of Scott Kramer, LSU Press had agreed not to exercise the stage rights for a period of three years after the release of the first motion picture.[6] However, with the help from their attorneys, LSU Press received the right to produce a stage version of the source novel. The drama department then had to obtain the rights from LSU Press, which acted as a separate entity.

Frank Galati had been contacted by Gresdna Doty and had verbally agreed to be responsible for the production as director. Galati remembers: "I had heard of the novel. I had friends at that time who were teaching at Louisiana State University in Baton Rouge and I had heard from them that the university press at LSU owned the rights to the novel. Because my whole artistic life has pretty much involved the adaption of fiction for the stage, as soon as I read the book I realized, 'Oh my God, it's a classic comedy, a picturesque adventure with indelible comic characters and it would really play on stage!' I was sharing this observation with my friends at the university there and one woman, Dr. Doty, said that she knows the publisher and maybe they could make an arrangement with the university press to make a stage adaption that they would sanction."[7]

Following successful negotiations with LSU Press, the Chicagoan took off the term from his teaching job at Northwestern and fully devoted himself to work with the students on the proposed musical.

III

Galati brought some talent from Chicago with him: he wanted Scott Harlan to play Ignatius, the only professional actor in the whole production. Not only was he an experienced actor and singer, he matched Ignatius in his looks and could do a "brilliant" job, Galati was sure.[8]

While the director wrote the script and the lyrics himself, he contacted a composer, Edward Zelnis, who he had worked with before. Zelnis had a special talent for jazz and pop music, but was also a musicologist and experienced choral conductor who for years had served as Eartha Kitt's musical director. He was perfect for the job.

Giving regular updates to the author's mother was the farthest thing from Galati's mind in these hectic times, although he remembers reading her scathing letter. The fact was, though, Thelma didn't hold any rights whatsoever. Defensively, Galati shares: "I and the theater department got permission from the publisher, the university press, so we didn't do anything inappropriate. It would have been most appropriate to get in touch with her first, but that wasn't done and I didn't know how to do that. That was that."[9]

IV

Galati and his colleagues didn't have much time to get *A Confederacy of Dunces* on stage. The production was supposed to premiere in February of 1984. For Galati, that meant he had only six months to put everything together, which included six to seven weeks for rehearsals.

Before anything could be written, a decision had to be made about how to transform Toole's complex, multi-layered, comic masterpiece into a musical. Although Galati loved the book, he struggled with it: "I was particularly careful in carving this novel into a production. It was essential to maintain Toole's characters intact while translating the story line and plot into stage terms. This was an incredible challenge, as the book's length and complexity of plot made it necessary to 'collapse' a lot of the action into a manageable time frame for theater. [...] One of my major concerns was the numerous locations in the book and how quickly the action moves from one to the other. I had already rejected the idea of a narrative figure or chorus to bridge the necessary setting changes, and I offhandedly mentioned that if it were a musical the problem would be solved, as music turns the gears in a story on stage."[10]

In order not to confront the audience with a five-hour production Galati decided to trim the role of Dorian Greene, the homosexual character with whom Ignatius has a run-in. Apart from that, he remained faithful to the novel and its ideas, calling his approach to *A Confederacy of Dunces* and his general philosophy on stage adaptations "pretty conservative."[11] To stay as true to the source as possible was the motto.

Galati decided to shorten Ignatius's musings on life and philosophy as put on his Big Chief tablets and transform the essential elements of these into songs the obese hot dog lover could bark out. In the playbill, Galati wrote: "Ignatius J. Reilly says the last truly great composer was Scarlatti and yet he admires Batman. These kinds of opposites at work in one character or another, as they are in all people, are what endears them to us, makes them real. So, we want to hear Ignatius Reilly sing, we want to take him, and Mrs. Reilly, and Santa Battaglia, and Miss Trixie, and Mr. Levy and Lana Lee and all the others ... we want to take them and dress them up in a musical comedy. But how? I suppose by asking musical questions of the characters themselves: 'Excuse me, Mr. Reilly, what is your vocal range?' 'I beg your pardon. Of course, I am a tenor, I read comic books; all tenors read comic books, but I am a low tenor, with rich dark colors in my bottom register.... I also read Boethius.' And, of course, Mr. Reilly enjoys singing anything in the Baroque repertoire—but he does have his favorite 'musicomedy' stars, as he calls them, and he does watch a lot of TV, drinking Rock and Roll like Dr. Nut."[12]

V

Galati wrote both the script and the lyrics before handing them over to Edward Zelnis, who quickly realized what a beast he had on his hands. Ignatius is fascinated by medieval philosophy but loves Batman, too—he therefore doesn't reject the modern age outright. He lives and breathes New Orleans, which is famous for its Dixieland jazz. What music to write for such a *sujet*? Surely, Zelnis could do it all—and indeed he decided to do it all—dividing the musical moods of the show between three groups of performers: a Baroque ensemble, a rock combo and a Dixieland band.

By this time, the LSU drama department had already invested a large chunk of money into the production, and they would have to invest even more. It was clear that *A Confederacy of Dunces* would be extraordinarily expensive, especially for a semi-professional student production.

Galati and Zelnis auditioned approximately 200 actors, actresses, singers and dancers from Louisiana State University. Sixty of them were cast for the show. The various musical ensembles would perform Zelnis' colorful and diverse score, while three stage managers and a backstage crew of more than 25 people would guarantee a smoothly run production. The costumes were designed by the LSU theater faculty, while Victor Klimash from the music faculty served as musical director and Peter Amster as choreographer.[13]

It was a mammoth production which would last nearly three hours. Galati found the whole experience both frightening and at the same time deeply satisfying. He says: "I didn't get any money but it was a fabulous learning experience. I didn't know anyone to write the lyrics, so I wrote the lyrics myself. I didn't know how to structure the songs but I found my way and learned a lot about the process by having to do it myself."[14]

VI

Certainly, other playwrights and lyricists might have found the experience just as fulfilling. In 1983, *A Confederacy of Dunces* was a hot property, and the announcement of a stage adaptation led aspiring writers and composers to get in touch with Louisiana State University to pitch their talents. When the original announcement for the show had appeared in early 1983, Frank Galati was named as director but was quoted as saying he hadn't started with the adaptation yet. A young man named Erroll Miller saw his chance.

Miller was an aspiring playwright and lyricist, although he worked as a lawyer in Pittsburgh, and had his own ideas for the musical—a friend of his had written a spec script for *A Confederacy of Dunces*, which in turn had inspired Miller to write lyrics for it. After talking to Dr. Doty's secretary on the phone—who told him that a stage adaptation was already in the works but suggested he might share some of his ideas—Miller sent Doty a letter with various suggestions. Among his ideas for songs was a *Lament for Ignatius*—"'Forced to Function in a Century I Loath': this song could perhaps detail some of his past job-hunting experiences. It would give the audience some background to understand his character."[15] Miller added a suggestion for a song called "'You Simply Have to Organize,' a song to be sung at the madhouse political rally. There could be verses for many of the special interests including 'Pederasts to Power,' and others suggested by the book." None of his ideas were considered by the LSU drama department.

VII

When the end of rehearsals was in sight and the date for the premiere was looming, Dr. Doty finally replied to a letter Thelma had sent a few weeks before:

Dear Mrs. Toole:

[...] Work on the stage production of *A Confederacy of Dunces* is occupying us nearly full time, but the progress on it is exciting. I hope that you are planning to attend the Chancellor's reception and the opening night performance of the play. If you are I shall be pleased to meet you just before the reception and arrange for your transportation to the University Theatre from the Faculty Club. Just let me know your wishes.[16]

Of course, Thelma wouldn't pass up the opportunity to attend both the reception and the opening performance. She even came to one of the last rehearsals.

Opening night was on 24 February 1984 at 8 p.m. in the theater of the LSU Music and Dramatic Arts Building. The show was already a success by the time the date had been announced: audiences lined up in front of the building and LSU added additional performances, totaling twelve shows, running until 4 March.[17]

Despite the limited time Galati and Zelnis had had at their disposal, and the fact that Thelma hadn't been informed about the production, she loved the staging. Although frail and stricken with cancer, Thelma stood up at the end of the first show and, under rapturous applause, proclaimed: "This has been a beautiful evening in the American theater."[18]

Everything went well. Thelma was satisfied with Galati's approach, and when she was happy, she could be the most charming person on the planet. As the director observed: "I was terrified to meet her, if for no other reason than because she was responsible for getting this thing published. The poor man never saw his own dream realized. But she was a very passionate and funny and wonderfully odd lady. She came to the rehearsal once and then to the opening night. She was quite elderly, probably in her 80s, and she had problems with her feet and her legs, so she wore bedroom slippers. I knew she wasn't well. It was a real privilege to have met her. She was very enthusiastic."[19]

There were many enthusiastic members of the audience in the theater, one of which was a young man who would later play a pivotal role in trying to get *A Confederacy of Dunces* off the ground as a feature film: Steven Soderbergh. He was only a few years away from making a big splash with his debut feature, *sex, lies and videotape*, on the strength of which he would go on to become one of the most acclaimed and prolific directors of his generation. Of course, when he watched the events around Ignatius unfold on stage, Soderbergh had no idea that the same subject matter would one day drive him into crisis.

Though as great as the reviews were, Galati knew his version of the show would never be staged again. A proper production would cost $5 to $6 million, a sum hardly any theater in the world would spend on the extravaganza. Nor is it true to say that the director was over the moon with every aspect of the show. In fact, if he had another opportunity, he would change a few things. First of all, he admits that a running time of nearly three hours was way too long.[20] And although the cast members were great, the production could have been better had there been time for more rehearsals.

He didn't know it at the time, but Galati would get another shot at an *A Confederacy of Dunces* adaptation ten years later. But it wouldn't be for the stage, and it wouldn't amount to anything.

Part II
The Film That Never Was

We stand at a crossroads. One path leads to despair, the other to destruction. Let's hope we make the right choice.

—Woody Allen

In the film business you hate for things to be fucked up at the beginning. They'll end up there, it goes without saying. You're a writer and you're not stupid, so you know this. Nor is your own relative insignificance in the overall scheme of things in doubt.

—Richard Russo, "Milton and Marcus"

4

The Story of Scott's Life
aka Patient Zero

How a young producer finds himself first in the queue and subsequently embarks on a quest that would keep him busy for the next decades

Thelma Toole had many reasons to be happy in the years following the publication of *A Confederacy of Dunces*. Her son's novel had won the Pulitzer Prize, and a stage adaptation in 1984 proved to be a big artistic success. Though the icing on the cake for every fan, and, of course, for Thelma, was the prospect of seeing Ignatius on screen, raving about the modern world. Occasionally, Hollywood smells success from miles afar and production companies don't waste any time optioning the rights to a book—fiction and non-fiction alike—that might turn out to be a promising bestseller. The case of *A Confederacy of Dunces* was slightly different, since initially no one expected John Kennedy Toole's work to become a smash hit. After all, LSU was not a major publishing house for fiction and had only agreed on an initial print run of 2500 copies.

Nevertheless, one of the first people to get their hands on the book, and who fell in love with it immediately, was Scott Kramer, a Twentieth Century–Fox executive in his early twenties. He had worked as an assistant for director Paul Mazursky, whose best-known film was *An Unmarried Woman*.[1] By the early '80s, Kramer was under contract at Fox. He wanted to be a big-shot producer in his own right, "one of many people who dream of making movies in Hollywood," as Carson Productions president Marcia Nasatir puts it.[2]

It was a lucky accident Kramer got his hands on the novel in the first place. Originally, he had only wanted a copy of *Flora of Louisiana* by Margaret Stones which was published by LSU Press. Excited about giving a copy of that book as a present to his mother, who was deeply passionate about gardening, he got in touch with the publishing house, only to learn that *Flora of Louisiana* was sold out. LSU Press hated to be the bringer of bad news and suggested the young executive might be interested in its upcoming publication *A Confederacy of Dunces*. The work wasn't yet available in stores, but Kramer was pleased to find the manuscript on his doorstep in Los Angeles one day in early 1980.[3] Despite its complex structure, he was convinced it would make a great movie and put him on the map as one of Hollywood's major producers.

II

It would be a Twentieth Century–Fox production, if Kramer had his wish. Therefore, he forwarded the manuscript to his colleague David Madden, another executive at the studio. As a junior executive, it was Madden's job to evaluate the blistering satire and help his colleague acquire the rights to it. "Scott was very passionate about it, [but] the conundrum has always been how to turn the voice of this literary novel into a screenplay," remembers Madden.[4] Madden liked the book, but he was painfully aware that the novel was not one which could be adapted easily into a feature film. The former junior executive explains: "It had a tone that was not a typical film-tone. It needed to be handled the right way."[5] Despite being unsure about whether the story would work as a movie, Madden supported his friend and thought Twentieth Century–Fox shouldn't pass on the chance of optioning the rights. Kramer felt at home at the company and was sure his property would be in good hands.

> He who would build a sturdy
> house he intends will last,
> that will not be destroyed
> by the force of the winds and waves,
> would do well to select his site
> with a certain degree of prudence,
> avoiding the mountaintops
> where the gales buffet and rage
> and the desert dunes where the sands
> will erode beneath his foundation.[6]

Before he had a contract with Twentieth Century–Fox to make the film locked down, Kramer enlisted ICMP (International Creative Management Properties) to buy the rights for him. In July 1980, a little over two months after *A Confederacy of Dunces* had been published, a proposal was designed that would guarantee Kramer a twelve-month exclusive option on the property. He was represented by Jeff Berg, who would spent 40 years at ICM before a bitter internal power struggle prompted him to leave the company in 2012.[7]

The contract signed between ICMP—on behalf of Kramer—and LSU Press was industry standard, guaranteeing the Payer the sole, exclusive, and worldwide motion picture, television and allied and incidental rights to *A Confederacy of Dunces*, including theatrical, television, cassette and other compact devices, as well as sequel, remake, advertising and publicity rights. For said rights, ICMP paid $10,000 to the university press. If the film didn't commence production during the twelve months specified in the proposal, the agency would have to pay another $10,000 to renew the option.[8]

III

The contract was not agreed upon for quite some time. After an arduous negotiation with LSU's attorney Gene Winick, Scott Kramer initially rejected and subsequently accepted the deal.[9] While Les Phillabaum oversaw these negotiations, he also had to battle with Thelma who, of course, scolded him for allegedly not paying the royalties owed on the book in time and meanwhile expected constant updates about a possible movie deal.

Thelma was furious that LSU had been approached by Hollywood and not let her know about the possibility of a feature film adaptation of *A Confederacy of Dunces* immediately. Rather, in summer of 1980, she had learned through Walker Percy that LSU Press was in touch with a young producer named Scott Kramer who would be coming to New Orleans soon. Shooting was supposed to commence the following year. This was news to her.[10]

She picked up pen and paper and in July 1980 wrote a letter to Phillabaum, informing him that "if any executives visit Baton Rouge, I want to be included—especially those connected with the movie. The theater is my field as a performer, teacher, and director. I am also an expert casting director."[11] Although no contract between LSU Press and ICMP had been signed at that point, Phillabaum quickly reassured Thelma: "I have informed [Kramer] of your interest in the movie and your desire to be consulted. It is my impression that he would indeed like to discuss the matter with you, and I am therefore confident that he will contact you at the appropriate time."[12]

Thelma not only wanted to be consulted, she quite fancied the idea of directing the film, as she proposed in an interview: "This book is going to be very [difficult]. Not for me. Let me be the director! I'd have to join the Actors Guild and what-have-you but I'd do anything that's necessary. I have an idea how to open [the film]. I would be the narrator and the camera would start at D.H. Holmes without any characters. Passersby, customers, shoppers. Jackson Square. [Ken] mentions Jackson Square, Pirate's Alley, Royal Street and his magnificent description of Dorian Gray's [sic] three-story [...] home in the French Quarter."[13]

For Scott Kramer, there seemed no way around contacting Thelma and consulting her about his proposed project. Meanwhile, the contract between ICMP and LSU Press was signed at the end of 1980. In January of the following year, Thelma was paid her share from LSU Press. Phillabaum made the money transfer promptly, anxious not to upset the author's mother again. Of the $10,000 for the movie rights, Thelma received $4,486.52.[14]

IV

In the months prior to finalizing the deal, Kramer had kept himself busy with various pre-production tasks, confident that he and Twentieth Century–Fox would eventually agree on a deal. This proved more difficult than he had envisioned, though. Fox was not willing to take on the project without some guarantees. As David Madden remembers, Fox would only sign an agreement with Kramer if they were presented with a script or, at the very least, a screenwriter who had been enlisted by Kramer and with whom the upper echelons at Fox were happy: "We were open to him coming in with the right writer, but we wouldn't have moved forward without the right writer in place. That's not unusual. As a studio, you wouldn't want to commit to it without knowing that there was a writer who had an approach you liked. That's standard practice now and was back then when things were developed in the 80s. You wanted some guarantee. There were cases when a studio bought the rights to a book without a writer attached, but *A Confederacy of Dunces* didn't feel like one of those books."[15]

Kramer had one writer in mind for the project and even reached a (verbal) agreement with Alan Ormsby who had made a name for himself writing a handful of exploitation movies (among them *Deranged: Confessions of a Necrophile*) before joining the A list with his screenplay for Tony Bill's charming hit family comedy drama, *My Bodyguard*. He would go on to write Paul Schrader's now classic *Cat People* (1982) as well as pen "additional story material" for Disney's *Mulan* (1998).

Ormsby wasn't necessarily an obvious choice for *A Confederacy of Dunces*, but he had read and loved the book even before Kramer approached him. The writer explains: "I felt it was a very idiosyncratic novel that needed an offbeat approach—which is probably why it's never been made: its tone is unique, and its characters are not—as I recall—politically correct."[16]

Ormsby wanted to give it a try and lend his distinctive style to an adaptation of *A Confederacy of Dunces*. As soon as he had read the novel, he inquired about the rights, eager to secure them for himself. In order to find out if they were available, Ormsby had called up Thelma Toole, who had to break the news to him that the rights had just been sold by LSU Press to a young producer named Scott Kramer. Heartbroken, Ormsby had started working on other projects. Only a short while later, though, he was surprised to hear from Scott Kramer himself. Looking for a screenwriter, Kramer rang Ormsby, who was over the moon to be considered for the job of screenwriter for *A Confederacy of Dunces*. The pair met several times to discuss an approach, but Ormsby was soon disenchanted. As he remembers: "I know I was annoyed that he'd beaten me to the rights since he didn't seem to have much feeling for the material."[17]

In fact, Kramer and Ormsby didn't agree on much and no contract between them was ever signed. The latter never delivered a screenplay—he didn't even start writing. He and Kramer didn't see eye to eye, and Kramer was having problems setting up the project up with a studio—Kramer didn't have a deal with a writer, and Fox wasn't willing to sign a contract without a writer in place. A verifiable conundrum. Kramer and Madden only ever got as far as discussing two possible actors for the leading role: John Belushi and John Candy.[18]

V

While discussing his ideas for the film with Ormsby, Kramer kept both LSU Press and Thelma updated, finally contacting the latter at the beginning of 1981. Before that, the mother of the novel's author had sent him a letter, urging him to consider her as a consultant:

Dear Mr Kramer,

The writer, mother of John Kennedy Toole, whose novel has gained wide acclaim, has experienced a strong urge to communicate with you about the forthcoming movie. This is based upon my sixteen years of Dramatic Art Training, and a successful career as performer, teacher, and director. When you formulate plans for the movie, would you please give me an opportunity to speak with the director? I am hoping to be of substantial assistance to him because I have a keen insight into the characters, which my son drew so brilliantly.

My observation would be quiet and not intrusive. May the movie bring rich financial rewards for your astute judgment in securing the movie rights.

Looking forward!
Thelma Ducoing Toole[19]

Indeed, Thelma had quite a few ideas about how a movie of *A Confederacy of Dunces* should look and sound, and Kramer was to learn that Ken's mother was a force to be reckoned with. When he could get through to her at her home in Elysian Fields, that is.

Although her brother Arthur had moved in with her, there was no love lost between the siblings. Thelma despised Arthur and would consequently ignore him much of the time. Even when she had visitors, she instructed them to do the same. When *A Confederacy of Dunces* fan John Schulte, along with two friends, entered her home in 1983, he experienced firsthand the contempt Thelma had for Arthur: "Thelma shocked us by referring to Arthur Ducoing as 'the devil.' Arthur didn't appear to be the devil; he was just a spooky doppelgänger to his *To Kill a Mockingbird* literary counterpart, Arthur 'Boo' Radley. Once he skulked away, she told us that Arthur had been quite the writer himself back in the day, when he penned poetry while working at the Standard Fruit Company, which ultimately was purchased by Castle & Cooke Corporation, owners of the acquired Dole Food Company. 'Yes,' she said with tongue in cheek, 'Arthur is the Poet Laureate of pineapple.'"[20]

Their mutual contempt resulted in scenes straight out of *What Ever Happened to Baby Jane?*, the chilling Robert Aldrich-directed classic starring Bette Davis and Joan Crawford about two siblings living under the same roof who despise each other. Whenever Scott Kramer tried calling Thelma and Arthur was the first to answer the phone, he would put it down immediately. With the hook off its cradle, Thelma was impossible to get in touch with. Another attempt would have had to be made after she saw what her brother had done and put the hook back.[21]

Therefore, it was often Thelma who phoned Kramer in Los Angeles, despite the cost at that time for long-distance calls. From the producer's point of view, talking to her was just as enervating as not being able to phone her: as soon as Kramer greeted her, he was barraged with a host of questions about his proposed movie. Thelma would then go on to read to him the latest reviews of the book, imitate characters from it and give readings, as well as rant about her enemies, such as Les Phillabaum, often leaving the producer little time to say anything at all.[22]

Obviously, Thelma was impatient to see the film in theaters, and with little to no knowledge about the film industry, she grew frustrated when after a few weeks the shooting still hadn't started. She didn't lose hope, though, and believed in Kramer as her savior who would bring her son's vision to cinema screens across the country. For months, Thelma kept calling Kramer and sending him notes. One of such read: "Dear Friend, Fantasy Sweetheart and Secret Ally: May the future loom brilliantly for the illimitable far reaching epic motion picture. Love, Thelma."[23]

Even more importantly, Thelma was desperate to get in touch with any actors cast—in order to teach them elocution lessons. The New Orleansian accents had to be pitch perfect, after all, and nobody could be trusted to imitate them properly without training from the former elocution teacher.

VI

Scott Kramer was wise enough not to tell Thelma that *A Confederacy of Dunces* was not the only project on his plate. In 1981, he was toying with the idea of filming a script titled *Take a Flying Leap,* a biopic about Russian ballet dancer Alexander Goudonov.[24] At the time, Kramer's then-fiancé Loree Rodkin was Goudonov's personal manager. The plan was that Goudonov would play himself. He therefore enrolled in acting classes with respected coach Stella Adler in New York.

The adaptation of *A Confederacy of Dunces* proved to be a bigger undertaking and fraught with more complications than Kramer had envisioned, taking up most of his time for the next few years. Rodkin then worked a talent manager and as such helped to launch the careers of stars like Brad Pitt and Sarah Jessica Parker before becoming a celebrated jewelry designer and providing the jewelry worn by Michelle Obama for the inaugural ball in January 2009.

5

Probably, Maybe Definitely

How Scott Kramer fights to save "his" project and enlists the help of a new studio, in which a carpenter had just been named vice-president of special projects

Even though no actors were committed to *A Confederacy of Dunces* when Kramer was in touch with Thelma, he very much liked the idea of casting Richard Pryor as Burma Jones and Shelley Winters as Irene Reilly.[1] The big question, though, was who could play Ignatius? Thelma had her own ideas and was not shy about mentioning them to anybody who would listen: "It was *Whatever* [sic] *Happened to Baby Jane*. He was so good."[2]

The actor in question was Victor Buono. He had played the pianist Edwin Flagg, who helps Bette Davis' character relaunch her career in what was one of Thelma's favorite films. For some reason, this picture about an aging control freak who once dreamed of making it big but now leads a lonely and grim existence in a dark house with a sibling she despises appealed to a frail matriarch who once hoped to become a celebrated star of the stage but now lived an insular and gloomy life locked in rivalry with a sibling she detested.

Buono's sweet on-screen persona had completely enchanted Thelma, and in her mind there was no actor better suited to portray Ignatius J. Reilly. Buono certainly had the physical stature to portray the big-boned hobby philosopher, but in 1981 the actor and poet was already in his early 40s, and with a bald head and full beard looked considerably older. Although he kept himself busy with various television roles, he was not, anyway, the big star Scott Kramer had in mind. Any hopes Thelma might have had of seeing Buono in what could have been the role of his lifetime were dashed on January 1, 1982, when the actor suffered a fatal heart attack.

The search for a lead actor continued. Kramer was eager to find a new production company that would back his vision and put money into the production. Fox wasn't too happy with Alan Ormsby as the scribe attached—disagreements between him and Kramer led to the latter's doubts about Ormsby as the right choice. Time was running out—since he only had a twelve-month option, finding the right writer and a studio were on top of Kramer's to-do-list. If the film was not in pre-production by the end of 1981, he would have to renew the contract with LSU Press and pay another $10,000 as his contract stated.

II

A *Confederacy of Dunces* had, by this time, already proven to be a hit with readers and critics alike. Luckily, Hollywood is not short of production companies. One such was Carson Productions, its eponym none other than legendary talk show host Johnny Carson, a television personality who had precious little interest in producing films.[3] None of his associates had any interest either. Carson, though, had a distribution arrangement with Columbia, which was then run by Frank Price. The studio helped finance the television programs Carson and his associates produced, paying their overheads and development costs as part of their collaboration. As part of the deal Columbia was required to distribute two motion pictures as well.[4] Thus Carson had to produce feature films, whether he wanted to or not.

Although it took a few years until Carson Productions had their first film shown in theaters and despite his own personal lack of interest, Johnny Carson was smart enough to hire Marcia Nasatir, a powerhouse of an executive, as co-president of his company.

Nasatir had spent four years at United Artists before, in 1978, she joined Orion Pictures as vice-president. She swiftly accepted Carson's proposal to work for his new company and in 1981 began soliciting manuscripts. Despite her being a major league player already—she was one of the producers who had brought Sylvester Stallone's *Rocky* to the screen—Nasatir was starstruck by Carson. She remembers: "[My colleagues and I] went to have a meeting with him. He was on the Columbia lot. We went to Johnny's house one time, too, and met with him. I remember how thrilled we were to be able to meet Johnny Carson. He lived in Beverly Hills, and I remember the room, it was an outdoor porch, absolutely lovely. Here was Johnny Carson who you could see every night! But he wasn't interested in producing movies."[5]

Before Carson Productions was up and running, a head of production had to be found. Johnny Carson relied on his attorney, business partner and fixer Henry Bushkin, to go head hunting. Bushkin explains: "The problem always with any Carson related company was, 'Will that person get along with Carson?' On the film side we interviewed a lot of people. Carson had to meet them, of course. For whatever reason we could never find that person."[6] That was, until Bushkin suggested a friend of his, Wallace "Wally" Wolf.

Wolf was an experienced motion picture lawyer who at the time represented Bill Cosby, among others. He was also an Olympic champion who had competed in the 1948, 1952, 1956, and 1960 Summer Olympics as a swimmer. In 1948 and 1952, he won the Gold Medal. Would Wolf get along with Carson? The deciding factor was his proficiency at tennis. Bushkin continues: "Johnny knew Wally because I got him to play tennis with Carson. There was another person to play with Carson who Carson liked. I then didn't have to play. If I was doing five times a week, maybe I am down to three times a week [playing tennis with Carson]. That's a funny way of looking at it. But that's how I was looking at it. Wally was an acceptably good tennis player, certainly for Carson. So we agreed to hire Wally Wolf as head of the film company."[7] Hollywood has always run by its own rules.

III

Little did Alexander "Sandy" Ignon, who just wanted to make it as an actor in the industry, know that he would play a notable role in the turmoil that would bring Carson Productions nearly to a standstill, turning the prestigious offices into a metaphorical Western saloon where the major forces would face each other, hands to their guns, ready to shoot until no one was left alive. Scott Kramer's story is also partly Alexander Ignon's story.

Like most other aspiring actors, Ignon needed non-acting work to supplement his income. Therefore, he worked as a carpenter. As it happened, he got a job remodeling Henry Bushkin's office in Beverly Hills, Paul Newman's former home— Ignon's girlfriend worked for one of Bushkin's partners and had recommended her boyfriend as a talented carpenter. A friendly relationship between Ignon and Bushkin was forged. Ignon remembers one particular afternoon when he was working on Bushkin's office: "[Henry] drives up in his Ferrari. I am covered with terracotta dust because I had been grinding a terracotta threshold. I was really pissed off and I said: 'Henry, there has got to be a better way to earn a living than this!'"[8] A few weeks later Ignon received a call from the attorney.

> INT. Cabin in Topanga. DAY
> SANDY is on the phone.
>
> HENRY (V.O.)
> Sandy, we want you to come to the office.
>
> SANDY
> Who is we?
>
> HENRY (V.O.)
> John McMahon and me. Johnny and I just formed a movie company
> and we want to talk to you. Wear something nice.[9]

From the small cabin where he lived in Topanga, Ignon traveled to Century City and took a meeting with Bushkin and head of the television department, John McMahon. He walked out of the office as Vice-President of Special Projects at Carson Productions. As such, he worked for Wally Wolf. The young actor was flabbergasted. So this was how Hollywood worked! Ignon recalls: "It was a sort of favor for me. I didn't really know what the fuck to do because I didn't know what I was doing. The mandate was: just go find material and put things together."[10]

This was what he did. Ignon found his first project for Carson Productions through his friend Keith Carradine, an actor who had starred in Robert Altman's *Thieves Like Us* and *Nashville*. The deal which was struck made Ignon the golden boy at Carson Productions. But one project wasn't enough, and being the golden boy comes with its very own set of expectations. Ignon continues: "Still not knowing what to do, I was at a bookstore in Westwood, looking at book titles for movies." A saleswoman determined the course of his life when she recommended the young producer take a look at John Kennedy Toole's *A Confederacy of Dunces*. He had asked her for a book which would make a "good movie."[11]

He sat down to read and soon found himself agreeing with the bookstore employee. "I liked the book," continues Ignon. "I inquired around. I called the publisher and I found out that Scott Kramer owned it."[12] And because Hollywood is a small community, Ignon knew Scott Kramer—Paul Mazursky, who Kramer worked for, was a friend of Ignon's. Kramer at that time was dating Mazursky's daughter Meg. Everything is connected.

IV

Ignon sought the approval of Wallace P. Wolf to take on *A Confederacy of Dunces*. As it happened, Wolf didn't share the salesgirl's opinion that Toole's novel would make a terrific movie, and opted against it. This didn't deter Ignon. He liked the book enough to take a risk on it in his role as Vice-President.

During a meeting with talent agents from CAA (Creative Arts Agency), with which Carson Productions worked with closely, Ignon proposed *A Confederacy of Dunces*. Wolf gave him dagger stares. Fortunately, the agents didn't notice. They were well-aware of the book, its success and marketability. They gave Ignon the go-ahead, much to the consternation of Wolf, who had no love for Ignatius J. Reilly or any other characters in the book. Nevertheless, his colleague didn't waste any time in phoning up Scott Kramer who, after finding himself in deadlock with Twentieth Century–Fox, was only too happy to talk about partnering up. They had made the gamble without considering Frank Price of Columbia, though.

V

After being given the green light from CAA, Wolf approached Price. The latter made it clear to Wolf in no uncertain terms that the book in question would never make a movie and that Carson Productions better forget about the idea as quickly as possible. In a surprising, devious act of double-cross, and despite his loathing for the novel, Wolf went ahead and optioned the rights anyway, paying for them out of Carson Production's discretionary fund. As Ignatius J. Reilly said, "We must stay to watch the corruption. It's already beginning to set in."[13]

Marcia Nasatir, on the other hand, liked the book and was open to Kramer's ideas.[14] She was shocked, though, to see him arrive for a meeting—the young man didn't look like a prestigious producer. As Ignon remembers, Kramer wore a different haircut than "conventional people," a baseball cap and an earring in one earlobe: "He really put off Wally, his style did. Wally was very conventional."[15]

Nasatir and Wolf weren't the only people in film business who weren't immediately enamored by Kramer. As his colleague David Madden remembers, Scott Kramer had already upset a few important people in Hollywood: "He was smart and charming, but he never made it into the mainstream. As close as he got was working with Mazursky, but even those people didn't get a lot of things made.

"I liked him, but he was a little bit of a pugnacious personality. Some people found him a little difficult, which comes out of passion frequently. It's not necessarily a bad thing if you are passionate about something. He didn't take 'No's for an answer, which didn't always ingratiate him to everybody. He was always coming back with the same kind of thing. Tenacity is really important for a producer, but when you say 'No' about something and he comes back five months later to ask again and you say, 'I have already read it and I have already said I didn't like it,' [then it becomes problematic.]

"He was pushy in a way. Producers have to strike a balance between being tenacious and knowing when to walk away if you want to be successful. I am not sure Scott had that kind of sensitivity."[16]

Sandy Ignon has a slightly different take, although he can understand why some people were put off by the young producer: "[He is] a very bright man, and very astute. I always found him to be honest and probably too honest for this business. He was very straight-ahead. I liked him a lot. He is incredibly intense, and perhaps he is so intense that it could be construed as arrogance a little bit."[17]

Kramer's appearance didn't deter the decision makers at Carson Productions. *A Confederacy of Dunces* was a go. In the summer of 1981, a deal was struck—one which, necessarily, involved Thelma.[18] Since she was the deceased author's next of kin Carson Productions insisted Thelma sign a copyright assignment—in order to avoid unpleasant surprises later on, the executives wanted to make sure she was aware of the agreement that had been entered into for the motion picture rights and that it met with her approval.[19] Thelma signed the document promptly, over the moon that a prestigious, famous and highly respected star such as Johnny Carson would be involved in bringing Ken's work to the screen. Little did she know that her much admired talk show host had nothing to do with any of the films that bore his name. Bushkin explains that Carson was never asked to give his consent regarding optioning *A Confederacy of Dunces*: "Obviously Carson would never get involved in a decision like that. You would never discuss something like this with him. He would look at me and say, 'What do I know?' He would be absolutely right."[20]

VI

Nine months prior to striking a deal with Carson, Kramer had already unsuccessfully approached Columbia. In late 1980, they had passed on the property as Kramer remembered when a deal was eventually struck with Carson: "I originally brought them the book. Nine months later, they asked me if I would do the book [as a film]."[21]

By now, Scott Kramer had become an Ignatius himself, running around town, trying to get a job, trying to sell *A Confederacy of Dunces*, all without much success at first, but encountering many shrewd characters along the way—with him maybe being the shrewdest of them all. Now, after many trials and errors, it seemed that Kramer was finally successful, that thanks to Wally Wolf's daring he had convinced a company to back his project. Carson Productions replaced ICM Properties as Kramer's backers, shortly after the twelve-month-option was running out. ICM had purchased the option for the young producer in July 1980. In June 1981, Carson Productions signed a deal with LSU Press which Kramer enthusiastically communicated to the press.

The problem was, Frank Price hadn't been informed about the deal. Columbia was outraged that negotiations had successfully concluded behind its back and announced to journalists. A spokesperson for the studio declined to comment, only grimly stating that "we haven't announced it yet."[22] It was a deal which would nearly lead to the implosion of Carson Productions as a whole.

6

Slices of Doom

How Scott Kramer learns that getting John Belushi to commit to take a meeting is an undertaking not to be underestimated, and is then confronted with several tragedies at once

The question of who could play Ignatius was a constant. Ignatius was a slob. And who, at that point in time was the most famous slob in movie history? Bluto from *Animal House*! The 1978 frat comedy was the big breakthrough in cinema for John Belushi, who had already made a name for himself as a highly talented comedian as part of the *Saturday Night Live* troupe. He had also been a fixture in Kramer's and Ormsby's meetings when they discussed a possible approach for the screenplay.[1]

Kramer was aware of Belushi's reputation, that the comedian had experimented with drugs in his teens and had never stopped. Indeed, his heavy use of cocaine was an open secret, and as a result he had been found difficult to work with. During the shooting of John G. Avildsen's *Neighbors*, Belushi had been so heavily under the influence that he more than once wasn't able to leave his trailer to shoot his scenes.[2] He began throwing temper tantrums in the offices of studio executives, and despite the fact that *Animal House* had been his only feature film hit, his ego ran amok.

By the end of 1981, his manager Bernie Brillstein had become desperate. His client needed another big box-office success as soon as possible and Brillstein wanted him to commit to star in the comedy *The Joy of Sex*.[3] Belushi had other ideas and didn't want to be pressured into projects which simply required him to read lines from a script. He wanted to bring more of himself into the films he made. He wanted to be in charge. Also, following the success of *Animal House*, he had often been hired to play lazy, foulmouthed slobs, and he was now eager to escape this typecasting.[4]

Towards the end of 1981, Belushi had started using heroin in addition to cocaine and Quaalude and was lacking the concentration his manager desired from his client. This became evident to Scott Kramer soon enough: Brillstein had read about the plan to bring *A Confederacy of Dunces* to the screen and he seized on the chance, calling Kramer to inform him that his client was interested in the lead role. This was great news for the young producer, who followed Brillstein's invitation to meet the actor in New York where Belushi was filming *Neighbors*.

Kramer turned up early at the Odeon restaurant before John and his wife Judy came in to take their seats.

However, it soon became clear that there had been a case of miscommunication. Belushi was puzzled to find a person unfamiliar to him at his table and in no uncertain terms asked what Kramer thought he was doing there.

The producer quickly informed the actor that Bernie Brillstein had invited him to discuss a project. Although Belushi allowed Kramer to stay, the following laid-back meeting amounted to nothing. Not only had Belushi not read the book, but also he knew nothing about this supposed adaptation.[5]

That the heavy-set actor hadn't even read the book and therefore didn't seem overly excited about *A Confederacy of Dunces* was disappointing for Kramer, but not to Thelma. She was not impressed with the idea of Belushi as Ignatius, mainly because she wasn't familiar with any of his work and still favored Victor Buono. "Some mentioned Bulosi [sic]. What do you think? I don't keep up with TV. [...] Someone else told me Bulosi [sic] wasn't intelligent enough. [Ignatius] was seven foot tall," Thelma mused.[6]

II

Kramer didn't give up hope. Luckily for him, Brillstein called him again in Los Angeles a few weeks later to assure him his client had finally read the book and was ready to discuss the project.

It was too early to celebrate, especially as after Kramer had traveled to New York again he learned that Belushi still hadn't read the book. The producer sought an ally in Judy Belushi who, by then, had indeed studied the novel. She liked it enough to recommend it to her husband, who simply hadn't gotten around to reading it yet.[7] Even so, Judy's praise for the book was by no means a guarantee she would urge John to sign a contract—she wasn't too keen to see her husband as the novel's antihero.

"Ignatius was a messy kind of guy,"[8] as she puts it, and in that sense quite similar to Bluto from *Animal House*, a role that John had tried to escape for a number of years. Judy was tired of seeing her intelligent partner playing slobs. It was for the same reason she and John agreed he should turn down the role of Arthur in the movie of the same title: "The film would have been full of debauchery and drinking, while John wanted to be in something more sophisticated and play somebody more sophisticated," says Judy Belushi.[9] *Arthur* was eventually made starring Dudley Moore and became a smash hit. Meanwhile, John was interested enough in *A Confederacy of Dunces* to finally read the novel and agree to a meeting in Los Angeles.

III

In September 1981, Hollywood and New Orleans were buzzing with excitement about the possible casting of John Belushi as Ignatius J. Reilly. Even the actor was astonished about the word of mouth: "Cab drivers, people like that, ask me whether I'm going to play Ignatius. A guy last night asked me that question. A lot of people seem to know about it."[10]

But Belushi had demands. He only wanted to play the leading role if his friend Michael Apted would direct. The duo had recently wrapped *Continental Divide*, a romantic comedy starring Belushi and Blair Brown. Although the film didn't meet the studio's expectations at the box office, the actor and director had worked well together and were keen to continue their working relationship. This became public knowledge when Apted asserted in an interview that he would only direct *A Confederacy of Dunces* if Belushi played Ignatius: "[It is a] brilliant book, full of genuine comic observation, but it's poorly structured. It'll be very, very tough to do. It's so difficult getting good material in Hollywood. [...] There's always a lot of people associated with it, and it's difficult ever to get the right people together. But I think John is the only person in the world who could play it, and that's the only way I'll do it. It's a question of whether we maneuver so we get within striking distance of it."[11] Talks between Michael Apted and John Belushi would remain informal, though. The director never "took a stab at adapting the book."[12]

IV

The hope for Kramer was that *A Confederacy of Dunces* would reunite Belushi with one of his colleagues from *Saturday Night Live*: Buck Henry. One of their acts had been particularly memorable: a 1976 episode in which Belushi had played his most beloved character, the samurai, and injured Henry with his katana. Henry had promptly started to bleed from the forehead. There was no animosity between the two, though.

Belushi thought his colleague would be perfect as the screenwriter for the adaptation, as did Scott Kramer who could slowly see the crew of this dreams assemble. While Belushi would play Ignatius and Henry would write the script, Mike Nichols could be the perfect director for a vehicle such as this. It would be a formidable triangle.

The German-born director Nichols had already succeeded in adapting another modern comedy classic in his 1970 version of *Catch-22*, a book which had been thought to be unfilmable until Nichols—with a script by Buck Henry—proved the doubters wrong.

To Kramer's surprise, though, Henry wasn't impressed with the idea of adapting *A Confederacy of Dunces*, despite his admiration for the book. As he remembered it, "I actively voted against it. The book breaks down into two tones that don't go together: wild social satire and Southern Gothic."[13]

V

Even though an adaptation of the novel had at no point been a priority of his, the assessment by his trusted friend Henry did nothing to heighten Belushi's interest in the project. If he had accepted the role, his widow claims, he would have delayed the project for several years because there were during these months other ideas bouncing around in his head that were far more important to him.[14] Two of the projects Belushi was more passionate about were Louis Malle's *Moon Over Miami* and Jay Sandrich's *Sweet Deception*. *Sweet Deception* was suggested to Belushi by director Jay Sandrich, who thought the actor would be brilliantly cast against type as a young, honest, attractive man who, in the midst of a wine contest, becomes involved in diamond smuggling. Belushi liked the idea but wanted to make the project his own, and hence he rewrote the script with Don Novello. In a frenzied drug-haze, they changed the title to *Noble Rot* and heavily altered the screenplay, much to Sandrich's dismay. Sandrich, Paramount executives, as well as some of Belushi's friends, hated the result: the humor was ill-judged, it was vulgar, the story didn't make any coherent sense and, above all, it wasn't funny. But Belushi remained passionate about the film and was determined to make it his next project.[15] *Moon Over Miami* was written as a political farce, based on the Abscam scandal. A conman (to be played by Belushi) had introduced an undercover FBI agent (to be played by Dan Aykroyd) to congressmen who were subsequently filmed taking money from a fictitious company set up by the FBI. The investigation into political corruption led to the conviction of, among others, seven members of the United States Congress. Belushi died before shooting was to begin and Louis Malle then lost interest in the project.[16]

Despite his reluctance concerning *A Confederacy of Dunces*, Belushi found taking a meeting with Kramer couldn't hurt. You never knew. But the scheduled meeting never took place. Only days before talks about the adaptation could begin in Chateau Marmont in Los Angeles, John Belushi passed away from a drug overdose.[17] It was March 5, 1982, and Belushi was 33 years old.

For years, Kramer would recount to friends and acquaintances how he learned of the comedian's death. Attorney and producer Michael Arata explains: "As Scott was about to leave for the meeting, his partner switched the television on and said, 'Have you seen the news?' 'No, what's the news?' And they were carrying John Belushi out of the hotel on a stretcher."[18] Hollywood was devastated to lose one of its most talented, beloved performers. So was Scott Kramer, and although Thelma Toole hadn't been wild about seeing the *Saturday Night Live* star as Ignatius, she was impatient to see her son's work on screen.

> *You have had a sharp bump, and you think that Fortune's attitude toward you has changed. But you're wrong. She hasn't changed a bit. She was always whimsical, and she remains constant to her inconstancy.*[19]

VI

There was, however, one positive development. It was clear to everybody involved that a feature film of the definitive New Orleans novel would have to be filmed in the Big Easy. Fortunately, at that very moment the city was rapidly expanding its involvement with the movie industry. In the early '80s, New Orleans hatched plans to become a second Burbank, the place where most Hollywood productions were shot. In 1980, films produced in Louisiana had had an estimated $200 million impact on the state economy, and projects were planned to increase this amount. So, of course, the Louisiana Film Commission would only be too happy to have a Hollywood crew in New Orleans to shoot *A Confederacy of Dunces*.

The director of the Film Commission was Jo Beth Bolton, who had taken up the post in the spring of 1980. In July 1982, she said: "My idea is to have a Burbank situation in New Orleans with the major studios merging operations to establish a filming center. I would like the World's Fair [of 1984] to be the impetus for New Orleans to become a major filming center in the nation."[20]

Bolton was successful during her tenure. *The Toy* with Richard Pryor and Paul Schrader's *Cat People* were shot in Louisiana.

Carson Productions obviously needed an experienced location scout who knew their way around Louisiana and could recommend parts of New Orleans for certain scenes. One such location scout was David McCarty, whose father worked for the Film Commission at the time. Like almost everybody else in New Orleans, McCarty was familiar with the novel and delighted to be asked to scout locations for a film based on it: "This is one of the most famous books written about New Orleans, one of the few books that really keep true of the New Orleans feeling. It was a two-week scout and a long time before digital. I used to send out file folders."[21]

In these two weeks McCarty went around New Orleans, took many photographs of places that he thought might provide locations for the film, and sent his folders to the production company. Unusually, he was left to his own devices, as a production designer who was supposed to join him in Louisiana never turned up. McCarty found quite a few places he deemed suitable for the adaptation, as he remembers: "Cliff's Lounge was one of them, although it's not in the Quarter. It was in the central business district. The Old Absinthe House [was another place] which was very similar to what would have been the bar where he and his mother would drink. The tie factory Wemco [would serve as the pants factory]. I scouted a lot of the Ninth Ward, [looked at] homes as if they were his homes. You get references to the streets where Ignatius' home was but you never got a specific address where he lived."[22]

It would have to be a pretty grim, shabby building, that much David McCarty knew from the novel's descriptions of Ignatius's and Irene's house: "The address that Patrolman Mancuso was looking for was the tiniest structure on the block, aside from the carports, a Lilliput of the eighties. A frozen banana tree, brown and stricken, languished against the front of the porch, the tree preparing to collapse as the iron fence had done long ago. Near the dead tree there was a slight mound of earth and a leaning Celtic cross cut from plywood. The 1946 Plymouth was parked in the front yard, its bumper pressed against the porch, its taillights blocking the brick sidewalk. But, except for the Plymouth and the weathered cross and the mummified banana tree, the tiny yard was completely bare. There were no shrubs. There was no grass. And no birds sang."[23]

"I scouted the streetcar, the buses, the bus barn," McCarty continues. "I remember specifically scouting the Elysian Fields bus route because that's where he would have gotten from the Ninth Ward to Elysian Fields, downtown to go to D.H. Holmes and the bars.

"Mancuso's house was to be located in a similar area to the Ninth Ward. [I scouted] shotgun style doubles that were not well-kept. I did scout a few others. D.H. Homes at the time didn't have the bakery that they had in the book.

"McKenzie's Pastry Shoppes, I scouted for that. They were a famous New Orleans bakery. In the book, Ignatius even carries something from McKenzie's in a box. In the 80s D.H. Holmes didn't have a bakery anymore. Obviously, [I scouted] all of Canal Street because that was a shopping district in the 60s when he was young."[24]

Since John Kennedy Toole had been very specific with the descriptions of places in *A Confederacy of Dunces*, it was an easy job for McCarty, and one he took great joy in. He was even more delighted that he received encouraging feedback from Carson Productions for the materials he had sent. Then a short while later, he received the fateful call telling him that the project was canceled.

McCarty received a check and moved on to new projects.

VII

It was one of the last location hunts Jo Beth Bolton oversaw—and she would never see *The Toy* released. Before the film's premiere, the Louisiana Film Commission was in a state of shock: on 16 August 1982 Jo Beth Bolton was found dead in her home in New Orleans. Her husband Jim had first shot her and then aimed the gun at himself.

Commerce secretary Ben James said, "Jo Beth's death can only be described in terms of tragedy. Her record of accomplishment reflects the enthusiasm and dedication with which she pursued her work."[25] In December 1982, a special screening of *The Toy* was organized with the proceeds going to the Bolton Educational Trust to benefit her daughters. Upon her death, David McCarty wrote an editorial celebrating Bolton's life and work. This piece touched one of her daughters so much that she thanked McCarty profusely for his kind words. The two of them later started dating and found love that lasted for five years before their relationship ended.[26]

VIII

This, however, wouldn't be David McCarty's last encounter with *A Confederacy of Dunces*. A little more than ten years later, when the project was at Paramount under Scott Rudin, the scout received another call to look for locations for a possible adaptation. This time around, though, McCarty wouldn't even get two weeks to scout locations. Unusually, he did not even receive any paperwork related to this version of *A Confederacy of Dunces*. Nor did he ever see a script, which was at the time still being developed. That was fine with McCarty, who felt assured after his contact at Paramount said: "It stays close to the book. We want to see what your interpretation is of the book."[27]

The location scout was satisfied with that piece of information, and he immediately sent a copy of the files he had put together for Carson Productions. Not much had changed in New Orleans since then—or at least not enough to warrant choosing new locations for every sequence depicted in the novel. For example, the bar McCarty had chosen—the Absinth House—was the same, and the tie factory would still serve as Levy Pants.

Shortly thereafter, McCarty received another phone call from Paramount, informing him that the project had been postponed indefinitely: "I think I only got three days on it. That was very quick because it was like, 'Oh this again.'"[28]

Paramount sent his file folder back, which was lost to Hurricane Katrina in 2005.

IX

But why was *A Confederacy of Dunces* abandoned by Carson Productions in 1982? Already a few months before, the pressure on Kramer was mounting: not only was Thelma Toole getting restless, but so were executives at Carson Productions, as was the director of LSU Press, Les Phillabaum. As early as February 1982 he had confided in Thelma: "We are not too pleased with what little information we have been able to pry loose from Scott Kramer recently. He seems to have made precious little progress."[29]

A few months later pressures involving the film resulted in a full-scale crisis at Carson Productions, an upheaval which would eventually lead to several departures at the company, the sale of the rights for *A Confederacy of Dunces*, and a lot of heart-break for Scott Kramer.

X

Now at Columbia, Frank Price learned about Carson Production's involvement in *A Confederacy of Dunces*, a project he had expressively forbidden them to take on. Feeling betrayed by Wallace Wolf, who had bought the rights behind his back, Price turned to Henry Bushkin to issue a stark warning: Columbia would no longer work with Carson Productions as long as Wolf was employed there. Bushkin took Price's threat seriously and fired Wolf.[30]

The president couldn't simply be let go without severance pay, though. As Sandy Ignon would soon find out, said severance included the film rights to *A Confederacy of Dunce*s: "I happened to look at [Wolf's departure contract] and it said, 'In no way is Alexander Ignon to have anything to do with *A Confederacy of Dunces*,' and [Wally] took it. He was trying to take it. I hit the roof."[31]

INT. HENRY's office. DAY.
SANDY storms in. HENRY is sitting behind his desk.

SANDY
Henry, what the fuck is this?

HENRY
I don't know, I haven't really looked at it.

SANDY
Wally is trying to steal *A Confederacy of Dunces*! He has always
hated it and the only reason he bought it is Frank Price hated it!

SANDY walks down to WALLY'S office.

SANDY
You motherfucker, you chickenshit![32]

"I went into carpenter mode," admits Ignon.

Henry Bushkin was concerned: "Sandy could have thrown the guy out the window, that's how aggravated Sandy became in those days. Sandy also threatened to kill my ex-partner Arnold Kopelson at one time. Actually, I was suspect as whether he would actually carry it out. He has matured. 30 or 40 years later you look at things a little bit differently than you did back then. The emotions don't run that high."[33]

> *If you cannot remember the goal of all things, then you suppose that wicked men have power and luck. And because you have forgotten how the world is ordered, you imagine that there is nothing but the vicissitudes of Fortune. [...] The best cure there is for such a disease as the one afflicting you is a correct understanding of the governance of the world, which is not merely a string of random events but the result of divine reason.*[34]

There was precious little Ignon could do. Wallace Wolf would take the rights to *A Confederacy of Dunces* with him, and with them he would be free to set up production at another studio. Alternatively, he could also make some money by selling his option, avoiding any obligation to engage further in the adaptation of a work he wasn't passionate about anyway.

By this point, Carson Productions had held the rights to the novel for less than a year and already everything was in turmoil. Sandy Ignon left the company shortly after his altercation with Wolf—in any case, working as a vice-president for a studio didn't suit his artistic sensibilities. He was repulsed by how *A Confederacy of Dunces* had been treated, and would grow even more disgusted when he learned what Wolf, an experienced entertainment lawyer, had been able to pull off: Wolf had stripped Scott Kramer of his ownership of *Dunces*.

7

The Two Texans

How two old childhood friends with precious little knowledge of the film industry come together to break into Hollywood for their love of Ignatius J. Reilly

Wallace P. Wolf soon learned that an entrepreneur from Texas was interested in purchasing the movie rights to John Kennedy Toole's book.

John Edward Langdon was the offspring of a wealthy family that had made its fortune in the oil industry. His grandfather was George Munsey Langdon, the first mayor of Van Horn, a small town in Texas. John's father was Jack M. Langdon, a prominent judge, rancher and congressman who sat on the 17th District Court and the Court of Civil Appeals for Tarrant County in Fort Worth.[1]

Born in 1944, John Langdon initially followed in his family's footsteps. He earned a law degree from South Texas College of Law but subsequently became an investor and inventor who, among other things, in the 1960s had come up with the idea for Gropax, a seed starter kit.[2] A specialized machine which planted seeds in compost, and was designed by John and his brother Brian, became his biggest financial success. Moreover, he began founding companies involved in cancer research and treatment, technologies for the recovery of oil, and biomass re-generation.[3]

Yet more than anything, Johnny Langdon wanted to make movies. Much later in his life, in 2007, he founded the Lone Star Film Festival in Fort Worth, where he set up the Johnny Langdon Film Education Initiative to provide training and experience in screenwriting, acting, directing, editing, sound and set design.[4]

His interest in pursuing a career as film producer perplexed some of his friends. His business associate Susan O'Connell recalls: "He really had not seen many movies in his life. It's ironic that he wanted to make movies, but he wasn't a film buff."[5]

But incompetence never prevented Langdon from plunging in with enthusiasm, and thus he founded Bumbershoot Productions, a company with the general goal of investing in art, including music, novels and films. From the beginning, it was clear to him he couldn't undertake this venture by himself and so he included his attorney, Phil Dixon, and also approached an old friend, Maidee Walker.

II

Walker was also from Fort Worth, the daughter of another wealthy family, and a childhood friend of Langdon's. After spending her childhood in Texas, she had

49

traveled the world and experienced many adventures. For a year-and-a-half she had lived in Sydney, before embarking on a tour through Europe.[6] She fell in love with Greville Plugge, the son of British businessman and politician Captain Leonard Frank Plugge, who created the International Broadcasting Company and was a pioneer of long motoring holidays on the European continent. It was to be a love story with a tragic ending: in summer of 1973, while Walker was skiing in Aspen, Greville died in a car accident on the way to Essaouira in Morocco. Maidee Walker and Greville Plugge had planned to get married that autumn.[7]

In the aftermath she moved to Boston, where she was surprised to hear from her old friend Johnny Langdon, who had once also proposed to her. He informed her that he was about to start a production company, but couldn't possibly undertake the venture without her. In 1980 he begged her to come with him to Fort Worth and work on some projects he was toying with.

To say Walker was reluctant is to put it mildly. Considering herself to be a writer first and foremost, she confesses: "I wasn't interested in the whole process of making movies. It didn't interest me. It was laborious and a lot of heartbreak."[8]

There was another reason for her caution: she was aware of the fact that her childhood friend had little to no knowledge of the film industry. "After a long time thinking about this I said, 'Okay.' I went back and got involved in it, but I never thought that this venture with Langdon was going to work." She also feared Langdon was too involved in other undertakings to dedicate himself fully to his new studio: "It was a small operation, and he had other companies to do with oil and gas, some inventions that he liked to invest in, cancer treatments and so forth. He had a lot going on. The movie thing was just something he wanted to do."[9]

It was indeed a very small operation, with Walker (who was named Vice-President of Bumbershoot Productions) and Langdon (the President) the only creative forces on board to devote themselves to any particular project.

III

While Maidee Walker was skeptical about John Langdon's business venture, she also saw Bumbershoot Productions as an opportunity. She had read *A Confederacy of Dunces* and recommended it to her new business partner. He loved it. Langdon found the novel hysterically funny, and the character of Ignatius reminded him of a dear childhood friend who had since passed.

George had grown into a free-spirited, rebellious young man, full of mischief, and the subject of many funny stories who became a constant source of amusement. Langdon would regularly tell his children about his friend George—he was similar to Ignatius in that he was a rebel, an anti-authoritarian, someone who didn't try to fit into society. As a boy, with his parents out of town for the weekend, George got rid of all the furniture in the house, selling parts of it and putting the rest in storage. When his parents came back, they found the house empty.[10] "George was a brilliant, talented person who went into the wrong direction," says Anne Livet, Langdon's third wife. "He couldn't stand the hypocrisy of people. It was worse in the time he grew up in. He saw through things."[11]

While in the prime of his life George one day traveled to Vegas. Following his stint in a casino, he was roughed up by gangsters associated with the mob who tried to collect money from him. During and after an extended stay in a hospital the young man suffered excruciating pain for months. Eventually, he decided to take his own life. Driving fast on the freeway, he turned into an access road and met a premature death.[12] John Langdon never came to terms with his friend's passing.

IV

As an admirer of the book, Maidee Walker knew how hard it would be to turn it into a film. She recognized multiple challenges early on, the most obvious of which being Ignatius himself. How to capture the anti-hero in all his complexities and contradictions? It is a difficult challenge, as stage director David Esbjornson wrote in his character breakdown of *A Confederacy of Dunces*:

> A complex and contradictory character driven by insecurity and a profound need to be accepted on his own terms. Extremely over-weight with an eccentric and somewhat baffling approach to fashion. He is self-aggrandizing and aggressive in his world-view and his ego often spins out of control. He loves words and the sound of his own voice. The role requires skills in language, an innate sense of timing, good physical skills.[13]

It was vital that Ignatius be blisteringly funny on screen. After all, he had become a cultural, comic icon because of his contradictions, flaws which have made many readers empathize with this bumbling anti-hero, confident that there is an Ignatius J. Reilly in all of us.

V

Ignatius is a more complex character than he might initially appear, for he is not just a possibly autistic hobby philosopher so much as a modern-day Don Quixote. Despite the impression Ignatius gives in his interactions with people—he can't help but lecture, demean and insult—he clearly desires to be liked and can't help but become emotional as the possibility of achieving that goal becomes increasingly distant. When a group of women make fun of him he is suddenly at a loss as to what to say, "his lips quivering" while he prepares "another hot dog to quiet his trembling nervous system."[14] He also clearly wants the factory workers at Levy to like him when he—uncharacteristically—starts to dance for their amusement.[15]

At certain times, mostly in his writings, Ignatius shows a surprising degree of self-insight and self-reflection: "Myrna was, you see, terribly engaged in her society; I, on the other hand, older and wiser, was terribly dis-engaged."[16] At other times he appears blind to social conventions. Ignatius may not have deserved the severe beating he received at the hands of the three lesbians at Dorian Greene's party, but he certainly could have prevented the attack had he been able to read the room and stand back, rather than insist on spelling out his political talking points. Clearly, nobody was interested.

Ignatius is deeply unhappy, and while he would never admit as much to other people, he is at least open about it to himself, writing at one point: "To be quite honest, I must say that since then things have been getting worse and worse. Conditions have deteriorated. Minkoff, my passionless flame, has turned upon me. Even my mother, the agent of my destruction, has begun to bite the hand that feeds her. My cycle is dipping lower and lower. Oh, Fortuna, you capricious sprite!"[17] And while Iggy allegedly has an "eye on the magazine market,"[18] and is clearly proud of his written work, it appears that deep down he doesn't want to succeed as a published author. He doesn't have enough self-knowledge, though, to face this question head-on. Instead, he only wonders briefly "why he had failed to send any of [his essays] off, for each was excellent in its own way."[19]

VI

Ignatius is not easy to pin down as a character. So well-drawn is he that beneath the shell of a bumbling fool is a complex character full of contradictions—and one which hasn't been as carefully drawn in any of the screenplays as in the novel.

The difficulty of capturing Ignatius in any adaptation becomes clear in his choice of literature: as a devotee of Boethius, Ignatius constantly references *The Consolation of Philosophy*. Yet what an odd choice the philosopher is for a character like Ignatius. As Jonathan Haidt and Greg Lukianoff point out in their book *The Coddling of the American Mind*, *The Consolation of Philosophy* is, in essence, an early example for Cognitive Behavioral Therapy (CBT): "In *The Consolation of Philosophy*, written in his jail cell, [Boethius] describes his (imaginary) encounter with 'Lady Philosophy,' who visits him one night and conducts what is essentially a session of cognitive behavioral therapy (CBT). She chides him gently for his moping, fearfulness, and bitterness at his reversal of fortune, and then she helps him to reframe his thinking and shut off his negative emotions."[20]

CBT teaches positive thinking and, therefore, optimism—something Ignatius does not have any patience with. As he says to Irene: "I refuse to 'look up.' Optimism nauseates me. It is perverse. Since man's fall, his proper position in the universe has been one of misery."[21]

Lady Philosophy clearly still has a lot of work ahead of her, as much as Ignatius may believe in the role of the Wheel of Fortune.

VII

While Ignatius immerses himself in reading philosophy and writing articulate intellectual essays and sarcastic diary entries, he occasionally displays the sweetness of a child. He might not want to admit it, but there is a gentle playfulness in him that wants out and sometimes does emerge—when he takes a bath, for example: "Occasionally he held the soap dish down until it filled with water and sank. Then he would feel for it on the bottom of the tub, empty it, and sail it again."[22]

Similarly, he enjoys watching Yogi Bear on television[23] and is up to date with pop culture—far from rejecting out of hand phenomena which capture the zeitgeist and the mainstream's attention: "I recommend Batman especially, for he tends to transcend the abysmal society in which he he's found himself. His morality is rather rigid, also. I rather respect Batman."[24]

His childlike sweetness is not only expressed when he is alone, but also in his fondness for some animals, although there is a creepiness expressed in his affection when he "tried to trap the cat in the bun compartment and take it home for a pet."[25]

While tender moments with his mother Irene are rare and brief (when he kisses her goodbye and expresses concern about her going bowling despite her arthritis),[26] Ignatius seems to find an ersatz mother in Miss Trixie. Finally he has found somebody who he can care for, and does so with great tenderness, even going "on his knees changing Miss Trixie's socks."[27] Surprisingly, the man who does not appreciate being touched suddenly has no qualms about letting the octogenarian wear his beloved cap—"for she has taken to wearing it rather than her celluloid visor on occasion."[28]

Ignatius is a devoted moviegoer—much like John Kennedy Toole was himself—and always excited to catch the newest products shown at the Prytania. More often than not this involves a fair bit of masochism, for he likes to watch Doris Day's films only in order to complain loudly about them. He doesn't appear to respect Hollywood's efforts to any extent: "I have sought escape in the Prytania on more than one occasion, pulled by the attractions of some technicolored horrors, filmed abortions that were offenses against any criteria of taste and decency, reels and reels of perversion and blasphemy that stunned my disbelieving eyes."[29]

But an intellectual like Ignatius cannot be satisfied with arthouse fare either: when the local cinema decides to show a Swedish drama our hero is outraged and decides to "speak with the manager of the theater about booking such dull fare."[30] Indeed, Ignatius is hard to satisfy, and little besides hot dogs, Batman and Yogi Bear can tame his aggression for an all too brief moment.

VIII

His relationship with Myrna Minkoff is just as complicated as his relationship with his mother. Again, it is impossible to summarize in a single sentence, or even in a few. Myrna and Ignatius experienced great satisfaction humiliating Dr. Talc at university, showcasing a mean-spiritedness which contributes greatly to the novel's bleakness: "Your total ignorance of that which you profess to teach merits the death penalty. [...] Pray to him, you deluded fool, you 'anyone for tennis?' golf-playing, cocktail-quaffing pseudo-pedant, for you do indeed need a heavenly patron."[31]

Although he wouldn't like to admit it, Ignatius is influenced by Myrna a great deal, and they are more similar than they think. She egged him on when it came to humiliating their professor and clearly inspired him in his protests ("A recent communication from her was bolder and more offensive than usual. She must be dealt with on her own level, and thus I thought of her as I surveyed the sub-standard conditions in the factory. Too long have I confined myself in the Miltonic isolation and meditation. It is clearly time for me to step boldly into our society, not in the boring, passive manner of the Myrna Minkoff school of social action, but with great style and zest."[32])

When Ignatius isn't busy getting politically educated by his "dear friend,"[33] he actively contemplates means of "destroying" her.[34] Moreover, while Ignatius is repelled by Myrna's sexually liberated lifestyle, he clearly wants to impress her, taking a camera with him to his protest at Levy's Pants, pondering: "Myrna would choke on her espresso when she saw this."[35] A little later, Toole gives his readers a variation on that exact thought, writing, "How Myrna would gnaw at her espresso cup rim in envy,"[36] as Ignatius "for a wild and very fleeting moment, pondered an affair." Is he not that asexual after all? When he discovers the pornographic pictures distributed by George on behalf of the Night of Joy, and ogles them with wonder, the stimulus is clearly Boethius, while visions of his beloved Rex finally make him decide to grab his erect penis and masturbate feverishly.[37]

IX

Part of Langdon's affection for characters such as Ignatius (and George) came from his own upbringing on the hands of his father, and served as a reaction against it: Jack M. Langdon was a judge feared for his strict rulings, while his mother was a philanthropist who provided scholarships to musicians. His father, upholder of law and order, couldn't have been more different from his artistically minded mother.[38] Their son would continue to support artists throughout his life.

His friend, John Holt Smith, a lawyer working in Los Angeles at the time, remembers Langdon's ranch in downtown Fort Worth, which seemed to him an especially curious art gallery: "His house was very eclectic and full of odd collections of art from local artists; people who you might admire but mostly rather say, 'Well, that's not art.' John liked eccentric things."[39]

Langdon's assistant, Analisa Garcia, concurs: "He was sort of eccentric, very moralistic and idealistic. He was a really good guy. He had a lot of passion and a lot of optimism. He always thought he would get everything done. He wasn't someone you would see and immediately call eccentric. Maybe his idealism and his commitment to the things he found important were rare. He wasn't a quitter. He kept on with his passion projects for years without any defeatism. He just kept going."[40]

Susan O'Connell, who joined Bumbershoot Productions in 1992, found similarities between Ignatius and Langdon himself: "He was an amazing, wonderful, crazy guy. I think he was attracted to Ignatius because he was kind of like Ignatius. He understood the lunacy, the wonderful optimistic lunacy of people. That's who Johnny was."[41] Unfortunately, it would take more than lunacy to succeed with an adaptation of *A Confederacy of Dunces*.

X

Initially, Langdon was lucky: John Holt Smith mentioned to him that, following a tumultuous and rather short period at Carson Productions, the rights to the novel which he loved so very much happened to be available. Thus in the early summer of 1982 Smith introduced Langdon to Henry Bushkin, who in turn put him in touch with Wallace P. Wolf. Wolf then drafted a contract between himself and Langdon.[42] Scott Kramer's name was not mentioned anywhere—Carson had entered into an agreement with LSU Press in July 1981 and they therefore had the option and, for a limited period of time, could do with the rights whatever they desired.

With Langdon's signature, Wally Wolf had unburdened himself from the project—its destiny was now in somebody else's hands. Wolf continued to work as an attorney, also in 1982 serving as the co-founder of the Los Padres Savings Bank in Santa Ynez Valley. In March 1997 he committed suicide, jumping off the Cold Springs Bridge on Highway 154 at the top of the San Marcos Pass. He was 66 years old.[43]

XI

In autumn of 1982 a deal between Bumbershoot and Carson was struck, though already in May, the entrepreneur from Texas and his associate producer Harry Friedman had traveled to New Orleans to speak with natives about their plans to further develop the by then already famous novel.[44]

Langdon paid $130,000 for the option. Kramer was furious. He was convinced he had been cheated over the rights to the property. Nevertheless, there was precious little he could do. What Kramer had hoped would be a smooth ride had degenerated into a nightmare, and he felt defeated by the setbacks. Although he loved the book, he also wanted to pursue other projects. After all, he was still employed as an executive at Fox, a job which took up a considerable amount of his energies. However, his time at the company would end soon.

By 1983 a lot of the executives at Twentieth Century–Fox had changed. Paul Mazursky had already left the company, and Scott Kramer's contract would only last for a few more months,[45] and by that point the rights to *A Confederacy of Dunces* were no longer his.

Sandy Ignon felt bad for Kramer and, in hindsight, regrets ever putting him in touch with Carson Productions: "He became bitter over it because of the Carson film thing. I guess I am tainted by the Carson thing because I am the one who got him in."[46]

Was that good fortune so dear to you, even though you should have understood that it couldn't be trusted and was, therefore, never really yours? You should have recognized that it was never in your control and that the visit of the unreliable goddess is a sure sign of misery to come.[47]

XII

Langdon, on the other hand, was over the moon about his recent acquisition. As the president of his own company he could rely on the help and expertise of various friends who knew their way around the film business. This group included John Holt Smith—who had brokered the deal between Langdon and Wally Wolf—and Roderick Taylor, a young screenwriter.

Taylor, born in 1950, had been introduced to Langdon through their mutual friend Gary Burton, who had given Langdon a script of Taylor's called *Empire Man*. The film-to-be told the story of a Texas underdog, a televangelist who wants to lead his fellow Americans to self-actualization and ends up being elected to the U.S. Senate.[48] Langdon loved the script, committed to making the film with Bumbershoot Productions, and became close friends with Roderick Taylor. Since the writer had already garnered a lot of experience in Hollywood, he took on an unofficial position as adviser to Langdon.

Taylor quickly became aware that his new friend had a naivety that on the one hand endeared him to the screenwriter forever, but on the other made it an uphill battle to produce a movie with him. Taylor remembers: "John had actual tenacity on an incredible scale. You couldn't beat it out of him because of all the years he stayed involved in all these projects. That was an incredible virtue. If he would have only been a bit more aware of the way these situations work.... John stood in awe and amazement at the injustice that confronts you in the Hollywood system. He would say, 'That's the best script!' Yeah, they don't care."[49]

While being under contract at Universal, the writer had experienced how the system is run: "The first time I did television I thought I am going to revolutionize the business. 'These people have seen nothing!' I was astonished to find out they don't want that. They want the same old thing. They want the same thing in the same way from the same people. It is a business. At the same time I thought I could cheat them and do something that would enhance the human race. They were not interested in that dimension."[50] Rather than rallying against the injustices of the film industry, as Ignatius would have done, Taylor quietly accepted the way things work in Hollywood.

John Langdon was very different from the typical Hollywood producer. He was an idealist, always eager to support artists and their projects if he became enamored with them. Despite—or because of—the Texan's ignorance about the conventions of La La Land, Roderick Taylor loved working and spending time with the entrepreneur: "He was a wildcatter and he would take this wild, wild chances. I miss the hell out of his presence in the world."[51]

In traveling to Fort Worth for the first time to visit Langdon at his home, Taylor got introduced to the Texan lifestyle. At Langdon's place, a ranch near the now defunct Carswell Air Force Base, the California-based screenwriter also met Maidee Walker for the first time. After a few days in Fort Worth, though, Taylor felt like having been put through the wringer. Walker, Langdon, and a business associate of Langdon's consumed alcohol, nicotine and cocaine as if they were oxygen.[52] A few days of this and Taylor felt like checking himself into a rehab clinic. Despite this, Taylor found the Texans welcoming people of great intellect and interest in other people's lives and work. They, on the other hand, were not interested in listening to Taylor's advice.

8

Manufacturing Dissent

How John Langdon decides not to listen to good advice, he and Maidee
Walker feel the wrath of Thelma, and a script finally begins to be written

When Bumbershoot Productions was formed Langdon hired several high-profile attorneys from Los Angeles and set up a board meeting in Dallas. Their plan was to entice Hollywood's Creative Artists Agency (CAA) to come on board, using the company to package talent and negotiate deals between Bumbershoot and the Hollywood studios. It was not an unusual approach at the time, a period when CAA grew to become the most powerful talent agency in the film business.

In Roderick Taylor's view, though, this was the wrong approach—it would unnecessarily complicate Bumbershoot's plans to break into the motion picture industry, especially since Langdon's knowledge of how Hollywood worked was next to non-existent. He wasn't shy to voice his concern at the board meeting. As he remembers: "[I said to John]: 'I want to say something that's going to be unpopular here, but I don't think you should be spending all this money to court CAA. Just take a million dollars and make this movie. Then you will understand everything and people will come to *you*.' It was the best advice I ever gave anybody. But he wouldn't do it. Too many people talked to him."[1]

Instead of following Taylor's advice, Langdon decided to pursue another idea to finance *A Confederacy of Dunces* as well as other projects he was toying with for Bumbershoot. He decided to go on tours to collect money.

The first of these tours was devoted to *Blind Faith*, a Roderick Taylor-scripted comedy of which 15 minutes had already been shot and which starred a young Daryl Hannah. In order to finance the rest of the picture Langdon and Taylor traveled through New Orleans, New York City, Los Angeles and Texas. With events hosted to promote the project, the duo showed the available footage and gave out private placement memorandums (a funding round of securities sold through private offerings) to the attendees.[2] Through Robert Strauss, then chairman of the Texas Democratic Party, Langdon arranged to gather some of the richest people in and around Houston. They were supposed to buy $10,000 shares which would enable the producer to finish *Blind Faith*.[3]

Although the auditorium was packed and potential investors were intrigued about the film, few people would bite after having inspected the private placement memorandum more closely. They had a good reason, as Roderick Taylor explains: "The reality is that the fathers, bankers or trust lawyers of younger people, who would get enthused about it, would say, 'In the movie business they won't promise you a thing.' They would read the private placement memorandum which was nothing but a monument to disclaimers by the attorney who created them. It's not something that encourages anyone to invest. They would say, 'I love it,' but the memorandum says, 'We are not even going to promise we will make the movie, much less distribute it.' It makes it very hard because you rarely meet people who don't have somebody else offering their opinion."[4]

Although *A Confederacy of Dunces* was already a beloved book by 1982, the same problem would arise when Langdon tried to get funding from private investors for an adaptation of Toole's work. Nevertheless, late that year he was still euphoric about the project and convinced he could raise the necessary money. He estimated the budget to lie between $5 million and $7 million, saying, "We'll be able to do it for that [...] because it will be shot almost entirely in New Orleans where the novel is based. New Orleans is like a set anyway."[5]

He went on to explain that all the rights were in order, contrary to Scott Kramer's impression: "We're exercising our option with the book's publisher, LSU Press. Then we'll raise pre-production money to get the screenplay written. [...] We keep hearing that nothing has been done in the past because it's too difficult to create a screenplay from this work. Our feeling is that, with the people we have in mind, the story already exists. And it's incredible. The writers have to understand the South, however, and that's what we'll insist on. It will be a great screenplay."[6]

II

Although John Langdon didn't know much about the inner workings of a film studio, he realized that he was in no position to pay for every aspect of the production out of his own pocket, and so the Texan busied himself with preparations for his *A Confederacy of Dunces* tour. Indeed, a large chunk of 1982 was devoted to securing financing, and Langdon approached his friend, entrepreneur Johann Bultman.

With others, Bultman was, in 1998, to found the New Orleans Musicians' Clinic, which would provide health services to artists in need. Bultman knew his way around New Orleans and had many influential friends, which was just what Langdon needed. So the entrepreneur asked Bultman to recruit 30 people who were willing to invest at least $5,000 each in his *A Confederacy of Dunces* project.[7] The Bumbershoot president wanted to travel to New Orleans in June to speak with potential investors and convince them of his project. Similarly to his approach to his other (unfinished) feature, he planned to give out memorandums and show a clip from *Blind Faith*.

However, shortly before the meeting with wealthy individuals was to take place, Langdon first postponed and then canceled his trip. Only a few days before he was due to make his appearance in New Orleans, he had to concede that he had failed to sign the necessary papers required in order to conduct his business in the state of Louisiana. This was a problem that hadn't been sorted when he announced his trip to the local press.[8]

John Langdon had no better luck with another idea: after his plan to get investors in New Orleans involved had failed, he and Maidee Walker decided to try sell $10,000 limited partnership units in the film.[9] Langdon wanted to rely on wealthy friends in Texas, where he was well connected to businessmen and successful, established artists.[10] However, not enough money could be collected, despite Langdon knowing several millionaires and billionaires who lived in Fort Worth.

> *You ascend? Fine! But you must acknowledge that it can't be wrong for you to have to descend again. You were not unaware of how a wheel works.*[11]

Still, Langdon wasn't yet ready to approach big studios. He wanted to keep *A Confederacy of Dunces* close to his chest and not let busybodies from Los Angeles interfere in his creative vision.

III

Langdon would have found a backer in a studio had he been open to it. News travel fast in the film industry, and most literate studio heads were aware of the fact that Bumbershoot Productions held the movie rights to Toole's novel.

One producer who was desperate to get his hands on the rights was Robert Chartoff, who, in 1983, would produce *The Right Stuff*. Before that, he had fallen in love with the tale of a medievalist waddling through New Orleans like an elephant in a glass menagerie.

Chartoff was aware it would be a difficult novel to adapt, but he knew just the right man for the job: Stephen Geller had written the script for *Slaughterhouse-Five*, George Roy Hill's 1972 adaptation of Kurt Vonnegut's classic novel. Like *A Confederacy of Dunces*, *Slaughterhouse-Five* was challenging for any screenwriter, for reasons that are obvious to everybody who has read Vonnegut's dark satire.

Chartoff called up Geller, confident the writer would be able to handle an adaptation of Toole's novel, but the producer ran into a wall soon enough.

Geller remembers: "There were a pair of Texans who had bought the rights to the book for [what was] a considerable sum at that time. That was in the early 80s. Bob wanted to get the rights and asked me whether I wanted to write the script. I met with [Maidee Walker], the woman who was the partner in that transaction, and she said, 'We are not selling it until we get what we want!' She was adamant about it. I didn't understand what all the emotion was about. Bob Chartoff never got the rights. It didn't make any sense to me. I only assumed they didn't have any background in making films."[12]

IV

As it turns out, Stephen Geller was right: the pair of Texans didn't have any background in making films. John Holt Smith tried to help his friend as much as he could by introducing him to attorneys and producers in Hollywood, but he soon realized that John Langdon wasn't willing to compromise. Hollywood executives and a Texas entrepreneur were chalk and cheese, says Holt Smith: "It's very hard for a non–Hollywood guy, or a guy who is not really connected, to get things done. They are happy to sell you rights, but it's very hard for you to become the producer of a film in Hollywood. It's a local boy's club, just like if you went to scout oil in Texas. You better get a Texas partner, otherwise you are just a target. It's similar in Hollywood. It's a local club. My advice for him was [to say]: 'You need to find a producer who has done things.' But John was very independent."[13]

Hoping to find an independent backer, in 1984 Langdon met with Steve Tisch in Los Angeles. Tisch, born in 1949, was a producer who had left Columbia Pictures in 1976 and financed Tom Cruise's first big success, *Risky Business*, seven years later. Over lunch, Langdon managed to interest Tisch in his vision for *A Confederacy of Dunces*. The businessman agreed to produce the venture and then waited for further instructions from his Texan counterpart.[14] The collaboration between them would never take a place—an agreement was never drafted. Tisch would remain busy with other projects. In 2005, he was named chairman and Executive Vice President of the New York Giants football team.

V

Money aside, the biggest obstacle at this time was that John Langdon, despite his pompous announcements to the press, still didn't have a script to show. He toyed with the idea of commissioning his friend Roderick Taylor to pen a draft, but never broached the subject with him.

Although Taylor would have been happy to give *A Confederacy of Dunces* a try, he was aware that transforming the novel into a screenplay would be a massive challenge: "That book is so expansive in a way, full of rich characters, it may be difficult for most writers, most screenwriters even, to thread a needle. A lot of the non-essential secondary plot observations in the book are very amusing and enriching. If you pair it down you got to really work hard to keep it all together."[15]

Roderick Taylor stayed involved in Bumbershoot for a while in other capacities, using his deal with Universal to discuss a co-venture with Langdon's company. Sean Daniels was president of Universal at the time and, as such, regularly sat down with Taylor as his writer to discuss future projects. Roderick Taylor remembers one of his meetings with Daniels:

INT. RESTAURANT. LOS ANGELES. DAY
RODERICK and SEAN sit at a table,
lunch plates in front of them.

RODERICK
I know some guys who just bought the rights to
A Confederacy of Dunces.

SEAN
Yeah, I have heard a lot about this book.
Who do you see starring in it?

RODERICK
(beat) John Candy would be great.

Camera pans to the door. JOHN CANDY walks in,
sees SEAN, comes over.

JOHN
Hey, what are you talking about?

<u>SEAN</u>
A Confederacy of Dunces.

<u>JOHN</u>
(laughs)

<u>SEAN</u>
Would you be interested in being in it?

<u>JOHN</u>
I would love to be Ignatius J. Reilly![16]

"We had a brief chat and then he walked away," Taylor commences. "Sean gets that serious bearing-down-on-you look and says, 'You have those guys call me today!' In other words, we were sitting there with a movie. We had the book, the star, the studio!"[17]

Taylor was as excited as if he himself had just received the Pulitzer Prize. Immediately, he called up Langdon to tell him the good news: with John Candy as Ignatius J. Reilly, Universal would finance *A Confederacy of Dunces* and their project was a go!

Langdon was less excited. Politely, he informed Taylor he didn't like John Candy and had no interest meeting with him or anybody at Universal.[18]

The writer was dumbstruck. Instead of slamming down the receiver, Taylor politely asked who would meet Langdon's approval for the role. Without missing a beat, the entrepreneur mentioned Robin Williams, then an upcoming star who had entranced audiences nationwide with his portrayal of Mork in *Mork and Mindy*.

Taylor was less sure about Williams as Ignatius, but that wasn't the biggest issue for him, as he explains: "Sure, Robin Williams was great and he could put on a fat-suit, but it was even harder to get Robin Williams to read something. We didn't have a script! A guy like that is always going to say to you, 'I would like to see a script.' That's the first level of reality."[19]

It was the first time John Candy had been suggested in relation to *A Confederacy of Dunces*, but it wouldn't be the last. In fact, until his unfortunate passing, the actor would from now on remain associated in one way or another with the project.

VI

While the script—or rather, the absence of one—remained a problem, Langdon had another challenge on his hands. He hadn't foreseen that, regardless of any other steps he took, there was one person he would inevitably have to deal with: Thelma Toole.

Thelma was less than pleased about the fact that a company from Fort Worth had bought the rights to the screen adaptation of her son's masterpiece. For her, Bumbershoot was clearly a step down from having Johnny Carson associated with the project. Now she would have to deal with a company from Fort Worth that she had never heard of. Furthermore, "bumbershoot" was a slang for "umbrella" and certainly didn't have an elegant ring to it.[20] Worst of all, Thelma had a sense of déjà vu all over again because the person who had bought the rights to her son's work had failed to get immediately in touch with her and—much to her outrage—hire her as a consultant on the film. Instead, she read about Bumbershoot's acquisition in a newspaper article. In an angry letter sent to Bumbershoot Productions in 1983, she vented:

The trite expression "Let me introduce myself" is not apropos, because we are affiliated with a masterpiece novel and Pulitzer Prize winner to be made into an epic picture.

I am Thelma Ducoing Toole, mother of the scholarly and literary genius, John Kennedy Toole. It was surprisingly unpleasant that you did not contact me when you visited New Orleans for publicity and fundraising. You must remember that I am "Owner of the Book" by inheritance and the valiant search I made for ten years seeking publication. With the espousal of Dr. Walker Percy we succeeded triumphantly. You did not tender the courtesy and respect due.

Based on sixteen years of Speech and Dramatic Art training and fifty years of highly professional teaching, I am requesting to be made consultant to the director. I know and love New Orleans. I can be of estimable value.

It is with eagerness that I await your reply.[21]

You are unhappy because you have lost those things in which you took pleasure? But you can also take comfort in the likelihood that what is now making you miserable will also pass away. You enter this situation in life for the first time, a newcomer and a stranger. But part of you always knew that there is no constancy in human affairs, and that time brings change inevitably.[22]

John Langdon and Maidee Walker were dumbfounded to receive Thelma's angry letter. It was true, they hadn't contacted her, but that was because they hadn't seen any need to. After all, they didn't need Thelma's permission to adapt *A Confederacy of Dunces*. "She didn't like that. It's a tough world,"[23] recalls Maidee Walker, but she and Langdon decided to pay her a visit after all, to "tender the courtesy and respect due."

Visiting the elderly lady at her home in Elysian Fields was a sight to behold for Walker and Langdon, who were used to vastly different lifestyles.

"The whole thing was a complete shrine," remembers Walker. "It was all *A Confederacy of Dunces* and John Kennedy Toole and Ignatius. There were posters and pictures everywhere. The manuscript was there. The whole thing was a shrine to *A Confederacy of Dunces* and her son."[24]

It was not a pleasant visit per se, although the vice-president of Bumbershoot found herself highly amused by the "Owner of the Book by inheritance." Walker continues: "We went over there and met with her to tell her that we wanted to make this movie. She was enthusiastic, but she was also very hands-on. It was all about, 'Mine, mine, mine!' In her mind she was trying to decide if she wanted us to be involved in her movie. I don't know that that decision was ever made, to tell you the truth. I could see her kind of looking at me [as if she was saying]: 'I am not sure if I like you or not.' She was almost comical in the way that she was sassing you out, seeing whether she liked you or not. I would not have wanted her in my life, I'll put it that way."[25]

Thelma had pretty clear ideas about who she wanted to be involved in the project. Not only did she want to be a consultant on the film, but she suggested John Huston as the director. It was an idea that was never seriously considered by Bumbershoot.

Walker and Langdon left Elysian Fields both bemused and nervous. They were bemused because Thelma *was* funny and certainly had kept them entertained. They were nervous because the tiny house in New Orleans with its shrine to Ken and Ignatius was grim and gloomy, and because they knew Thelma would be tenacious in her efforts to get her way. Although neither one of them kept Thelma updated about every small step they took, Walker sent her a kind letter—in which information regarding her plans for *A Confederacy of Dunces* was so vague as to be non-existent:

Dear Mrs. Toole,

It is inexcusable that I have taken so long to write to you ... please accept my apologies. I had wanted to write you a very special note rather than the usual "business type letter" for your gracious hospitality ... and the time somehow slipped away. That always seems the case when there is more to say than is possible. You are such a wonderful and genteel lady.... I wrote you many letters in my mind that never made it down on paper. Please forgive me....

After our delightful visit in New Orleans, Johnny and I have been working like mad between Texas and Los Angeles. We have been working very hard and, with a little luck, we should have some news to report to you very soon. You would be so pleased at all of the applause and acclaim we hear at every turn about *A Confederacy of Dunces*. It is truly one of the most important literary works of the century.... Therefore, the motion picture must do the work justice at every turn. I am honored to be associated with it ... and with you.

Again, Mrs. Toole, thank you so much for such a lovely evening with you and your friends. And, please know how much it meant to both Johnny and me ... and how very special you are to us. I hope this letter finds you well and happy and I will be in touch very soon. Here's to our success together!!

With love,
Maidee Walker[26]

VII

Following the publication of the novel, Thelma spent a large part of her time giving interviews and receiving her son's fans. By the time John Langdon had optioned the rights to the novel, she was used to being invited onto television shows, to elegant dinner parties, and to receiving friendly phone calls from admirers of *A Confederacy of Dunces*—hence her initial wrath directed at the two Texans.

Certainly, there was no shortage of writers who wanted to try their hands at an adaptation of *A Confederacy of Dunces*. Throughout the '80s and early '90s, many fans wrote scripts on spec and sent them to Bumbershoot Productions. One such writer who sought to transform his love for Toole's novel into professional work was John Schulte.

Schulte came from Ohio but moved to Oklahoma as part of his father's quest to eventually settle in California. His son moved to the state in the mid–'80s where he worked as a freelance writer. Later, he started working for Playmates Toys.

Schulte became part of the group that made *Teenage Mutant Ninja Turtles* popular worldwide: along with friends, he pitched the idea of turning the comic book heroes into toys and an animated series.[27] Since the original comic books were dark and gruesome Schulte conducted a market study and tried to figure out how to best reimagine the franchise for kids.

It wasn't something the U.S. market was ready for in the '80s. And so *Teenage Mutant Ninja Turtles* became an entertainment property through an initial miniseries that became a sleeper hit when it was re-run in syndication. Schulte's true passion, though, was writing scripts, and his freelance status allowed him to devote a good chunk of his time to develop ideas for films.

The biggest place in Schulte's heart was taken by *A Confederacy of Dunces*: "I fell in love with the novel immediately. The thing that grabbed me the most was the satire that is prevalent throughout the book and the abundance of adjectives. It was so over the top and effusive. It was quite cinematic. There were so many incongruous and seemingly disconnected scenes that didn't particular amount to anything but that made it to this groundbreaking piece of literature that really wanted to be a movie. But I understood completely why it might not work."[28]

9

A Fan Gets Involved

How a young writer makes the trek to New Orleans and gets his first impression of what he imagines the film business must be like, while Maidee Walker clashes with John Langdon

Initially, John Schulte wrote a few scenes for an adaptation of *A Confederacy of Dunces* but, since he didn't have any rights to the novel, didn't dare to develop a full script. Already in late 1982, he wondered whether it was possible to buy the rights.

One way of finding out was to contact Thelma Toole, something he had wanted to do anyway, simply to satisfy his curiosity. After all, it was Ken's mother who had managed to get the book published, and surely she had many interesting things to say about the novel and her deceased son.

Schulte was hopeful when he called Thelma in New Orleans. It was February 1983, and the young fan was immediately dumbfounded by what he heard her say—or what he didn't hear her say: "She told me that the rights had been reverted back to her because nobody had come up with the option money on it, and her agent had a first right refusal out to a couple of different production companies. I wanted to seize that opportunity and get down to see her. As it turned out she was either ill-informed or I didn't understand what she was saying because it was long distance and she was talking a mile a minute about everything else under the sun."[1]

By February 1983, the rights had already been acquired by Bumbershoot Productions, a fact Thelma did point out to Schulte when he went to see her in person a few weeks later. A visit on which he brought two close friends.

Jacques Louis was an aspiring writer who, battling suicidal thoughts himself (and whose actual name was Jack Lewis), was fascinated by Ken Toole's life, while Tim Boggs, a college friend of Schulte's, simply sensed an exciting opportunity for an interview. All three of them found themselves in Elysian Fields, and shared the same impression of the tiny house as Michael J. Nathanson, Maidee Walker and John Langdon had before them.

Schulte later wrote, "The hothouse atmosphere of Thelma's domain was immediately and oppressively evident the moment we stepped into her diminutive, overstuffed, and rundown parlor. Ken's mother had turned this squalid room into a shrine to her posthumously famous son. Posters of anti-hero Ignatius and photographs of John Kennedy Toole covered every wall, sprinkled with pictures of Thelma herself."[2]

The way she was dressed, Thelma wouldn't have appeared out of place in *The Wizard of Oz*: she wore a gold lamé caftan with a round white-yellow hat and waved a golden fairy wand that she had been given when she was named Queen of the Krew of Klone's at Mardi Gras. She couldn't have been more affable towards Schulte and his friends, though, who were all fans of her son's work.

Thelma was only too happy to help: Schulte asked again about the movie rights, and she informed him about Bumbershoot Productions. For her guests, there was no doubt she didn't appreciate the name, but she suggested Schulte get in touch with John Langdon and Maidee Walker—it was the latter who was supposed to be working on an early draft of the adaptation.

Schulte seized this chance and, a little later, met with Maidee Walker in Fort Worth. He had several things on his chest, as he remembers: "One of the reasons why I met up with Maidee Walker was the notion about how do you crack this nut and get to the core of what *A Confederacy of Dunces* is all about. It's one of the reasons why Hollywood has continually fumbled and failed. It completely missed the secret ingredients of what *A Confederacy of Dunces* is all about, and it's that sense of chaos, a collection of really eccentric characters that are all at a common place at a common time. The ringleader is of course Ignatius. It didn't have a Hollywood ending. None of the ingredients are there that make it a typical Hollywood movie. But the way it was written was quite cinematic. That dichotomy of how to address the creative [aspect] of it was what compelled me to do something with it."[3]

II

Naturally, writing a script for the film was a difficult undertaking. Before Walker tried her hand at an adaptation, Langdon had inquired about several other writers who might be suited to the material.

John Holt Smith, his friend with a deep-rooted love for literature, had suggested Roy Blount, Jr., a writer and humorist. Blount was a Southerner who had been Smith's roommate at college, and who would go on to write several acclaimed novels, essays and short stories, as well as a screenplay for *Larger Than Life*, a comedy starring Bill Murray which premiered in 1996. Smith explains: "I always thought that the guy who could write this was Roy Blount, Jr. It always seemed it would take a Southerner to write the screenplay."[4] Langdon, however, never consulted Blount.

Of course, Roy Blount, Jr., had already read the book. In fact, he had already been contacted by somebody else who had his own plans for an adaptation of *A Confederacy of Dunces*: Henry Gibson.

By the early 1980s, Gibson was a regular American film and TV presence. The actor had appeared in Robert Altman's *Nashville* and in John Landis's *Blues Brothers* alongside John Belushi and Dan Aykroyd. As soon as Gibson had read Toole's novel, he was certain that Toole's writing offered first-class material for a film. But in order to make that project a reality, Gibson needed to acquire the rights and find a screenwriter—and these were just the first two steps on a long and winding path.

While looking into the matter of rights, Gibson inquired about a talented Southern writer who could pen a feature film adaptation of the novel. Revered film critic Pauline Kael immediately suggested Blount and forwarded his number to Gibson. In a short conversation over the phone, the actor asked the writer whether he would be interested in working on the project.

"I said sure, but expressed doubt that a screenplay could capture the book's voice," remembers Blount.[5] "To me the book works as a prose confection. I wonder how well live actors could deliver those lines or answer to those descriptions. Think of Huston's *Wise Blood*, Altman's *Popeye*—the verbal magic is missing. Not that Toole is as good as Flannery O'Connor...."

As the rights were not available at that time, Blount never heard from Gibson—who died in 2009—again.

III

Since Maidee Walker loved the novel and knew it intimately before she started working on an adaptation she already knew how tricky it would be to transform the multi-layered adventures of Ignatius J. Reilly into a full-length feature film. She was also aware that every reader of the novel favored different aspects of it.

Lurking beneath the slapstick and satire was a dark undercurrent; the story of an obese, unemployed man who still lived with his mother, didn't have a girlfriend and spent his time thinking about Boethius and the Wheel of Fortuna whenever he was not masturbating onto his stained bed sheets. He was a man who is deeply dissatisfied with the society he lives in, who is an outcast and whose mother wants to send him to "chariddy," an institution where professionals can take care of his troubled soul.

Maidee Walker saw all of this and struggled with it. The book was "complicado," as she puts it: "It was very satirical, but underneath there was a lot of hidden depth there. It was supposed to have that veneer of comedy over it, but to me it was very dark. Doing the screenplay, trying to do it on these different levels, was very hard."[6]

The temptation for John Langdon was to focus on the comical aspects and turn the adaptation into a straightforward slapstick farce. As Walker remembers: "I don't think anybody could fully understand what the book was saying without taking away everything from it and making it into a stupid movie as a straight comedy. That's what I thought they wanted to do. I don't think anybody was particular willing at that point to make it into this very tiered movie like the book was. Everything that John Kennedy Toole did in this book was quite extraordinary. The way he could keep the satire here and the deep, dark things there. You have this overload, a bit of comedic stuff only because of Ignatius wearing funny clothes and walking around in his bathroom slippers. I had tried to hit on all of those things instead of making a slapstick comedy that so many people wanted to do. I didn't agree with that at all. I did the best I could."[7]

IV

It was a battle for Walker to come up with a script that honored the novel and satisfied her childhood friend—a childhood friend and now would-be movie producer who had a completely different take on *A Confederacy of Dunces* than she did.

Although, since Ignatius reminded him of his friend George, Langdon could see the tragedy in the novel, he wasn't particularly interested in the darker aspects of it when it came to the feature film—as a huge fan of *Saturday Night Live*, Langdon wanted to turn the plot into a slapstick comedy, and he never changed his tune.

When Susan O'Connell started working at Bumbershoot several years later, she had no qualms about Langdon's idea for the *A Confederacy of Dunces* script: "Johnny in many ways was Ignatius. Johnny was always thinking in a way that anything is possible. He was an inventor. He supported inventions and thinking that basically the world was off-kilter and that it needed strong, crazy, innovative, unstoppable people to make it right. I know he didn't see it as dark."[8]

Langdon did not wish to focus on or even portray any of the sleazier characters and their adventures. A born-again Christian who disdained anything dark and nefarious, John Langdon even had a Pat Robertson bumper sticker on his car. (Something which, incidentally, Ignatius certainly wouldn't have appreciated, exclaiming after the hot dog vendor informs him that he reads Father Kelly and Billy Graham every day, "Oh, my God! [...] No wonder you are so lost.")[9]

Langdon's life and views were deeply influenced by a tragic event that had rocked the family home twenty years earlier. In March 1963, his 21-year-old sister Jane had been traveling from Texas to Arizona to meet her parents. She never got there. On her way she was kidnapped and abused before being shot and fatally wounded. Her body was found in an abandoned prospector's tunnel near Arizona. She had been shot twice in the chest, once in the head.[10]

It was a shocking, grim and gruesome episode that made headlines for weeks. Jane's killer was never found. The crime constitutes the oldest unsolved murder in Maricopa County.[11]

Prostitutes (along with guns) proved to be an issue for Langdon, a subject he didn't feel comfortable tackling. Unfortunately for the entrepreneur from Texas, prostitutes and strippers do play an important part in John Kennedy Toole's novel, as does the underworld and a large circle of gay dandys, exactly the people who were regular targets for the televangelist Robertson.

Over the years several writers, including Maidee Walker, would focus on different characters in the screenplay. Some writers shared more affection for several of the minor characters than other writers or producers did, so there would be regular back-and-forths between Langdon and "his" writers concerning how to treat some of the less central characters. Oftentimes, a writer would reduce the part of a character, only then to be instructed by Langdon to create longer and stronger scenes for them, or vice versa.

John Langdon's son, Clay, remembers his father's apprehension concerning some of the darker themes and characters in *A Confederacy of Dunces*: "[There was] some discomfort on how to treat and cast and characterize the prostitutes and how to treat some of the minor characters who had a nefarious, criminal underworld-like background. My father was funny in that he would romanticize a lot of the parts of the story. There is a lot of darkness in the book. He would choose to ignore it. He had some pretty thick rose-colored glasses, and he wanted to see Ignatius as a hero but didn't really want to dive too deep into the darkness. He loved the absurdity of the protest and the picketing and all the stories of Ignatius making mischief."[12]

In 1987 John Langdon would get upset when he saw Alan Parker's *Angel Heart*, a New Orleans–set film in which Mickey Rourke played a private detective hired to track down a missing singer—coincidentally, David Ross McCarty worked as a location scout on the picture. Langdon hated the story; hated Mickey Rourke and his character; hated how New Orleans was portrayed; hated the violence, the sleaziness, the darkness; and, most of all, hated the success of the film.[13] If Langdon got his wish, *A Confederacy of Dunces* would be the opposite of *Angel Heart.*

V

The depth, darkness and sadness which Maidee Walker described is palpable in some of the novel's strongest moments and does not only concern minor characters such as the prostitutes. At the heart of any story there always is a conflict, and the main conflict at the heart of *A Confederacy of Dunces* comes out of Ignatius's fractured relationship with his mother.

It is a complicated relationship and psychologically intricate. Irene Reilly suffers under her son daily, more often than not feeling humiliated by him in front of other people: "'Oh, he treats me bad sometimes,' Mrs. Reilly said loudly and began to cry. 'You just don't know. When I think of all I done for that boy...' [...] 'You don't appreciate me. [...] You treat me like garbage. I been good.' [...] Mrs. Reilly had collapsed, sobbing, on the bar, one hand clenched around her beer glass."[14]

The humiliating treatment Mrs. Reilly receives at the hands of her son, a conflict worthy of a Tennessee Williams play, makes her dependent on alcohol, and hence *A Confederacy of Dunces* is also a portrait of an alcoholic who lives from moment to moment and has long since given up on any of the big dreams she might once have had for herself. But like every serious subject in the novel, Irene's alcoholism is treated in a lighthearted manner. She keeps her muscatel in the oven where her bottles are nearly baked more than once. Yet at other moments, there is a raw tenderness in the descriptions of Irene's loneliness: "She sat at the kitchen table sipping a little muscatel and blew away the one baby roach that was starting to cross the table."[15]

It is this loneliness that makes Irene dependent on Ignatius, for he is the only person she has regular contact with. As soon as she meets Santa Battaglia, and when Claude Robichaux proposes to her, Irene starts to ponder locking her son away. When she finally does make the call to the "chariddy," she has become emancipated and found a new life with reliable friends and a man who respects her. She has finally got what she had hoped for, as she professes to Ignatius in one of the novel's most touching, gut-wrenching moments: "'I'm worried about dying half-way decent. [...] I want to be treated nice by somebody before I die. You learnt everything, Ignatius, except how to be a human being."[16]

Certainly before Irene leaves the house on Constantinople Street that fateful evening she and Ignatius could not live with each other, but nor could they have lived without one another—their relationship is one which oscillates wildly between moments of violence and tenderness. Irene, who cannot support her son's intellectual quest and does not understand his world view ("'Go sit in your room and write some more of your foolishness.'"[17]), has given up on him ever being able to support himself. And yet she grabs any moment that can give her pause and lead her to praise her own flesh and blood—only a few pages after Irene had condemned Ignatius's foolishness, she expresses her pride. All it takes is Ignatius's announcement that he has prepared a speech for Dorian Greene's gathering: "'A political meeting? Ignatius! Ain't that wonderful!'"[18] But, again, soon thereafter the pendulum swings back and Irene "slapped her son flatly in the face [...] A slap struck Ignatius in the nose: another landed on his right eye. He waddled down the hall, pushed the long shutters open, and ran out into the yard."[19]

Irene, unable to endure any more humiliation, has finally lashed out physically, while her son regularly lashes out verbally as a reaction to frustration and perceived injustice. In this way *A Confederacy of Dunces* is, as much as anything else, a novel about humiliation. Irene isn't, after all, the only person who is humiliated on a daily basis. So is Ignatius, although he carries that burden very differently than Irene does, preferring to insult his opponents verbally and in his writing rather than striking out physically. However, he, too, reaches a point when he cannot carry this weight any longer. Dorian Greene's party becomes a grueling experience, the pinnacle of a long series of misfortunes, most of which Ignatius had brought upon himself simply because he cannot help himself.

VI

It is not only Ignatius's and Irene's relationship which verges on the hysterical. Mrs. Reilly's fragile relationship with Claude Robichaux is handled similarly by Toole, in that it oscillates powerfully between tender and violent emotions: "Mrs. Reilly screamed wildly, bursting into a crazy, loud tears that didn't subside until the frightened Mr. Robichaux took her maroon head and placed it carefully on his shoulder."[20]

Toole's work highlights how it feels to be shut out from society—and in the novel's grimmest moments the author doesn't even try to conceal the pariah's pain with humor: Ignatius is rejected by Dorian Greene and his friends; Irene seeks somebody who respects her; Mancuso is ridiculed by his superior; Gus Levy is little more than a checkbook to his wife, who constantly reminds him about missed opportunities and unrealized dreams: "You've thrown your father's business down the drain. That's the tragedy of your life."[21] (In an ironical inversion, Miss Trixie is the only character who does not want to be wanted and yet who is being kept in her job despite her desperate pleas. In this way she experiences a very different kind of cruelty.)

Early on, when they visit the Night of Joy, Irene and Ignatius are put in their place as pariahs in society, being told in no uncertain terms by Lana Lee: "Beat it. Trade from people like you is the kiss of death."[22] A few days later, the group of artists, after having had their work insulted by that Reilly kook, tell Ignatius flatly in his face: "We don't want you here,"[23] and he is further insulted and humiliated by Dorian Greene who exclaims: "That look on your face. Like Bette Davis with indigestion."[24]

Another kind of humiliation is experienced by Jones on a daily basis. Toole's novel is a social commentary as much as anything else; and while he includes jokes that are now deemed politically incorrect, he clearly sympathizes with African Americans and criticizes their treatment at the hands of the white society of the 1960s. As Jones says: "I wanna get someplace, man. Whoa! I want me a air condition, some color TV, sit aroun drinkin somethin better than beer. [...] I never go to school more than two year in my life."[25]

In order to give Jones more depth as a character, Toole includes extended scenes in Mattie's Ramble Inn. Says Watson to Jones regarding his job under Lana Lee: "'One thing I don like to see a colored man make fun of hisself for being colored. That what she be doin with you fix up like a plantation darky.'"[26]

VII

Unfortunately for screenwriters, *A Confederacy of Dunces* is made up of its various colorful and complex elements—take just one of them away and the whole structure falls apart. In order to produce a two-hour movie, Toole's work needs to be condensed heavily, and with that approach various elements and aspects of the novel are lost.

> *And you also know that everything that exists endured and perseveres as long as it is a unity but is destroyed as soon as it ceases to be a unity. [...] This is true and obvious about all living organisms.*[27]

Compared to the book, the social commentary in the adaptations is weak. Instead, they tend to focus on the comedic elements, the slapstick and on wry verbal jokes. But Toole extends his sarcasm to politics, when Ignatius discusses his ideas for a revolution he tentatively titles *Saving the World Through Degeneracy*, delivering an acid political satire worthy of writers Joseph Heller or Paddy Chayefsky: "None of the pederasts in power, of course, will be practical enough to know about such devices as bombs; these nuclear weapons would lie rotting in their vaults somewhere."[28]

Similarly, Toole lacerates psychoanalysis, most obviously in his depiction of Mrs. Levy's relationship with Miss Trixie, who snarls, after being subjected to a therapy session at the hands of her alleged benefactor: "I'll get even with you people. [...] Don't worry. You'll find out."[29]

VIII

Considering all the challenges the source novel presented, Maidee Walker was open to discussing her approach with John Schulte, the young man who had approached her following his visit to Thelma Toole's home.

Walker provided him with a copy of one of her many drafts. By and large, the hobby writer liked it, but he also had some concerns: "The characters needed to be pushed out more, they weren't fierce enough. The dialogue was not fighting to be faithful to the book. There were some general notions that were thrown out to her, as well as some very specific instances related to structure and scenes."[30]

And so an exchange started: Schulte and Jacques Louis provided Walker with some notes and Schulte sent her the script he had been working on. By this time Walker had set up shop at North Las Palmas Avenue in Hollywood, where she would work on all things related to *A Confederacy of Dunces* when she wasn't in Fort Worth.[31] She received Schulte in her office and also kept in touch with him via phone.

Eventually, Walker—having received feedback from the uber-fan—felt confident enough with her work to send a draft of her screenplay to Thelma Toole. The first version of her adaptation, though, was finalized only in December 1984, close to five months after Thelma's death.[32]

Ken's mother died of cancer in late August 1984. Joel Fletcher stayed close to her until the very end, remaining her trusted confidante in the last years of her life. Even in her final weeks, Thelma was a fighter. Although she refused to undergo dialysis after she had been diagnosed with a cancerous growth in her kidney, she never gave up on the dream of seeing *A Confederacy of Dunces* on the big screen. Fletcher wrote in his diary, recounting the last time he saw her alive: "I mentioned the premiere of the movie and reminded her that I would be one of her escorts. We talked about it and what we would wear to it. It made her happy to fantasize about this future event which grows less likely all the time."[33]

IX

After going through nearly 20 drafts, Maidee Walker finally had a version of the screenplay that she was happy with, which she delivered it to Langdon. And so, Ignatius would finally transcend the pages of John Kennedy Toole's novel:

A green hunting cap squeezed the top of the fleshy balloon of a head. The green earflaps, full of large ears and uncut hair and the fine bristles that grew in the ears themselves, stuck out on either side like turn signals indicating two directions at once. Full, pursed lips protruded beneath the bushy black moustache and, at their corners, sank into little folds filled with disapproval and potato chip crumbs. In the shadow under the green visor of the cap Ignatius J. Reilly's supercilious blue and yellow eyes looked down upon the other people waiting under the clock at the D.H. Holmes department store, studying the crowd of people for signs of bad taste in dress. Several of the outfits, Ignatius noticed, were new enough and expensive enough to be properly considered offenses against taste and decency: Possession of anything new or expensive only reflected a person's lack of theology and geometry; it could even cast doubts upon one's soul.[34]

BLACK SCREEN
THEME SONG from original soundtrack BEGINS.
FADE IN
"When a true genius appears in the world, you may know him by this sign,
that the dunces are all in confederacy against him."

Jonathan Swift
DISSOLVE TO
EXT—CITY OF NEW ORLEANS AND THE MISSISSIPPI RIVER—AFTERNOON
Approaching New Orleans from down river, an aerial shot plays on the bulging
curves of the winding Mississippi River. MAIN TITLES BEGIN. As we descend on
Canal Street, crowded with people in the 5:00 rush, the focal point becomes a green
hunting cap moving slowly through the masses.

CUT TO
BACK VIEW OF AN ENORMOUS MAN
The camera zooms in and follows the bulging backside of an enormous man.
As he waddles squarely down the middle of the sidewalk, his trousers
billow around his gargantuan rump as he rolls forward—making him
look like a baby elephant from behind.

CUT TO
CLOSE UP OF THE ENORMOUS MAN'S FACE

Underneath the visor of the green hunting cap, which is squeezed down
on his fleshy fat face, the man's huge supercilious eyes look down
on the crowds of people. Full, pursed lips protrude beneath
a bushy, black moustache and, at their corners, sink into little
folds filled with disapproval and potato chip crumbs.
The angle slowly widens until it includes all of him.
CUT TO

FULL FRONTAL VIEW OF THE MAN
He is dressed in voluminous tweed trousers, a plaid flannel shirt and
a woolen muffler ... the earflaps on the green hat stick out like turn
signals indicating two directions at once. As he lumbers along,
he is taking handfuls of potato chips from a huge bag
and stuffing them into his mouth.

DIFFERENT ANGLE
As the man plows through the people like the prow of a ship, the shot begins to
widen to include the bustle on Canal Street....

EXT—CANAL STREET—D.H. HOLMES DEPARTMENT STORE—AFTERNOON
The TITLES END and the MUSIC GIVES WAY just as the man reaches
the front of the department store. Then, suddenly, right at that moment,
the doors fly open and a YOUNG BLACK MAN in a bright yellow shirt
and space-age sun glasses bursts out onto the sidewalk,
and whams straight into the waddling mass.
(Excerpt from Maidee Walker's script)[35]

10

Can You Pass the Rorschach Test?

How Maidee Walker structures her screenplay to stay true to John Kennedy Toole's vision, but John Schulte disagrees with aspects of her approach

Although Walker stayed true to the depiction of several characters in the novel, she made some changes which she considered essential, the most glaring of which is her take on Ignatius. While he is not the most pleasant person to know either in the book or in the screenplay, he is incomparably more likable in Walker's adaptation. Various scenes depict a sweetness in him that is absent from Toole's work. He is kinder to his mother—although still far from loving—and even defends her in front of other people when they talk to her in a tone that Ignatius deems insulting.

While some future screenwriters would omit the tragedy of Rex, Ignatius's dog, Walker gives the backstory sufficient room to explain Ignatius' abrasive behavior and in this way make him more sympathetic to the audience. As is explained in the novel, our favorite medievalist is only the obnoxious pariah he is because he witnessed the death of his beloved dog when he was a teenager. Since neither the church nor Irene showed any understanding for Ignatius' deep sorrow, he retreated into himself until he became the person he now is. (In the screenplay, said explanation is given by Ignatius's mother, as opposed to Miss Annie in the novel.)

The difference between Toole's and Walker's approach is that the former skillfully hints at Ignatius's tragedy early on by telling a whole story in one short sentence ("Stopping by the grave, he read REX in faded letters on the cross")[1] long before Miss Annie elaborates on the sad plywood cross. Walker lets Irene explain the tragedy in detail, leaving nothing to the imagination and therefore at least partly excuses Ignatius's abrasive behavior from the start. Toole displays none of that sympathy.

There are more radical changes in the screenplay. While Claude Robichaux, who is infatuated with Irene Reilly, is a shy and socially awkward man in the book, he becomes someone more like Renfield from Bram Stoker's *Dracula* in Walker's script, a lunatic who might have even more severe problems than Ignatius does. When Robichaux makes his entrance at Santa Battaglia's house, he sees a scurrying cockroach and quickly pops it in his mouth and devours it with great delight.

Several of the challenges that Toole's novel present are, though, solved rather elegantly. Ignatius's philosophies, which he writes down in his Big Chief tablets, are expressed in his dialogues with other characters. Events only recounted by Ignatius in his tablets—such as him entering the Levy Pants factory and starting to dance— are dramatized to comic effect. Myrna Minkoff appears very early on when she turns

74

up at the Reilly home and tries (unsuccessfully) to seduce a disgusted Ignatius. This leads her to believe that her friend has indeed "become" gay and cannot be saved. As in the novel, she tries once more, when she drives to the Reilly's toward the end of the story. Ignatius not only gets into the car—desperately trying to escape the hostile people from the "chariddy"—but, in Walker's screenplay, at least appears to be sincere about his desire to start a new life in New York City with Myrna.

As a feather in her cap, Maidee Walker is the only writer who affords Mr. Watson an entrance in Mattie's Ramble Inn—a setting which is noticeably absent from future screenplays. Artists subsequently tasked with adapting the novel for the screen dispense with Watson altogether. This allows Walker, through dialogue between Jones and Watson, to infuse the script with a commentary on the racial politics of the 60s. It also enables her to bring out one of the smaller yet no less impressive delights of the novel, in that several people—such as Watson—cross paths with Ignatius without literally ever crossing paths with him. Here, he is a spirit hovering over everything and everyone.

Although several slapstick elements are taken directly from the novel and inserted into the screenplay, it is not the light-hearted *Saturday Night Live* lovefest her friend and employer favored. It was a difficult balancing act from the start, and Maidee Walker, at least, was happy with the final version of her script: "I just liked the fact that I was seeing that it was multi-leveled, that it wasn't just a comedic thing; that it was gloomy, [had] grim things and the satirical angle. That's hard to make. That's a *very* hard film to make."[2]

II

After long and arduous discussions about the approach to the screenplay John Langdon reluctantly accepted Maidee Walker's final draft. It was good enough to commence pre-production, although he was never crazy about the script, as Susan O'Connell claims: "I wasn't asked to have an opinion on it because Johnny just said, 'This doesn't work.' They took it out into the world and it didn't get a good reception. [In the '90s] he wasn't about to do that again. He wanted to find another writer."[3]

Although John Schulte had discussed Toole's novel with Maidee Walker at length, the young man wasn't enamored with her final script either. Schulte and his friend Jacques Louis took a detailed, in-depth look at her screenplay and still found certain approaches to the work problematic. In a letter to Maidee Walker they laid out their qualms. Although they start praising her for doing an excellent job at adapting such a dense novel, a close examination of the book's, and therefore the script's, challenges followed swiftly:

> We share your opinion that the screenplay must be faithful to the spirit of Toole's great novel, and we are confident that the very qualities of the novel that turned it into a world-of-mouth best-seller and cult literary classic have the potential of generating a cinematic smash hit on the order of *Rocky Horror*, although, of course, much better in quality and execution. Unfortunately, the more we study Toole's novel the more we find ourselves compelled to confront, head-on, some very real drawbacks it has as a cinematic property.
> Filmgoers are not going to sympathize as literary buffs did with plight of a fat, lazy male who mooches off his mother and insults her with cruelty and abuse. Filmgoers, again quite

unlike sophisticated readers, are going to squirm with boredom and indifference if subjected to 2½ hours of episodes beating the essentially dead horse of Iggy's utter unsuitability for "nine to fiving."[4]

As great admirers of the source novel, Schulte and Louis were careful not to suggest too many changes. Nevertheless, they did propose to alter at least some elements of Toole's work for the screen adaptation.

One main challenge for screenwriters has always been the character of Myrna Minkoff. After all, in *A Confederacy of Dunces* she is only seen through the letters she exchanges with Ignatius until she eventually turns up in the flesh right at the finale of Toole's novel. While other scriptwriters would find a way to enhance her role, Walker struggled with Minkoff.

Although she does appear towards the beginning of the screenplay, visiting Ignatius at home and trying to liberate him sexually, she then disappears altogether only to turn up again when her old friend attempts to flee the employees from the "chariddy." Schulte's and Louis's suggestion to Walker was to enhance Myrna's role and with it the "upbeat and redemptive love theme she represents."[5] They go on from there:

> We recommend deleting altogether Iggy's crusade among the homosexuals, greatly downplaying the material about Gus Levy and his wife, ditto the tedious material about Lana Lee and Burma Jones (a dangerously racist stereotype, in any event, especially if you buy another idea of ours, which is a transposition of the action of the film *Dunces* from circa 1962 to 1986).[6]

Future writers who would attempt to adapt *A Confederacy of Dunces* paid heed to at least one, and in some cases several of these ideas, without having read the letter in question. It suggests a similar view about a film version of the novel. Schulte and Louis continue:

> All of these major cuts will bring brevity and fast pacing to the film, which should zip along gleefully like a Howard Hawkes [sic] roller coaster of laughs, but stop well before the slightest trace of boredom sets in (100 minutes running time, max). We have to keep reminding ourselves what even poor, brilliant John Kennedy Toole forgot: Brevity is the soul of wit.[7]

Warning that "too many sub-plots and digressions will only damage the film" and "too much texture can wind up amounting to no texture at all,"[8] Schulte and Louis emphasize their plea to concentrate on what they perceive to be a love story between Myrna and Ignatius. In Walker's screenplay, the latter at one point even cries out "I am a virgin," when the liberated hippy simply won't leave him in peace.

The biggest problem for any screenwriter to tackle, though, was how to make Ignatius J. Reilly relatable to the audience, which naturally would not only include fans of the book. "Iggy" is a rude, obese, asexual slob with a love for medieval philosophy and a hatred towards most elements of pop culture. The only way to make the audience feel warmly towards Ignatius, or so Schulte and Louis were convinced, was to portray his foes—the Levys, the Mancusos, the Gonzalezes—as utter morons, too stupid to tie their own shoelaces. In order to reflect Ignatius's status as an intellectual giant, his contemporaries should be much smaller in size. Maidee Walker's acquaintances even went so far as to suggest casting "the midget from *Poltergeist*"[9] as Irene Reilly.

III

The fact that a screenwriter like Maidee Walker was so open to suggestions and ideas from a fan like Schulte surprised him at first, although he quickly found an explanation for Walker's attitude: "Maidee put her ego in her pocket. She didn't have any illusions about it getting green-lit by any studio. Her script was going to get thrown away or wholly adapted by somebody with a bigger name. I was trying to be a bridge between what she had done and what we could do, and then collectively wait and see what happens."[10]

Since John Langdon had made it clear that he had issues with her script for *A Confederacy of Dunces*, Walker was not at any point sure her work might make it onto the screen. She therefore welcomed suggestions from fans, as Schulte continues: "She was not only open but also encouraging that we could do something together. I never got the sense it was competitive. She was very forthright in telling me at the time: 'Whatever is best for the book.' She was very much into that."[11]

Even so, Maidee Walker read Schulte's and Louis's letter but did not alter her final script. She was done with changes.

IV

Although Schulte never met John Langdon, he kept sending notes to Maidee Walker, and meanwhile she was busy talking to potential actors and directors in Hollywood. For John Schulte, a heartbreak was to follow in 1992 when his friend Jacques Louis, who had worked with him on the *A Confederacy of Dunces* script, committed suicide.

Like John Kennedy Toole toward the end of his life, Louis was plagued by delusions—and he also found himself suffering in a job at the Environmental Protection Agency rather than fulfilling his desire to become a successful writer. Editor Robert Gottlieb, who had also encouraged Ken Toole to keep rewriting the tale of Ignatius, rejected Louis's novel. Disillusioned, unfulfilled, depressed and lonely, Jacques Louis stepped onto the balcony of his high-rise one afternoon and jumped off.[12]

The screenplay for *A Confederacy of Dunces* he and John Schulte had worked on had already for some time been collecting dust. It was never seriously considered either by Walker or Langdon, but Schulte was convinced of his and Louis's approach. So convinced, in fact, that in a letter to Walker they had written:

> We have enclosed an approach to the opening of *Dunces* that we think is funnier and more gripping than Toole's opening gambit. After this initial "hook" opening, we propose flashing back to a short series of altogether new episodes depicting the beginning of Iggy and Myrna's relationship at Louisiana State University in Baton Rouge. This approach, reminiscent of *Citizen Kane*, builds interest in New Orleans and Iggy as well as suspense that would otherwise be altogether lacking. We propose using this LSU material as a bridge leading to the Holmes Department Store fiasco and the basic Toole throughline you followed in your screenplay (minus the deletions recommended earlier). What we would wind up with would be a classic Hollywood comedy: very upbeat, witty, sexy, and bracing, with a simple Boy Mets Girl; Boy Loses Girl; Boy Gets Girl story. In this context, the mishaps of the tortured genius in the New Orleans job market become much more interesting than they are in the book because they are less numerous (carefully selected and milked

for laughs) and presented in a much less misogynistic context, in that our screen Iggy, unlike Toole's, will truly fall in love with Myrna, not just use her to facilitate his escape in the same manner that he walked all over Irene.[13]

FADE IN
EXT. MISSISSIPPI RIVER—DAY
CAMERA SNAKES along the Mississippi River. The classic
Paul Robeson rendition of "Ole Man River" swells in
the background. The booming voice of IGNATIUS JACQUES REILLY
comments on the majestic path.

IGNATIUS (V.O.)
The Mississippi River. Immortalized in the trashy novels
of Mark Twain and the repulsive songs of Jerome Kern.

CAMERA PANS OFF the river and FOLLOWS a winding
course into downtown New Orleans. High rise office
towers project proudly into the sky.

IGNATIUS (V.O.)
New Orleans. Louisiana. U.S.A. In any discussion
of America and how its people live, we must
begin with New Orleans, U.S.A.

CAMERA DIPS DOWN from the spires of the landmark
St. Charles Cathedral, JOURNEYS into the heart
of the French Quarter, and OPENS into a picturesque
SHOT of the jazz bars on Bourbon Street.

IGNATIUS (V.O.)
The French Quarter. The most civilized spot in America. Home to scores of
sodomites, prostitutes, drug addicts, pornographers, hot dog vendors, and
litterbugs.

The Quarter, like some deadly nightshade, blooms at twilight. Never is the bloom
more sinister than on one especially disgusting night: Fat Tuesday. Mardi Gras.
When the saints go marching in ... and the
sinners come crawling out.

This is New Orleans at its finest hour. A whole city convulsed in an orgy
of collective madness.... A confederacy of dunces in league
against the few heroic men of genius who hide deep
within the bowels of this depraved metropolis.
(Excerpt from John Schulte's script)[14]

John Candy Can Only
Have Half an Olive

*How an overweight actor mentors the saga, Jonathan Winters pretends
to be several people, and Shirley MacLaine expresses an interest in the
project*

While Maidee Walker was in Los Angeles, opening, reading and discarding letters from John Schulte, John Langdon stayed mostly in his native Fort Worth and
tried to conduct business related to *A Confederacy of Dunces* from there. Since he was
well connected with artists and entrepreneurs in Texas and "never knew a stranger,"
according to his daughter Kendall, Langdon didn't have any problem finding possible
crew members for his passion project.[1]

He was particularly fond of Dr. John, a singer, keyboard player and producer from
New Orleans who he contacted in the mid–'80s, and who immediately expressed an
interest in writing, recording and producing music for the adaptation. Meanwhile,
the Neville Brothers were also contacted by Bumbershoot Productions around the
same time. Like Dr. John, they were from New Orleans and had garnered much attention for their mix of jazz, blues and soul. They, too, were interested in contributing
musically.[2]

For the instrumental score, the Texas businessman would, in the late '80s,
approach Randy Newman, who was not only a beloved singer-songwriter but also a
talented composer of scores for films such as *Ragtime* and *The Natural* (for both of
which he received Academy Award nominations).

Many years would pass, and no film was ever shot that could be scored. That
hadn't changed in the late 2000s, when John Langdon approached yet another musi-
cian: T-Bone Burnett, a well-known guitarist and producer who was raised in Fort
Worth and who first caught the public's attention in the 1970s as a member of Bob
Dylan's band. Later he would leave his mark by producing the soundtracks for such
highly acclaimed films such as *O Brother, Where Art Thou?* and *Inside Llewyn Davis*.[3]

II

While John Langdon looked for musicians and tried to raise money, it was
mostly left to Maidee Walker, with her house and office in Hollywood, to find actors
willing to sign a contract to appear in *A Confederacy of Dunces*.

There was no lack of interest. Every semi-literate actor and director in

Tinseltown had read John Kennedy Toole's novel and picked up on the news in the trade papers that Bumbershoot Productions owned the rights to it. Although Walker was originally from Texas and hadn't lived in Beverly Hills for long, she was already well-connected, and soon found herself having lunch with "every fat actor in Hollywood," as she put it.[4]

A perfect facility to mingle with the rich and beautiful was the exclusive Pritikin Health Clinic resort. Maidee Walker never dreamed of becoming a member of Pritikin to lose weight. Weighing just 98 pounds, she simply wanted to "have fun" and exercise a bit.[5]

One day, she found herself in the same class as John Candy, the beloved actor who had already starred in *Blues Brothers*, *Vacation*, *Stripes*, and *Splash*, although his big breakthrough was yet to come.

Born in Toronto, Canada, in 1950, Candy had quickly made a name for himself in roles as a big—and big-hearted—teddy bear of a man, a bit shy, a bit awkward, somewhat lazy, not the sharpest knife in the drawer, but supportive of others and ultimately somebody to rely on. Throughout his life, Candy had been aware of his weight problems and associated health issues. The Pritikin was supposed to help him shed a few pounds.

Walker met Candy in their class and was soon bowled over by his exuberant charm. As she remembers: "We were in the same class together and became friends. When he found out that I had written a screenplay for *A Confederacy of Dunces* we became even better friends, because he was dying to be Ignatius. He was the sweetest man! He said, 'Maidee, we can go have two martinis, but we only can have one olive,' because it was fattening. He was really sweet. We exercised and ran on the beach and all of that."[6]

> It is like that with all things that men want, in which they are not so much interested in the things but in their goodness. And we have agreed that what men want is happiness, and in the same way, when they pursue various goals for the purpose of achieving happiness, it is the happiness that they want. It would appear, then, that goodness and happiness are one and the same.[7]

Walker and Candy met several times for lunch, and she found him as nice as any person could possibly be—a delight to be around, an enthusiastic and intelligent man, a perfect creative partner.

Candy was desperate to play the role of Ignatius and Walker would have been only too happy to sign him right away. She only had one faint glimmer of doubt in the back of her mind: her new friend *was* sweet and charming, but Ignatius, most definitely, was not. The Canadian had already made a name for himself as a goodhearted screen presence. Would he, Walker wondered, be able to pull off a character such as Ignatius convincingly? Would the audience buy it?

Walker's bigger concern was her business partner, John Langdon. Although Langdon wanted somebody "really likable"[8] in the role of Ignatius, the entrepreneur wasn't, as he had already explained to Roderick Taylor, too excited about the idea of John Candy in the leading role—something he now made clear to Walker.

III

Walker had the same understanding of the novel as Candy. He agreed with her vision and saw the story as a clever satire with a dark underbelly. Langdon, on the other hand, wanted more broad comedy and less subversive dialogue and conflict. Rather than John Candy, he had another actor in mind who would be just perfect, or so Langdon thought: Jonathan Winters.

Winters's comic acts had provided John Belushi's biggest inspiration and by the mid–80s Jonathan Winters was a legend in his field. For his comedy recordings, the talented writer and actor was nominated for eleven Grammys, appeared in films like *It's a Mad Mad Mad Mad World*, TV programs such as *Mork & Mindy*, and performed stand-up to standing ovations. The fact that in 1985, Winters was already 50 years old—as opposed to the 30-year-old Ignatius—didn't concern John Langdon. He loved stand-up, had never missed an episode of *Saturday Night Live*, and dreamed of casting Jonathan Winters in his movie.

Walker shared Langdon's plans with John Schulte, who as he explains, wasn't too excited by the idea: "She was very affected when she went to meet Jonathan Winters to get him to play the part of Ignatius, which I thought was interesting, but I also thought, 'Can we please think outside the box of not finding every actor or comedian in Hollywood? Can we think about whether they look the part and can act the part?' She had her heart set on Jonathan Winters."[9]

She had indeed, as soon as she met him. Just like Candy, she found Winters to be a delight: "I had lunch with him, and he was an absolute riot. I know a lot of people aren't, they get up there and are really funny and in real life they are not nice at all, but he was absolutely charming and just as funny. He was an artist. He painted down in his basement. He had an extremely attractive wife. He was painting and she heard all this commotion downstairs and said, 'Who is down there?' And he said. 'All of us,' and it was just him painting in his basement and talking to himself. He pretended there were other people down there. His paintings are around. He would go down there and paint all the time."[10]

IV

Langdon's hopes for Winters in the main role were dashed when the actor passed on the project. Other choices for Ignatius were Josh Mostel and Dom DeLuise, who had already been approached in the early '80s, before Walker's script was finalized.[11] Josh Mostel, son of actor Zero Mostel, shrugs his shoulders: "I would be interested in the role, but it never got anywhere. I was asked, 'Are you interested?' Of course I'm interested! It's a great part! I had read the book and liked it. It's a terrific book!"[12] After Langdon and Walker failed to show him a script, Mostel said he didn't expect to see the project become a reality.

With Candy and Winters out of the picture, Langdon and Walker brainstormed who else could possibly be cast as Ignatius. They came up with several actors, one of which was John Lithgow, a surprisingly skinny choice for the role (although in 2019 Lithgow would don a fat-suit to portray Fox News boss Roger Ailes in Jay Roach's *Bombshell*).[13] The American actor had recently demonstrated his versatility by playing Roberta Muldoon (and receiving an Academy Award nomination for it) in George Roy Hill's 1982 adaptation of *The World According to Garp*.

A similarly unusual choice was Irish-born actor Richard Harris, known primarily for starring in films such as *Cromwell* and *A Man Called Horse*, as well as for his legendary hard-drinking sessions with Richard Burton, Peter O'Toole and other British stars of the era. But Harris was slim and already in his 50s when Langdon threw his name in the ring. This didn't deter the entrepreneur from contacting the actor, who as it turned out, loved the book. Though without financing in place, Harris wouldn't commit to appearing in the film.[14]

Another choice was Stuart Pankin, an actor who had won acclaim for his performances in the HBO series *Not Necessarily the News*, and who had the right stature and was of the right age to play Ignatius.[15]

Louie Anderson—who would later play Mrs. Baskets in Zach Galifianakis's series *Baskets*—was, in the mid–'80s, at the start of his career as a comedian and actor when he expressed an interest in playing Irene Reilly's boy. But John Langdon wasn't convinced by him, just as he wasn't convinced by Bruce Vilanch, an American comedy writer, actor and singer who was currently penning jokes for the likes of Robin Williams and had acted in small roles in several films, including *The Ice Pirates*. He had been recommended by one of John Langdon's attorneys, Stan Coleman, but the suggestion wasn't met with much enthusiasm.[16]

V

While finding a lead actor was already difficult, finding supporting actors was by no means easier for Langdon and Walker. The president of Bumbershoot Productions toyed with the idea of casting newcomer Whoopi Goldberg, who in 1985 had starred in Steven Spielberg's *The Color Purple*, for which she had garnered an Oscar nomination. Langdon didn't want to cast Goldberg as a woman, though.[17] He found her to be the perfect choice for the role of Burma Jones and wanted to transform her into a man, just like Peter Weir had cast Linda Hunt as a man in his thriller *The Year of Living Dangerously* in 1982. Hunt had received an Oscar for best actress in a supporting role.

VI

Other ideas for supporting roles were less inspired by film history and more by Langdon's personal relationships. In the early '80s, he had met a businessman named Jim Rogers, whose girlfriend was Sharon Stone, a young model and aspiring actress. Rogers' father was a real estate agent and well connected. Jim, on the other hand, was a counselor in Scientology and had married Mimi Spickler in 1976.[18] They divorced in 1980 and Jim hooked up with Sharon Stone thereafter. (Mimi became a successful actress as Mimi Rogers and married Tom Cruise in 1987.)

Through Langdon, Walker was introduced to Stone, who was in Los Angeles waiting for her big break. Rogers tried to get her career going, as Walker remembers: "They lived together. He would come to Fort Worth. I met Sharon Stone out in Los Angeles, before she had done anything. She was just a pretty girl. She clonked on to me and was calling me all the time. We went to lunch all the time."[19]

John Langdon liked Stone's paramour and was open to casting his girlfriend in the role of Darlene.

*These are all things that men want—wealth, high office, power, fame, and pleasure—
because these are the things they think will make them happy. The good, then, is that which
men pursue by these various means and avenues.*[20]

Walker continues: "She was so naive at that point and young. We had a nice time. She
didn't have a leg in yet, she didn't have anything going for her. I had done something
which she seemed to like a lot. [There was] the idea that there might be this incredible film coming out."[21] Stone's first big screen role wouldn't be in *A Confederacy of
Dunces*, but as Richard Chamberlain's sidekick in the Indiana Jones imitation *King
Solomon's Mines* in 1985. She finally became an international star in 1992, famously
crossing her legs in *Basic Instinct*.

VII

Another acquaintance of John Langdon's was Shirley MacLaine, who the entrepreneur had met during an unusual outing. In the early '80s, both had independently
traveled to Hawaii to experience a supernatural happening that was supposed to
occur one night.[22] After waiting for several hours with hordes of people tense with
expectation, Langdon eventually tapped MacLaine on the shoulder, saying: "Shirley, I
don't think anything is gonna happen here. Would you like to go for a ride?"[23] The two
became fast friends.

By the mid–'80s, MacLaine had long been one of the biggest screen stars of Hollywood: *The Trouble with Harry* (1955) had introduced her to the world of cinema,
and *The Apartment*, and later *Terms of Endearment* had completed her image as a legendary actress. She read Walker's script and immediately fell in love with it.

Coincidentally, John Schulte and Jacques Louis got introduced to MacLaine
around the same time through a bizarre chain of events: following their visit to
Thelma Toole, Schulte and Louis wrote an article about their encounter with the
Grand Dame of Elysian Fields and sent it to their agent, along with a mini draft
of their script. Said agent, in turn, forwarded the documents to MacLaine's agent,
with whom he was friends. And so it happened that one day Schulte heard his
phone ring and when he answered it, Shirley MacLaine was on the other end of
the line. The writer remembers: "Shirley called us and was very excited and said
she wanted to be in the movie. We said, 'Golly, we don't have the rights to it.' We
are just horsing around to see if we can get ourselves involved more with Maidee
Walker. There were enough issues with her script. It needed help if it was going on
as it was."[24]

MacLaine conferred with her friend John Langdon, who in turn delivered the
news to Maidee Walker: one of the great actresses of the 20th century was interested in playing Irene Reilly! Walker then served as intermediary by phoning up John
Schulte and bringing him and Jacques Louis up to date concerning MacLaine's interest in the project. Schulte and Walker both were surprised by her explicit wish to
be cast as Irene.[25] There was no doubt for the two writers that MacLaine would be
pitch-perfect as Santa Battaglia—but as Irene Reilly?

In any case, it would be great news to welcome Shirley MacLaine as part of the
cast—no one would say no to a heavyweight like her. Schulte and Walker wanted to
go even further: they wanted Shirley MacLaine to direct the film. Langdon was also

taken with the idea of hiring her as director, although he had also considered several other candidates.[26]

As flattered and excited as the Bumbershoot people and Schulte were by MacLaine's interest in the property, it was the worst possible time to embark on a project with the legendary star, as they were soon to find out. The actress was deeply into her spiritual phase around the time, traveling the world to learn more about spirituality, metaphysics and, through that, herself. She was practicing Transcendental Meditation and would claim that she had been the brother to a 35,000-year-old spirit in a previous life.[27] In the mid–'80s, her spiritual quest was more important to MacLaine than her movie career, a fact her agent might not have been too thrilled about.

MacLaine tried calling Schulte again a few weeks later, but as the writer wasn't home, left a message on his answering machine. When he returned her call a little later, he had to do the same, although MacLaine would never reply. A disappointed John Schulte muses: "We left a message on her machine several times and nothing ever happened. I know she was embroiled in a lot of travel at the time and doing a lot of books she had coming out at the time. She was probably more engrossed in that. It was all about her. We were a bit of a blip, and maybe she had done her due diligence, and her agent had realized we were one step removed from the project. So don't bother."[28]

Following the unanswered calls, Schulte decided to send a letter to MacLaine's agent, reminding her that they had already spoken about *A Confederacy of Dunces* and were willing, along with Maidee Walker and John Langdon, to continue their talks. In March 1986, Schulte wrote:

> We understand you had shown an interest in the Irene Reilly part. We feel, however, you are more suited to play Santa Battaglia (we have several hours of videotape of Thelma Toole doing her versions of these Southern grotesques). Irene is a diminutive masochistic, alcoholic floozy. You're much more styled for Santa, with her comic excesses and rich diction. But, moreover, you should consider the best role of all—director! Especially if you're keen on some of our other casting ideas.[29]

The actress never responded to their letter. It was frustrating for Schulte and Walker not to have the chance to discuss their proposal with MacLaine further. They wanted her to direct the film, make her appearance as Santa Battaglia, and—if at all possible—talk to her brother Warren Beatty about *A Confederacy of Dunces*.

Why? Well, wouldn't he be perfect as Ignatius? The idea of casting Beatty as the medievalist in Toole's novel came to Schulte when he saw a paparazzi snapshot in the "Star Tracks" section of *People Magazine*. In the photograph, Beatty was walking through heavy snow with a thick coat, protected from the cold wind by a tartan scarf and a floppy hat.

Casting Beatty as Ignatius would have been an odd choice by any means. Early roles such as in *Splendor in the Grass* (1961) and *Mickey One* (1965) had transformed the actor into the quintessential Hollywood heartthrob of the '60s, an image that was cemented when Arthur Penn cast him alongside Faye Dunaway in the iconic 1967 masterpiece, *Bonnie and Clyde*.

By the late '80s, Beatty hadn't made a film since the hugely acclaimed *Reds* in 1981. Unfortunately for his return to the screen after a six-year break, he chose Elaine May's *Ishtar*—one of the biggest and most expensive flops of all time. Even before *Ishtar* premiered, John Schulte knew that Warren Beatty badly needed both a box-office hit and a critical success—and the screen adaptation of *A Confederacy of Dunces* would be both of those: despite the fact that no actors had committed to the project, financing was still in limbo, a director had yet to be signed, and issues with Maidee Walker's script remained to be solved.

All this didn't deter Schulte who, again, took matters in his own hands, sending a letter to Beatty's agent in March 1986, briefly laying out the project's history and including his article on John Kennedy Toole's life. Schulte concluded by writing:

> Would you consider starring in this comedy, and this co-starring for the first time with Shirley MacLaine? Recent photographs of you on the set of *Ishtar* matched up, quite uncannily, with John Kennedy Toole's description of his great comic character, Ignatius Jacques Reilly.[30]

Warren Beatty never responded to the letter. Schulte and Walker also suggested Elizabeth Taylor to Shirley MacLaine when they tried to sign the latter as director. It would be quite simple, according to the writer and producer: MacLaine was interested in playing Irene, but would instead portray Santa, while Taylor would be a brilliant "alcoholic floozy" as Irene.[31] Walker and Schulte tried to convince MacLaine by writing "Your chance to get even!"[32] when suggesting Elizabeth Taylor as a possible Irene Reilly, remarking on the fact that Shirley MacLaine would finally get her second Oscar. However, neither Schulte nor Walker ever reached out to Elizabeth Taylor.

12

Doctors Differ, Patients Die

How Bumbershoot tries to entice high-profile directors and eventually decides to let an experienced Hollywood producer take a look at their property

The script remained problematic, and therefore a priority. While some actors liked Walker's work, others were far more critical, as she found out over the course of her years in Hollywood. The writer admits: "I was very involved initially, and then there was so much criticism of my screenplay. People wanted to make it more slapstick. I wasn't interested in that. Langdon never missed one *Saturday Night Live* show in his whole life. He wanted this film to follow that road and it wasn't that. It was so multi-layered. The slapstick part of that wasn't what it was. I don't think John Kennedy Toole ever meant it to be. What he was writing about was very dark and deep and gloomy."[1]

Was there any director who could transform Walker's screenplay into a movie that satisfied John Langdon as well? Finding a filmmaker who could please both seemed to be a Herculean task from the start.

II

In the early '80s, Robert Wise was looking for an exciting movie to direct. The esteemed filmmaker, born in 1914, had directed a vast array of projects, from musicals (*West Side Story, The Sound of Music*) to horror (*The Haunting, Audrey Rose*), science fiction (*The Day the Earth Stood Still, The Andromeda Strain*) to historical epics (*Helen of Troy, The Sand Pebbles*), as well as westerns (*Tribute to a Bad Man*), biopics (*Somebody Up There Likes Me*), melodramas (*I Want to Live!, Two for the Seesaw*), comedies (*This Could Be the Night, Something for the Birds*), thrillers (*Odds Against Tomorrow*) and action-adventure films (*Run Silent, Run Deep; Destination Gobi*). There was no genre Robert Wise hadn't tackled, and he had succeeded in most of them, although comedy wasn't known to be his forte. Despite having won four Oscars in the course of his remarkable career, he had fallen out of favor by the '80s, having directed *Star Trek: The Motion Picture* in 1979, a hugely expensive big-screen adaptation of the beloved television show, which failed to win over critics and did only average business at the box office.

Wise, who had served as an editor on Orson Welles' *Citizen Kane*, needed a new project, one which would serve as his comeback. When he heard the news that a company had acquired the movie rights to *A Confederacy of Dunces* and that a script had already been written, he jumped at the chance. The director got his hands on Maidee

Walker's screenplay, which was circulating in Hollywood, and got in touch with her immediately after reading it.

Although his comedies had been some of his least successful films—both at the box office and with critics—Wise wanted to direct *A Confederacy of Dunces*. For him, it wasn't primarily a comedy. Walker remembers how excited the director was about the possibility of being brought on board—and how excited she was, likewise: "He really wanted to do it—really, really wanted to do it. He was such a charming man. Robert Wise was interested for a very long time. I think it would have been his last hurrah. He wanted it so much! I never met somebody that I liked as much—but you can say that about Jonathan Winters and John Candy as well."[2]

For Maidee Walker, a director had been found. Although she didn't have much experience in film, she was aware of Wise's cinematic range, which would suit their new project just fine, since Toole's novel and Walker's screenplay combine a whole number of topics and genres under the veneer of comedy.

The writer continues: "Robert Wise was across the board. He did all sorts of films. He did everything. He would take me to the [Brown] Derby for lunch, and he was great. Every time he would walk into this restaurant, they would start playing a tune from *West Side Story*. I still believe Robert Wise would have been perfect. He could have gotten it made. He would have done it beautifully, and every producer would have been happy. There would have been bidding wars."[3]

III

There were no bidding wars. To her great frustration, Maidee Walker found out that John Langdon didn't share her excitement for Wise. He didn't even want to meet the director of *West Side Story*. For Langdon, it would just be a waste of time.

Walker never understood her business partner's reasoning, and neither did his mother. "It just killed me that Langdon didn't want Wise," admits Walker. "Even Langdon's mother said, 'What more would you want?' He just didn't get it. He was too *Saturday Night Live*."[4]

Since Walker knew that Langdon harbored a great passion for *Saturday Night Live*, and since she was painfully aware that Langdon wasn't entirely happy with her script, it came as no big surprise to her to find out that the Bumbershoot president dismissed the idea of Wise directing the film outright. Maidee Walker had already been frustrated by Langdon's behavior and attitudes, which she found wholly unprofessional, but with his vetoing Robert Wise, he finally risked her departure from their joint endeavor. Yes, Wise had made a few suggestions concerning her script, and warned her he would change a few scenes, but Walker had always been open to that. She was convinced of Wise as the right choice and had become friendly with him. Who else now could make the film?

IV

Mike Medavoy was one of the producers whose interest in *A Confederacy of Dunces* had been raised when John Langdon tried to find financial backers for the prospective film. Medavoy was the producer who had brought Sylvester Stallone's *Rocky* to the screen—along with Robert Chartoff and Marcia Nasatir, who had already circled Toole's work at Carson Productions.

In 1978, Medavoy had co-founded Orion Pictures, where he stayed until 1990. After some toeing and froing with John Langdon, Medavoy optioned the rights to *A Confederacy of Dunces* in 1985.[5] By now, Langdon had become frustrated with his lack of success in raising the money he needed for his adaptation and was willing to strike a deal with a Hollywood studio, albeit a comparatively small one like Orion. Still, Langdon tried to protect his baby as best he could: if Medavoy wouldn't commence pre-production within the next 12 months, the rights would revert back to Langdon.

In fact, nothing much happened with the project at Orion. Medavoy concedes he had two problems with the film, problems he couldn't solve: "For me it always came back to the same question: Who's going to play that part? How will it be done? Then the next question would be, 'Okay, how much does that movie cost?'"[6]

Medavoy had serious doubts. He claims he loved the book, found it hysterically funny, and thought it would make a great movie. But he admits, "the lack of thinking about who could play Ignatius is probably what slowed me down."[7]

Surely there was no shortage of heavily built actors who could play Ignatius J. Reilly convincingly? Medavoy had already heard rumors about John Candy's interest and Robin Williams being a contender for the role. But neither of these actors felt right to Medavoy. Wouldn't it be an option to put a svelte actor in a bodysuit? For Medavoy, it was an idea he considered only briefly, as he remembers: "[Ignatius] is a large-sized individual and central to getting that done. Unless you put a bodysuit on him, it makes it nearly impossible to cast. It needs to be the right person. I never liked the idea of putting a bodysuit on somebody. That's been done. It was done by the British comic troupe Monty Python in their film *The Meaning of Life*. That was a sketch, though. This requires somebody to do the whole movie."[8]

Medavoy may, as a reader, have loved *A Confederacy of Dunces* enough to option the rights, but Barbara Boyle, then senior vice president at Orion, knew deep down the novel was not her boss's cup of tea. It wasn't commercial enough: "It's a very odd book. It's completely internal. Is the man mad or is Ignatius the only sane person around? He is very heavy and very ugly. Do you think on a standard reading list of the ten American novels you have to read you would actually see John Kennedy Toole? I don't. You would see Faulkner and Hemingway. You wouldn't even see Walker Percy. I don't think Walker Percy is on everybody's list. Fitzgerald is far more obvious. The marketplace reflects that. It isn't the kind of book that Mike was naturally drawn to."[9]

Boyle was much more enthusiastic about Toole's work than her boss was. She and her husband were big fans of Walker Percy and hence had discovered *A Confederacy of Dunces* shortly after its publication. It quickly became one of her favorite books, and she was intrigued by the possibility of seeing an adaptation on the big screen, as she remembers: "My interest was always in the film and the life of Ignatius, actually. How to make that a character in a film? I actually couldn't figure it out."[10]

Boyle even talked about the book and its adaptation with Kit Carson, a celebrated American writer who a few months prior had received much critical acclaim for his screenplay for Wim Wenders's *Paris, Texas*. Orion's senior vice president found

Carson the perfect voice to adapt *A Confederacy of Dunces*, but discussions remained informal.[11]

V

Negotiations with Mike Medavoy weren't off to a promising start. The producer felt a fat actor would make it hard for the audience to empathize with Ignatius, but at the same time he wasn't entirely comfortable with the idea of a bodysuit. Budgeting a movie like *A Confederacy of Dunces* was just as nightmarish, as Medavoy explains: "You would need to be faithful to the characters in the book in order to get an audience. You could have made the film cheaper. You wouldn't have been so dependent on the cast then. The idea of finding a way to do it became threefold: one is the budget. Who's going to play the role? Who's going to direct it? The right team didn't come along."[12]

VI

While Mike Medavoy kept thinking about an actor for the lead role, Barbara Boyle was pondering who could direct. One name immediately came to mind: Miloš Forman. Boyle had worked with the celebrated Czech filmmaker at United Artists on *Amadeus* (1984)—which had won seven Academy Awards, including Best Picture, and Best Director—and she found Forman the perfect choice: "If you look at Milos' films, they are pretty eclectic and relatively unpredictable film subjects. For me it's not about the actors because it's always about the material and the director. In all the years I have worked in the film industry I have never had a piece of material with a really good director that I had trouble getting actors for. Actors like working with great directors."[13]

Boyle, though, was in favor of Robin Williams for the lead: "I knew him from long ago, from my Berkeley days. Boy, Robin Williams! But I wouldn't have said, 'This is the man,' I would have said, 'Get a director!' If Mike thought about Robin, I would have thought about a director. Mike's way of approaching a project was always, 'Will Redford do it, will Streisand do it, will Robin Williams do it?'"[14]

Boyle sent Walker's script to Forman's agent Marion Rosenberg to no avail. Similarly, other directors either didn't respond or made clear they were not interested in the project. Over the course of 1985, Walker's script was sent to various high-profile filmmakers. It was a long list:

Robert Zemeckis had just done *Romancing the Stone* and in 1985 celebrated a smash hit with *Back to the Future*. Although he was sent the script, no meetings were taken.[15]

The same was true for John Hughes who was sent the screenplay but did not respond. It was his busiest period, after all: in 1984 he had directed *Sixteen Candles* and *The Breakfast Club*, while *Weird Science* followed only a year later. They were all written by Hughes himself.[16]

George Roy Hill had reached his zenith with *The Sting* in 1973 and by the mid-80s his heyday seemed over. *The World According to Garp* had proven to be an instant success in 1982, based on a novel famously difficult to adapt, while *The Little Drummer Girl* in 1984 was a flop. His next venture, *Funny Farm*, in 1988 would be his last film.[17]

Alan Parker, too, was approached. The British director had helmed, among others, *Fame*, *Midnight Express* and *Birdy* before he started work on *Angel Heart* in 1986, a film Langdon despised. Had the thriller set in New Orleans premiered earlier, the entrepreneur from Texas certainly wouldn't have dreamed about supplying Parker with a copy of Walker's work. In any case, the director didn't respond.[18]

Neither did Ron Howard, the young filmmaker who had started out as an actor and by the mid–'80s, had already directed *Splash* and *Cocoon*, two verifiable Hollywood hits.[19]

Although Arthur Penn, who had directed *Bonnie and Clyde* in 1967, *Little Big Man* in 1970 was seriously in need of a hit, he also failed to react to the script sent to him through his agent Martha Luttrell at ICM.[20]

Mike Medavoy didn't see a way forward, but that didn't mean he gave up. During his tenure at TriStar—from 1990 to 1994—when Susan O'Connell and John Langdon suggested the project to him (yet again), he toyed once more with the idea of producing *A Confederacy of Dunces*. He soon found himself confronted with the same, seemingly unsolvable problems, and finally passed on the property altogether.[21]

VII

While Langdon and Walker tried to set up an adaptation with Orion, Scott Kramer wasn't idling. He was still very much active and had anything but given up on his dreams.

Although the movie rights by now belonged to the oil tycoon from Texas, Kramer approached Robert Shaye to set up shop at New Line Cinema. The producer had founded the company in 1967, and first became known for re-releasing "classics" such as the infamous propaganda film *Reefer Madness*, an anti-marijuana documentary. New Line Cinema prided itself in supporting underground cinema, edgy productions that went against the mainstream.

In 1984, Robert Shaye struck gold with his production of *A Nightmare on Elm Street*, an imaginative low-budget horror film which spawned seven sequels and a remake and is now considered a cult classic. In 1981, Shaye had helped John Waters get *Polyester* off the ground, a comedy about a suburban housewife whose life starts to fall apart. Waters had earned the title Pope of Trash after the release of his legendary counterculture film *Pink Flamingos*, which was released in 1972. *Pink Flamingos* had been distributed by New Line Cinema, and Waters formed a friendly working relationship with Robert Shaye, who would continue his support for the filmmaker when Waters moved more toward the mainstream in the early '80s.

Waters had devoured John Kennedy Toole's *A Confederacy of Dunces* when it came out, and missed no opportunity to praise the book in interviews. He described Ignatius J. Reilly as his favorite fictional hero[22] and stated he could read the novel again and again, since it had never failed to make him laugh.[23] Moreover, Waters had lived in New Orleans in the '70s, only half a block from Thelma Toole, a fact he was unaware of until decades later: "Oh, my God! And of course I love that book—it's still the first book I send to anyone I know who gets sentenced to prison. 'Cause it'll make you laugh, and nobody feels much like laughing when you just started serving a prison sentence. It's a tradition."[24]

After the book came out, Waters was passionate about developing a film about the unlikely hero and his alcoholic, long-suffering mother. Since Robert Shaye was eyeing the project while the rights were still with Bumbershoot, Waters decided to pitch the idea of himself as director to his friend. Waters is weary about talking about his involvement: "I have already told the tiny story of my involvement many times in interviews and feel it would be redundant. I had one pitch and it wasn't successful."[25]

VIII

Waters had one grand idea for "his" *Confederacy*: casting Divine as Ignatius.[26]

Born Harris Glen Milstead in 1945, Divine was a born-and-bread Baltimorian who became an international star as a transvestite and actor, playing female roles in Waters's flicks from his short, *Roman Candles*, in 1966 onward. Until Alan Rudolph came along in 1985 to cast Divine as a bad guy in his neo-noir *Trouble in Mind*, Divine had never played a man in films before, and was at that time of her life desperate to become a celebrated, serious actor. Harris Glen Milstead, Waters was sure, would be perfect as Ignatius—he had the stature and the acting chops to pull it off.

In a way, *A Confederacy of Dunces* would have been a perfect vehicle for Waters. Ignatius J. Reilly is a person difficult to understand. He is not likable but certainly provides a spectacle, and outcasts had always inspired and interested Waters. As he noted: "The politics of all my movies are the same, which is 'Mind your own business and don't judge other people. You don't know the whole story. Wait until you have heard the whole story and then you can figure where people are coming from. Something causes everything,' and I am most fascinated by subjects that I don't really understand, that there is no easy answer to, that I'll never understand, and I am always drawn to subject matter like that. I like to bring my audience along with me to be surprised by it and made nervous by it."[27]

Robert Shaye was open to Waters's ideas, and the director left the meeting in which he pitched his vision for the adaptation in high spirits. What followed then, though, was a long silence, as Waters later wrote: "The meeting seemed to go OK; the producer listened politely to my ideas, but I never heard from him again. He never even gave me the official 'no.' It wasn't until about a year later that I figured out why."[28]

As it turned out, it all had to do with the Manson murders.

IX

On the night of 8 August 1969, Tex Watson, Susan Atkins, Linda Kasabian, and Patricia Krenwinkel invaded a house at 10050 Cielo Drive in Los Angeles, where Watson, Atkins and Krenwinkel subsequently killed Sharon Tate, Jay Sebring, Wojciech Frykowski, Abigail Folger, and delivery boy Steven Parent.

John Waters was immediately fascinated by the case, and his interest became an obsession when the perpetrators were caught and their pictures printed in the papers: "The Manson Family looked just like my friends at the time! Charles 'Tex' Watson, a deranged but handsome preppy 'head' who reminded me of Jimmy, the frat-boy-gone-bad pot dealer I had the hots for in Catholic high school, the guy who sold me my first joint."[29]

John Waters started visiting Tex Watson in prison, until Watson found Jesus Christ, although they have continued their correspondence via post. In his book *Shock Value*, the director wrote about his curious friendship with the mass murderer "rather inappropriately and with little insight," as he would later admit.[30] He even included a photo of himself with Watson.

Unfortunately for Waters, Tex Watson had killed one of the best friends of a New Line executive, though the director has never mentioned the person's name. "I felt really awful," wrote the director. "And, natch, I didn't get the job. It might have been the single most disastrous 'meeting' to ever take place in Hollywood, but then I guess that all directors have their stories."[31]

> *The fact of the matter is that ill fortune is better for men than good. When Fortune smiles, she is always false. But when she is inconsistent and whimsical, she shows her true self. The first aspect of Fortune will deceive people, but the second is instructive.*[32]

13

Fare Thee Well

*How John Langdon tries to steer his ship safely into the harbor with help
from Twentieth Century–Fox as well as Harold Ramis, and eventually
severs his ties with an old, trusted friend*

In hindsight, Waters was content that he didn't get the job. Had his pitch been
successful, he would have had to adapt a story which already existed, whereas Waters
preferred to come up with his own original ideas rather than shepherd a pre-existing
work. A few years later he noted: "I did want to make it at a time with Divine as Ignatius. I would never do that today, it's jinxed, I think. So many people have tried to
make it. [...] I never did it. I never want to do somebody else's work. They didn't write
it for me. The fun of it is to make it up and then make it real. I just loved the book so
much at the time that I did have meetings about it. It never happened."[1]

Since his pitch at New Line Cinema wasn't successful—and Robert Shaye
decided to pass on the property (for the time being)—Waters never discussed the
property with Divine's agent, Bernard Jay.[2] Then, just a short time after Waters's brief
involvement with the *A Confederacy of Dunces* film Divine died at age 42, in her sleep
due to respiratory failure.

One other project John Waters wanted to make with Divine before her unexpected death was a sequel to their cult classic *Pink Flamingos*. Tentatively titled *Flamingos Forever*, Waters sent his friend from Baltimore and her agent the script. They
were appalled by it, repulsed by scenes in which Divine's character was supposed to
float off to heaven on a giant turd. Shock tactics such as these, they were convinced,
wouldn't fly in the conservative Reagan years and would simply be considered bad
taste.[3] John Waters didn't pursue the project.

II

After his disappointing experience with Orion, John Langdon very much wanted
to keep the rights to *A Confederacy of Dunces*. At the same time, though he had
grown frustrated, to him there was no question that he would eventually succeed in
bringing the adventures of Ignatius to the screen. Still, Langdon had rejected Robert
Chartoff's offer. Mike Medavoy hadn't seen a way forward, and Robert Shaye—when
approached by Scott Kramer—did not wish to finance the project either. Universal
Pictures, approached by Langdon in 1986, had balked at his asking price of $250,000
for the rights and passed.[4] For years, Langdon had burned money on the project

without yielding any discernible results. He had approached directors, actors and even musicians left and right without having secured financing. Finally, in 1987, there was a silver lining: Harold Ramis got involved.

Ramis had worked with John Belushi on *Second City TV,* become friends with him and written the screenplay for Belushi's big breakthrough, *Animal House.* In 1980, Ramis had made his debut as a director with *Caddyshack,* a comedy about an exclusive golf course tyrannized by gophers. Although the film received mixed reviews, it was an instant smash hit at the box office. A future for Ramis as a director of hugely successful comedy films lay ahead of him. He would go on to direct *Vacation* (1983); *Groundhog Day* (1993); and *Analyze This* (1999), a film about a mob boss seeking a therapist's help which was released the same year *The Sopranos* premiered. He and Mike Medavoy were good friends—the latter had distributed *Caddyshack,* one of Orion's financially most successful projects.

As it was, after the financial debacle of his 1986 film, *Club Paradise,* Ramis was looking for new opportunities. His friend and producing partner Trevor Albert, with whom he had worked for years, gave him Toole's novel to read, and both fell in love with the work instantly. As Albert remembers: "We found it enthralling and funny, and it represented a lot of sensibilities that we admired in comedy and literature and storytelling."[5] The novel also felt oddly "cinematic," as if it was only waiting to be adapted for the screen. Thus, *A Confederacy of Dunces* was to be their next project after *Club Paradise,* an ill-fated comedy with Robin Williams and Peter O'Toole set on a Caribbean island.

III

In order to seriously consider taking on the project they needed to find out who owned the movie rights to the book. Albert and Ramis contacted Louisiana State University Press, which duly informed them that the rights rested with John Langdon of Bumbershoot Productions. As luck would have it, since he hadn't been able to find financial backers for close to four years, Langdon was currently looking for somebody to option the rights. Ramis and Albert had a first-look option at Twentieth Century–Fox at the time, which obligated them to show the studio everything they were planning to develop.[6] At the helm of Fox was a young, dynamic force stirring up Hollywood: Scott Rudin.

Born in 1958 in New York City, Rudin had been a casting director for Broadway shows before forming his own company, Scott Rudin Productions, and becoming president of production at Twentieth Century–Fox in 1986. A year later, *A Confederacy of Dunces* was brought to his attention.

Unlike most producers in Hollywood, Rudin was a passionate reader and knew his literature. As such, he was familiar with the novel and expressed his interest in getting the project off the ground.

After receiving the green light from Rudin, Albert and Ramis set up a meeting with John Langdon. They had to convince him they were the right people to take on *A Confederacy of Dunces.* Langdon was delighted, since Harold Ramis's work was right up his alley.[7] Therefore, the entrepreneur from Texas seemed willing to sell the rights to Twentieth Century–Fox, staying involved only as executive producer.

Although the meeting went well for Langdon, it was a disaster for Maidee Walker. Soon it would lead to a break between her and her business partner, as it became clear that the director's ideas were vastly different from hers. "Ramis was involved, and he wanted to do his own screenplay. He wanted to make it more slapstick. He wasn't going to take the essence of the book, the satirical side. He was going to make it funny, and I don't think it was meant to be funny like that. The book had nothing to do with *Saturday Night Live* and Harold Ramis."[8]

IV

For Walker, Ramis's involvement meant her screenplay was not going to be used—Langdon hadn't been too convinced that her script was going to work, and Ramis had his own plans anyway. Although Walker quite liked Ramis, she didn't appreciate his approach as a director, and things came to a head between her and Langdon. After several years of trying to secure financing and sign up actors for the various roles in the film, she decided it was time to leave Bumbershoot and dedicate her time to other projects. She explains: "I opted out and said, 'I can't deal with this.' [Ramis] would have made something like *Meatballs*, *Animal House*, or *Caddyshack*. Come on! Langdon and I did not agree on the way things should proceed. We parted ways because of that, because of the way he wanted to do it and the way I saw it. I saw it in a complete opposite way. I didn't want to have anything to do with it. It never happened."[9]

Walker and Langdon's relationship turned sour. It wasn't helped by the fact that Langdon didn't want to pay Walker for writing the screenplay: "He didn't offer me anything for the script. That was another not very nice note to leave on, because I had worked so hard. We didn't part on very good circumstances and we had been friends since we had been children."[10]

Maidee Walker decided to file a lawsuit against her old childhood friend in order to get what she deemed she deserved—a financial compensation for having written the script.[11]

Langdon's daughter, Kendall, concedes that her father could be difficult at times, and she wasn't surprised that things went south between him and Walker: "I know that despite my dad not having had a lot of very good business sense, he was a kind and compassionate person and he could get really heated. He could be an asshole sometimes, but then he would be over it and be back to being his kind, compassionate self. I am sure he rubbed people the wrong way over the years."[12]

The lawsuit, in which Langdon was represented by his Fort Worth attorney Phil Dixon, was eventually settled out of court.[13] The producer and his former friend and colleague made up several years later, after the storm had settled. Maidee Walker would continue to meet with Langdon, reminisce about old times, and attend his birthday parties. They remained good friends until his passing.

V

For Walker, what had started as an exciting project became cursed, a hopeless endeavor that had yielded no acceptable results. Yet in Walker's view, he hadn't been able to do anything the way it should have been done. If the film was made eventually, Walker would receive a credit as associate producer, regardless of her involvement. It would be a small victory. For Langdon, things were looking up, though, with Ramis and Twentieth Century–Fox as possible partners in crime. Even so, Bumbershoot had achieved nothing for the longest time.

"[Walker and Langdon] went through a whole bunch of money," remarks Susan O'Connell, "trying to get the script out there without knowing anybody in Hollywood. It was a fool's errand, although the book was known. Johnny's view was never ever negative. It was always kind of hopeful. He knew it was going to take crazy energy to do it. That's what he felt about Ignatius."[14]

VI

In order to sign over the rights for a finite amount of time, a couple of questions had first to be answered. Over the past seven years, the rights had reverted from Scott Kramer to Carson Productions to Bumbershoot Productions.

Setting up a contract between Fox and Bumbershoot was no easy feat, as Maidee Walker remembers: "It was even confusing back then. It was like, 'Who has the rights now and who is involved and who isn't?' It was a mess. It really was."[15] With all the paperwork on the table and the rights cleared—with Bumbershoot as the sole owner—Langdon, Albert and Ramis set up shop at Twentieth Century–Fox, which paid $150,000 for the option.[16] If the film wasn't in production within the next five years, the rights would revert back to Bumbershoot.

Of course, John Langdon and Scott Rudin were polar opposites. While Langdon was a free-spirited inventor and entrepreneur, his counterpart was a tough businessman in Studio City. Their approaches to projects and their understandings of the film industry were vastly different. Nevertheless, Langdon and Rudin were amicable with one another and remained so until Langdon's death.[17]

Although the president of Bumbershoot Productions had no creative input in the decisions Albert and Ramis took, he would receive credit as executive producer, since the rights had been his. The same went for Scott Kramer: although he no longer owned any rights to *A Confederacy of Dunces,* due to his earlier involvement he would receive remuneration as associate producer. In early 1987, the Toole Estate had requested he repay a loan he had received to push the movie adaptation of Ken's novel forward. As it stood, Kramer was unable to repay the money he owned, as for years he had worked without compensation and was now in dire straits.[18] He was therefore eager to see the cameras rolling—as soon as principal photography started, he would receive a cheque.

For the new creative team, it was important to get a feel for the environment depicted in the novel. Neither Ramis nor Albert had previously been to New Orleans, so the latter took an initial trip to the city before he and Ramis started thinking about possible writers for the script. "I tried to get a sense of the city and the people," explains Albert, "just so as we were developing [the film] we would have an understanding of it. I ended up spending probably four, five months over the course of the next few years in New Orleans, talking to people about the book and about shooting it there, what that would be like."[19]

Representatives of the Film Commission in New Orleans escorted the producer around to show him the sights that could be captured on film. As part of his research, Albert also talked to residents of the city who knew John Kennedy Toole and his mother.

Meanwhile, Harold Ramis had come up with a new idea for the script—he turned to somebody who had already pondered the idea of writing an adaptation of *A Confederacy of Dunces*: Stephen Geller.

VII

Geller seemed an obvious choice. Despite the obvious difficulties in making a movie out of Vonnegut's literary masterpiece, his *Slaughterhouse-Five* adaptation had been much lauded. Albert admits that *Slaughterhouse-Five* wasn't "much good as a film itself," but that the screenplay was tremendous: "You can't compare *Slaughterhouse-Five* to *Dunces*, but *Slaughterhouse-Five* was also very difficult to adapt, and Vonnegut also has very unique voice. Geller had done such a good job with that, maybe he is the right guy."[20] The only drawback was that Geller wasn't from the South, something that Ramis and Albert found important.

During the '60s and early '70s, Geller had lived in Italy, where he was under contract for producer Dino de Laurentiis. It was the best time in the author's life: he could pick and choose his projects, writing one script a year for the American film industry while enjoying Mediterranean food in Rome. When he eventually came back to the U.S., he found the film landscape changed completely: while directors were hailed as auteurs in the '60s and '70s, largely left alone by producers, due to several high-profile flops that nearly bankrupted the studios—*Heaven's Gate* (1980) most notorious among them—this had all changed. Suddenly, producers were running the show again, often developing five or even six projects at the same time.

Geller was dumbfounded about some of the tactics employed in Hollywood in the late '70s and early '80s. A producer would sign a contract to run a studio, only for the studio to then decide to fire said producer a few months later. Since producers couldn't be fired easily because of their binding contracts, the studio had to buy them out, earning them several million dollars for a few months of work. Geller understood quickly that everything was about "the deal," while the true artistic spirit had taken a back seat.

While this was not a pleasant environment for Geller to work in, he was quite intrigued when he received a phone call one day with an offer to write a script for *A Confederacy of Dunces*.[21] The screenwriter was surprised to learn that Harold Ramis would direct the film—Geller had "hated" *Caddyshack*, which he found an abominably silly film, and he certainly didn't share Ramis's sense of humor.[22] The writer was very careful to commit to the project on the spot, fearing difficulties along the way:

INT. STEPHEN'S HOME. DAY.
STEPHEN is on the phone.

HAROLD'S ASSISTANT
Would you at least meet with him and talk with him about it?

STEPHEN
Sure.

HAROLD'S ASSISTANT
What would you like to ask him?

STEPHEN
I want to know why he wants to do the movie. I can write it, but that's not the issue.
I am not sure that what I write would ever be done the way that the author had
intentionally intended it to be.[23]

Stephen Geller did have a pleasant meeting with Harold Ramis, who he found polite and soft-spoken. That didn't mean that Geller was convinced their project would be successful. He therefore asked the director a very simple question—why did he want to make this adaptation?

INT. HAROLD'S OFFICE. DAY.
HAROLD and STEPHEN sit opposite each other.

HAROLD
It's a terribly funny book.

STEPHEN
Yes, but everything you have done so far is very different from it.

HAROLD
Not at all!

STEPHEN
My experience in this town is that you are expected to perform a certain way.
I am not, which is probably why you asked if I'd be interested,
but you are going to be under a tremendous amount of pressure
to push the film a certain way that is unlike anything you have done.

HAROLD
I am perfectly capable of doing it and I love the book![24]

Finally, Stephen Geller agreed to give it a try, though he took some precautions to protect himself from the studio and the director not accepting his work. Geller explains:

I said, "I am going to do an outline first before I begin to write. I want to discuss it with you before I begin because you are not going to see me before I finish the first draft. I want to make sure we are in agreement about the film and its tone and intention. If we are not, before I start writing you better find somebody who agrees with what your vision is."

[Ramis] said, "Fine," and I went and did an outline. I came back and went through it with him scene by scene. We did this twice, and he agreed to the outline. I had him sign it, and he said, "Why should I sign it?"

I said, "Because when I turn the first draft in you'll probably claim this isn't what we talked about. I speak from experience."

"What happens if you change direction?"

"I'll call you. Any point along the way I'll call you and make suggestions. You are going to know every step of the way what I am doing, but I am not going to show it to you until it's finished."

He said, "Fine."[25]

Not everything was fine, though, and Geller soon got an inkling that a storm was brewing.

14

The Bad News Is There
Is No Good News

How Scott Rudin's departure from Twentieth Century–Fox puts the
project in jeopardy, and Stephen Geller wrestles with John Kennedy
Toole's masterpiece

In 1989, only shortly after Geller had agreed to pen the script, Scott Rudin left Twentieth Century–Fox for Paramount. While Amy Pascal was named creative executive of Fox, the new head was Joe Roth.[1] Stephen Geller had no high opinion of him, as he makes clear: "He was known for action movies and for a kind of blatant mediocrity. He was fabulously proud of his own mediocrity."[2] [Cue Ignatius: "Oh, good heavens! (...) What degenerate produced this abortion? (...) Just look at these smiling morons! If only all of those wires would snap!"[3]]

According to Geller, he was "[t]he kind of person who says, 'I know what people want and this is what I give them. I don't give a damn one way or the other.' It's stupidity and vulgarity, and when I heard that he had been made head of Fox, I said to Harold, 'We are really in trouble. This man is not going to get the book.'"[4]

Upon receiving the news of Roth's involvement, Geller might have very well said: "This is going to be even worse than I thought."[5]

Popular acclaim is not worth talking about. It comes randomly, for little or no reason, and it never lasts very long.[6]

Joe Roth hadn't read the book and was in unfamiliar territory with a comedy-melodrama about a heavy-set, chaos-bringing medievalist roaming through New Orleans. Geller also experienced a more general fear which was based on his experiences in the industry: whenever the head of a studio changes, a vast number of projects that were in development are dropped. This was as much the case in the '80s as it is today. There are several reasons for this, two of the most important being the new head's lack of passion for a production, and the possibility of a bruised executive ego: if a film that has been developed under a predecessor becomes a huge hit, it is clear to everybody that the praise will not be directed at the new head. In short: Geller wasn't hopeful for *A Confederacy of Dunces* surviving under Amy Pascal and Joe Roth. Nevertheless, he kept working on the script and turned in the first draft to Ramis and Albert. It didn't take long for Geller's fear to be confirmed.

II

One afternoon, the writer received a call from Harold Ramis. The director was clearly disturbed by a meeting he had just had with Joe Roth:

> INT. STEPHEN'S OFFICE. DAY.
> STEPHEN is on the phone.
>
> HAROLD
> I had the most surreal meeting.
>
> STEPHEN
> Yeah, I can imagine.
>
> HAROLD
> The first thing Roth said to me was, "This is a piece
> of shit. What the fuck is a medievalist?" I explained
> it and he then said: "Who the hell knows such a character?
> If I don't know what it is, nobody knows what it is.
> He can't be a medievalist! And I don't like
> the Jewish girl, Myra. It's antisemitic."
>
> STEPHEN
> Wow, first of all, he is very Catholic. Her love for him
> out of masochism and sorrow is very Jewish and very right.[7]

Geller was Jewish himself—as was Roth—and found his criticism ridiculous. The producer wasn't the only force to be reckoned with. While working on the script with Harold Ramis, Geller found himself at odds with the director's partner, Erica Mann-Ramis, filmmaker Michael Mann's sister. While the two men were working diligently on revisions of the script, Mann-Ramis would often chime in by asking what certain statements and metaphors meant. After Geller, impatient to get on with the work and tired of constant explanations, blew up one day, he found himself compared to Ignatius by Ramis's partner. He also didn't find it particularly helpful to hear her describe how her brother would stage a scene, painfully aware that *A Confederacy of Dunces* was not a project Michael Mann would ever touch.[8]

III

Although he was happy with the work he had done, things slowly began to sour for Geller. He followed his usual approach, which he had also taken for his adaptation of *Slaughterhouse-Five*. The writer explains:

> It was totally the tone and principal events of the book. But most importantly it was Ignatius's point of view. It was a fantastically paranoid vision of the world and rich in its medieval angst and fury. I had incredible fun. It was the book. One of the things I had learned early on is that in the screenplay as long as the characters are the characters of the author and the themes are the themes of the author, the least important aspect are the events—unless they are an intricate part of the character, which of course in *A Confederacy of Dunces* can't be any other way. In *Slaughterhouse-Five* that's exactly the way, but what I did there was imitate Kurt Vonnegut's tone so that you have a sense of reading and seeing Vonnegut in all of the scenes, when in fact there is so little dialogue in the book it gives the effect that you are reading and seeing Vonnegut. In effect you are seeing an approximation.

> It's not the real thing, but in terms of the texture of the work, the language, the scenes themselves and Kurt's intention, it was the book. The same was true with the screenplay of *A Confederacy of Dunces*, safe that it actually adhered much more strictly and strongly to the author's intention because the book is Ignatius. The dialogue was so easy because it wrote itself. It was there on the page. The characters are already there.[9]

In addition to his outline that had been accepted and signed by Harold Ramis, Geller wrote two drafts of the script. Although the director assured his colleague he loved his work, Ramis would later say Geller's script "didn't feel like a commercial movie,"[10] a statement that could have been made about the novel itself.

Susan O'Connell, who was not yet involved, but who started working on *A Confederacy of Dunces* a few years later, didn't consider Geller's script worth consideration, calling it "horrible."[11] She also didn't think Geller captured the darker side of the story: "[The book is] very well balanced in terms of its character development. It brings everything along. Then you have all of these wonderful surprises coming from Ignatius's imagination about how to solve that situation. Who would think of that? I agree it's not a comedy. But it's a dark comedy, if anything."[12]

Trevor Albert and Harold Ramis soon understood how tricky an adaptation of the book was—not because Geller's script didn't work for them, but because they realized that there were several aspects of it that would cause problems regardless of who tried their hand at a screenplay. Says Albert: "The first thing you realize when you take *A Confederacy of Dunces* and you turn it into a screenplay is it sounds so funny when you read it in a book, but those lines don't feel quite so funny when you read them in a screenplay. How much voice-over do you use? Can you present the voice-over in a different way, so it's not a matter of Ignatius actually talking, because that seems weird? That stuff quickly became challenging."[13]

There were other challenges as well which had to do with the passage of time, with changes in society since the book had been published. They also had to do with political correctness, as Albert resumes:

> One of the things that undermined certainly us was, "What's the plot?" A big part of it centers around pornography, and by the time we were developing the movie that was less scandalous than when the book came out. The idea of dirty magazines would be hard to explain to young people. Why was that such a thing? Machine guns may be more provocative than the ideas of illicit girly pictures. That seems mild now. A lot of the plot centers around that in a way. That was problematic. How do you portray Myrna Minkoff as the times are changing? Can you make that character relatable for contemporary audiences? [What about] Jones? How do you treat the line of not making it feel racist? He's hilarious and in that time subversive, but what does that feel like now? A lot of the things we didn't see when we optioned it. Until you start working on it you don't always realize where the problems lie.[14]

IV

There were numerous problems concerning the historical aspects. Doris Day, Ignatius's least favorite motion picture actress, was the one of the major stars of her time—the '50s and '60s—but would less sophisticated members of the audience, especially the younger generation which studios needed to attract in order to generate revenue, still understand Toole's numerous pop-culture references? Would it make sense to set a screen adaptation of *A Confederacy of Dunces* in the modern-day United States?

As if it were all so simple. Important plot points would either have to fall away or be replaced, such as Lana Lee's distribution of what in the 1960s constituted outrageous pornography. Nowadays, in an age when hardcore pornography in all its facets and with all its kinks can be downloaded with a single click, Lee's material is a mere trifle. Already in the late '80s, it provoked little more than a tired smirk or a weary shrug.

On the other hand, Ignatius's nature demands that he express his thoughts in an appropriately inappropriate manner which would certainly guarantee a restrictive R-rating at the box office. As shockingly politically incorrect these outraged musings are, they are what makes Ignatius in the first place. *A Confederacy of Dunces* is rich in examples: "The children on that program should all be gassed,"[15] "It is mechanized Negro slavery; it represents the progress the Negro has made from picking cotton to tailoring it,"[16] "I do admire the terror which Negros are able to inspire in the hearts of some members of the white proletariat and only wish (This is a rather personal confession.) that I possessed the ability to similarly terrorize,"[17] "How dare she pretend to be a virgin. Look at her degenerate face. Rape her!"[18] And so on.

How to even hint at Ignatius's warped sexuality, which he can only express when lying on his stained bed, thinking of his beloved Rex: "Ignatius touched the small erection that was pointing downward into the sheet, held it, and lay still trying to decide what to do. [...] At one time he had almost developed it into an art form, practicing the hobby with the skill and fervor of an artist and philosopher, a scholar and gentleman. There were still hidden in his room several accessories which he had once used, a rubber glove, a piece of fabric from a silk umbrella, a jar of Noxema. Putting them away again after it was all over had eventually grown too depressing."[19]

V

Given Geller's explanation of his approach to adaptations, it is not surprising his screenplay for *A Confederacy of Dunces* changed several aspects of the book. The most glaring difference is a very basic one: while John Kennedy Toole wrote his novel in the 60s and placed Ignatius in the New Orleans of the same decade, Geller updated the source material by putting it in the '80s.

Ignatius's passion for pop music is reflected in him watching television in his room, preferably programs with MTV-like dance parties. As in the book, he records his thoughts in the now-famous Big Chief tablets, and is not content sitting on them like J.D. Salinger, who refused to seek a publisher for the majority of his works. Quite the opposite, Ignatius is most keen on sharing his thoughts about medieval philosophy in modern culture with people who might not be the ideal target audience. Therefore, Ignatius is deeply upset when *People Magazine* and *SELF* refuse to publish his musings on "Fourteenth Century Abuses among the Carmelite Nuns" and "Modern Methods of Martyrdom."

The slackers of the '80s wouldn't be real slackers, though, if they didn't spend a portion of their time playing video games, which is exactly what Geller makes Ignatius do—in a video arcade, no less. There are even references to a well-known tech company when the main character rummages through his drawers at Levy Pants, only to proclaim that he just found a "Macintosh." This is not evidence, as suspected by Gonzalez. Said Macintosh is, of course, a mere apple, which Ignatius starts munching with great delight. His love for Dr. Nut, meanwhile, has given way to a desire for chicory coffee with boiled milk—a drink Ignatius tries to order repeatedly, only to be informed that instant coffee is the only coffee available.

Myrna Minkoff makes her entrance in a coffee house. As in Maidee Walker's script, she appears early on. Here, she is present throughout most scenes. In Geller's work, she serves as the moral backbone of a society that has fallen prey to rampant capitalism. Her fight for the disenfranchised is one Ignatius can fully get behind—or is, at least, willing to consider, since he respects Myrna a great deal more in Geller's adaptation than in Toole's novel. Ignatius even seriously ponders accepting her invitation to come to Manhattan with him in the quest for a better society.

Joe Roth might have had problems with the depiction of Myrna, but especially as a Jew, phrases such as "These children should be gassed," which is uttered by Ignatius as a reaction to an especially appalling TV program, wouldn't have sat well with him either. Since he hadn't read the novel, he had no way of knowing that this was John Kennedy Toole's phrase, in style with the rest of the book, a feast of political incorrectness.

As much as Ignatius likes Myrna, the object of his attraction in Geller's screenplay is none other than Darlene, who moves through the scenes like a ghost—or, rather, like a fever dream. Standing on street corners and trying to attract clients, the stripper and prostitute makes Ignatius's head turn more than once, and although he knows neither her name nor her background, he is hopelessly enamored of her, proudly announcing to his mother that he plans to make Darlene his wife.

He gets the chance to speak with her eventually, although the scenario is less romantic than Ignatius hoped. Lured into the Night of Joy, he spots Darlene dancing on the stage. Convinced that the club is not only a whorehouse but that its owners are also human sex traffickers, he tries to rescue her from the establishment. In the course of his ensuing escape, the big-boned hero accidentally encounters a group orgy in which people are putting roses into various bodily openings, while others are playing lutes, or with each other. Attracting the gaze of Mancuso outside the club, Ignatius exposes the Night of Joy for what it is and, along with Jones, becomes a hero in the press.

Burma Jones's relationship to Ignatius is different from that in the novel. In Geller's script, Jones works at Levy Pants until he is fired for his taking part in Ignatius's ill-fated protest for better working conditions. His job at the Night of Joy earns him less money than at Levy Pants, which had already made it next to impossible for him to provide for himself. Considering the state of the factory, this is not surprising, since Geller paints the company as a hellhole straight out of a painting by Hieronymus Bosch's (Ignatius's favorite painter)—the perfect working environment for the hot dog loving anti-hero.

Having already failed a job interview at an insurance company after insulting his potential new employer, Ignatius accepts Gonzalez's offer, only to wreak havoc on the premises. Ignatius's job as a hot dog vendor gives Geller yet more possibilities to turn up the level of mean-spirited rudeness on Ignatius's part. The screenwriter depicts Ignatius as a Larry David–like figure, a decade before *Curb Your Enthusiasm* premiered. When, for example, Ignatius refuses to sell a hot dog to a young boy, he is duly informed by the child that he is legally obliged to sell him the product. Ignatius replies curtly the young boy's mama is a cow.

In spirit, the script is not far removed from the book, in which Ignatius is already portrayed as the social assassin described by Geller and later modified by Larry David: "'Magnolias don't look like that,' Ignatius said, thrusting his cutlass at the offending pastel magnolia. 'You ladies need a course in botany. And perhaps geometry, too.' 'You don't have to look at our work,' an offended voice said from the group, the voice of the lady who had drawn the magnolia in question. 'Yes, I do!' Ignatius screamed. 'You ladies need a critic with some taste and decency. Good heavens! Which one of you did this camellia? Speak up. The water in this bowl looks like motor oil.'"[20]

For Ignatius, there is no shortage of opportunities to teach his fellow citizens about medieval philosophy, even if *People Magazine* refuses to print his observations. As in the novel, the New Orleanian once took up a teaching position at Tulane, only to be dismissed from his job after one day. Geller's depiction of Ignatius as a teacher echoes John Kennedy Toole's last weeks of teaching—not necessarily because Toole ordered his students to write a 500-page paper on Boethius's *Consolation of Philosophy*, but because his distraught students are immediately irritated and frightened by the raving scholar who seems to have lost his marbles.

Despite these sometimes radical changes, Geller stays true to the characters, and even provides Ignatius with an inner life and with emotions that were not evident in Maidee Walker's version of the story. His eyes after a day of work at Levy Pants, for example, are "weary and sad," and he is clearly deeply distraught by the news that his mother Irene has accepted the marriage proposal of Robichaux (spelled Robichaud in the screenplay). Geller has fun playing with these characters. For example, he has Mancuso taken away to "chariddy" by the attendants at the end of the story after a cunning Ignatius has convinced them that he was Professor Boethius and the clumsy policeman was the lunatic they sought.

VI

Harold Ramis and Trevor Albert didn't find Geller's throw-away lines such as "Welcome to the Night of Joy, Lazies and Genitals," as proclaimed by Lana Lee, particularly amusing. As the author had feared, Roth and Pascal as the people in power didn't "get" either the novel or his adaptation of it when it was described to them by Ramis and Albert, who were never happy enough with Geller's adaptation to show it to the studio head.[21] What Roth heard didn't please his ears. He had a problem: this shocking work was not a film for John Candy.[22]

15

A New Broom Sweeps Clean

How Stephen Geller exits the project and is replaced by a Pulitzer Prize-winning playwright from Mississippi

When Ramis informed Geller, the writer was perplexed—it was the first time he had heard John Candy mentioned as a leading man. In fact, Geller had a very different actor in mind for the role of Ignatius.

Before he had embarked on the script, Geller had watched a warmly received British miniseries called *Edge of Darkness*. One actor made a particularly big impression on him: Ian McNeice. Born in 1950 in Hampshire, England, McNeice had made a name for himself as a reliable supporting actor in British film and television. The heavy-set actor had already appeared in *84 Charing Cross Road* along with Anthony Hopkins and in *The Lonely Passion of Judith Hearne* with Maggie Smith. He would go on to star in *Funny Bones* with Jerry Lewis, *Ace Ventura: When Nature Calls* with Jim Carrey, and *From Hell* with Johnny Depp.

The suggestion of casting Ian McNeice in *A Confederacy of Dunces* fell on deaf ears with Joe Roth, although Geller remembers that Ramis was quite taken with this idea: "Harold kept saying during the writing, 'Who do you see playing Ignatius?' I said, 'Simple, it's the most obvious thing in the world! There is a fabulous British production called *Edge of Darkness*, a TV series with Robert Peck and Joe Don Baker.' The MI5 guy was played by the juiciest actor in the world who was perfect for Ignatius. 'Who is it?' 'Ian McNeice. He is ideal. You gotta see him!' It was a while ago and Ian was still young. Harold saw *Edge of Darkness* and he lost his mind. He said, 'Oh my God, he's perfect! That's our Ignatius!'"[1]

It wasn't "their" Ignatius, as far as Joe Roth could see it. Geller continues: "When Roth mentioned John Candy, Harold said, 'I know there is a person who is really wonderful for this, who has the intelligence, the lunacy and the snottiness and all the characteristics of Ignatius, and that is Ian McNeice.' And Roth said, 'I don't want to hear about it! Nobody knows who the hell he is!' 'Well, he is a big star in Great Britain.' 'Fuck Great Britain! He is not John Candy!'"[2]

II

By that point, Stephen Geller was thoroughly fed up, and the producer had already demanded a couple of other changes that didn't sit well with Ramis and Geller. Roth didn't want Ignatius to be a medievalist, Myrna was not supposed to be

Jewish, and Irene needed to be "nicer"—a harmless eccentric who could be played by somebody like Debbie Reynolds. Geller was furious: "So it's John Candy and Debbie Reynolds. At that time I thought, to say it with Samuel Goldwyn, 'Quote me out!' I am not the least bit interested in pursuing this. It's just ridiculous! It's not the book. He doesn't care about making this movie."[3]

It was clear that everybody involved in the production was at odds about the approach to the film, and Geller didn't see a way forward. He left the project. One last suggestion he made to Harold Ramis was to take the film back to Scott Rudin at Paramount. But Ramis didn't follow his colleague's advice, convinced that he could reach a compromise with Joe Roth. Geller was surprised, then, to see a certain movie trailer a few years later. The movie in question was called *Only the Lonely* and featured John Candy and Maureen O'Hara—as opposed to Debbie Reynolds— in the main roles and was a Twentieth Century–Fox production. The film revolved around a heavy-set man in his thirties who still lived with his mother, to whom he is deeply devoted—until he falls in love with a woman whom his mother views with disapproval.

For Geller, it was clear what had happened: Roth had taken the aspects of *A Confederacy of Dunces* he liked and commissioned a screenplay for a sweet-natured romantic comedy that was easily marketable. Geller recalls laughing: "The postscript to all of this, which is amazing, is that the film was never made, but Joe Roth did get his wish of making a film with John Candy. He took the idea of a fat man living with his mother, falling in love with a girl and having to choose between his mother and the girl. They basically stole from *A Confederacy of Dunces*—when you say the jewelry is in the safe, it's not in the cupboard, they will go straight to the cupboard and they will take the plates and they will miss the jewels. They are going to be wise-ass. They made that movie called *Only the Lonely*. That was Twentieth Century–Fox's answer to *A Confederacy of Dunces*. That's it. Isn't that funny?"[4]

It was clear to Geller that *A Confederacy of Dunces* would never be made under Joe Roth's reign—no matter who would replace him as screenwriter. And Geller would be proven right.

III

Even with Stephen Geller off the project, director Harold Ramis still had several options: he could shop the project over to Paramount, where Scott Rudin might bring it to life; he could simply give up and devote himself to other films; or he could stay at Fox and try to entice Joe Roth with a new writer. Ramis opted for the latter. Since he wasn't over the moon about Geller's adaptation anyway, he and Albert enlisted Beth Henley to pen a rewrite.

Albert explains: "Somebody recommended her and we thought that was an interesting idea, to get back the Southern sensibility and a sense of humor. Although Geller had a sense of humor, he didn't have the Southern sensibility. Maybe telling the story from a woman's point of view would change the dynamics of the script."[5]

Born in 1952 in Mississippi, Henley had an ear for Southern dialects and an understanding of the Southern way of life. In 1981 she had won the Pulitzer Prize for her play *Crimes of the Heart*, which in 1986 would be adapted into a feature film directed by Bruce Beresford. Originally, Jonathan Demme had been contracted to direct the film from a screenplay by Henley.[6] However, after she was fired, Demme quit in protest, only for the project to be revived by Beresford a few years later.

The year of 1981 was the year in which John Kennedy Toole had been awarded the Pulitzer for his novel—a further common denominator between Henley and Toole. Her success following *Crimes of the Heart* had intrigued Hollywood executives, who paid her to write several scripts, most of which were never filmed.

While Stephen Geller was writing his version of *A Confederacy of Dunces*, Henley had premiered *Miss Firecracker* in 1989, an independent comedy directed by Thomas Schlamme based on her play for which she had also written the screen adaptation. When Geller heard that she had committed to the job, he already knew that Joe Roth could never be convinced to make the movie, regardless of how brilliant Henley's script might be.

Henley did enjoy writing screenplays for films, though she was already aware that writing for film or television was much different from writing plays for the theater. In regard to writing for TV, she was quoted as saying, "You go in with a committee of people and each one gets one of their own ideas in. It's like nailing them all together and trying to patchwork the thing. And it comes out brown dishwater: non-specific, bland. I mean, they work at getting things bland for TV."[7] In regard to writing film scripts, her stance was slightly different. Asked what she enjoyed most about it, she replied: "Well, let's see. We wouldn't want to say money, would we? Actually, I love to work on a great book with a great director. It's like getting paid to go to some special Harvard class."[8]

IV

After being contacted by Harold Ramis and his producing partner Trevor Albert, who also loved *Crimes of the Heart*, Henley didn't hesitate to accept their offer to adapt John Kennedy Toole's novel.[9] Two reasons had convinced her: her love for the book, and money. Henley remembers: "It seemed like a lot at the time, but I wasn't used to getting a lot of money. If you are a playwright, you are just so grateful to get money. I was working with nice people on projects I loved."[10] At the same time, "*A Confederacy of Dunces* was like a self-taught masterclass. That's something I would have done for free."[11]

Ramis and Albert gave her free rein to "do what you do," which—without reading any of the previous screenplays that had been written for *A Confederacy of Dunces* and which Ramis kept her from studying—Henley set out and did. The playwright explains: "I was already a huge fan of the book. I am from Mississippi, so New Orleans is close to my heart. I loved doing the adaptation. It was one of the first times when you fell deeply in love with the author that you are doing the adaptation from. John Kennedy Toole got really under my skin. I really enjoyed writing it."[12]

That doesn't mean that she found it easy, as she confessed: "It's so sprawling and the tone so specific that it's hard to capture and dilute into a two-hour movie. The Reader's Digest version is not going to be the same."[13]

Neither was this particularly good time in Henley's life. While she was working on the first draft of the screenplay, she was also busy preparing for the production of one of her plays, which was to be staged at the Manhattan Theater Club. Unfortunately for everybody involved, the preparations turned out to be a disaster: the lead actress appeared three days late, only to quit after four days of work.[14]

Henley was a "mess," and it certainly didn't help that Ramis and Albert suggested some major changes to her first draft. The writer assured the duo she would oblige, but found herself dumbstruck when she went to a meeting with them: "They decided that for some reason they weren't too interested in the story of the book."[15] The director and producer were more intrigued by the characters, but weren't too concerned about following the adventures as described in the novel. When they suggested Henley let Ignatius work as a policeman in New Orleans, she nearly fell from her chair: "I was like, 'You know, I can't do that. I am a writer.' That's what I remember. They were very nice, though. They weren't going to do the book, they were going to use the character from the book. I didn't know where they were going with it, so I said, 'You better get somebody else.'"[16] (John Candy, who by then Ramis and Albert had in mind for the role, later played a policeman in the aforementioned *Only the Lonely*.)

V

In her screenplay, Henley reversed some changes made by Geller. Her work, written in 1990, avoids references to modern comforts such as MTV. For her, *A Confederacy of Dunces* was a period piece and should remain one.

In hindsight, Harold Ramis realized that Beth Henley was right. To him, it didn't feel like a movie either, and Joe Roth still had zilch interest in financing a venture that in his opinion had as much commercial potential as a five-hour, black-and-white film of a glass of sour milk sitting in a kitchen pantry. It simply was not the crowd-pleaser Roth had in mind. Trevor Albert confesses: "I don't think we ever figured out between Stephen Geller and Beth Henley what the three-act structure was in the story, and how much would be voice-over, and all that stuff. We ran into roadblocks with both those writers, not for any lack of talent, but as people before and after us have learned it's very tricky, translating the story into a screenplay. Well, there is certainly lots of funny stuff in both drafts but never as good as the book."[17]

Ramis had to stand by helplessly and watch the option at Fox run out. Several years had passed since Bumbershoot Productions signed over the rights, and neither Ramis and Albert nor Pascal and Roth were interested in renewing the option. Ramis and Albert "came to the realization that we didn't know how to do it," as the latter puts it.[18] Maybe it was best if Ramis, Albert, and Beth Henley concentrated on new projects. The trio would talk about other possible co-ventures, none of which would come to pass.[19]

During her busiest period as a screenwriter for Hollywood productions Beth Henley adapted Reynolds Price's novel *A Long and Happy Life* as well as *The Shipping News* by Annie Proulx (neither adaptation would ever be realized), and also worked closely with Jonathan Demme on a number of projects. One of these was *The Stopwatch Gang*, a script about a woman and two men who successfully pull off a heist. They only get arrested when they start spending the stolen money lavishly, but manage to escape from prison and start planning their next big operation. The production was supposed to start in September 1996, but as Demme and Henley discovered, no executive was willing to bankroll it.[20]

16

Back to Base

How John Langdon enlists the help of Susan O'Connell, who immedi-
ately starts to breathe life into the project by trying to find a director

In late 1991 the rights to *A Confederacy of Dunces* reverted back to John Langdon—and he couldn't have been happier about it. His passion for the project hadn't
waned, and he was now more determined than ever to make the film a reality.

In May 1992, he reported that the project was back at Bumbershoot and that
he had a script.[1] That claim wasn't a lie per se, but more than anything it was a PR
move designed to entice the press. Langdon still held the rights to Maidee Walker's
draft, but by then he had come to the conclusion that he would not use it. He had also
learned another lesson from his endeavor with Maidee Walker: it was a waste of time
trying to run a production company without at least one person knowing the ins and
outs of the movie business. He needed somebody to help him get the project off the
ground, and, as coincidence would have it, he soon met someone he thought could be
his ideal business partner: Susan O'Connell.

Before devoting more and more time to the stage, where she appeared in a
production of *The Miracle Worker*, among others, O'Connell had been an actress
who had starred in TV shows such as *Ironside*. Although she had studied acting at UCLA and spent most of her professional life in Los Angeles, she eventually settled in San Francisco in 1975 following a period of ill health. There
O'Connell retired from acting and set up Godmother Film Productions with two
friends. In 1980, she produced *Tell Me a Riddle*, an independent melodrama starring Melvyn Douglas.[2] However, securing financing for projects became increasingly difficult, and O'Connell eventually founded a new company, the Pacific
Film Fund, specializing in raising venture capital to develop scripts and future
film projects.

The Pacific Film Fund began after several of Godmother Productions' projects
had fallen through, among them *The Consultant*, a political film that was to star Jac-
queline Bisset. Bisset had backed out after disagreeing with the producer's choice for
director.[3] A similar problem occurred before filming on an adaptation of Rita Mae
Brown's *Southern Discomfort* could begin: Margot Kidder had been attached as the
star but was only willing to sign the contract with an experienced director at the
helm. Unfortunately, none of the directors considered suitable were available for the
next five years, leaving the project in limbo.[4]

II

By 1992, Susan O'Connell understood from direct experience that the struggle to attain financing was especially tough for professionals based outside of Los Angeles. Even so, she never dreamed of giving up on producing films, and when that year John Langdon asked her to support Bumbershoot Productions by becoming vice president of the company, they had already known each other for several years and struck up a close friendship.

In the mid–'80s, O'Connell had traveled to Texas with a friend in order to work on fundraising for the development of a book. They arrived without knowing a soul in the state, but her attorney knew Langdon and suggested she give him a call as soon as they arrived. This O'Connell and her partner did, and soon found themselves utterly charmed by the businessman.

As O'Connell remembers: "When we arrived in Dallas, my business partner and I introduced ourselves on the phone, and Johnny said, 'Come on over!' So we went there. Over a period of three months he hosted us in his guest house to use the time to raise money in Texas for this other project. We got to know him and got to know that he had tried to get *A Confederacy of Dunces* done, that he and his business partner had worked on a script and he had tried to raise money but hadn't been successful. From that point, Johnny Langdon and I became really good friends."[5]

III

As soon as, in 1991, the rights had reverted back from Fox to Bumbershoot, Langdon wasted no time in restarting the development process immediately, pitching the project to the Samuel Goldwyn Company that same year. Unfortunately for Langdon, the company was looking for smaller budget films and gave the entrepreneur a no.[6] Nevertheless, the next step for him in Texas and O'Connell in San Francisco was to find a director. Since the new vice president of the company knew the ins and outs of Hollywood, she set up meetings with various filmmakers who were thought suited to the material—though a viable script had yet to be written.

One such filmmaker was a young Tim Burton who had scored successes with *Beetlejuice, Batman, Edward Scissorhands* and *Batman Returns*, the last of which came out in 1992. When it came to *A Confederacy of Dunces*, his first foray into feature films—*Pee-wee's Big Adventure*—was the perfect calling card. The bright-colored comedy was about an oddball who if he had entered a psychiatrist's office might well have left in a straitjacket. *Pee-wee's Big Adventure* uses the slight story of the main character's missing bike as a reason to have him travel the country meeting various people who might or might not be odder than him, and who are in due course all changed by their encounters with the slightly intimidating boy in a man's body.

The meeting between Burton, O'Connell and Langdon came about via Glenn Shadix, a close friend of Burton's.[7]

Born in Alabama in 1952, Shadix had worked with the director on *Beetlejuice*, in which the actor portrayed the interior designer of the house into which Alec Baldwin's and Geena Davis' characters move. Shadix had fallen in love with Toole's novel and was passionate about playing Ignatius. He certainly had the physique, and convinced Burton to take a meeting with the producers. However, Burton passed on the property. He would go on to work with Shadix on *The Nightmare Before Christmas* and *Planet of the Apes,* before the actor died following a fall in his home in 2010.

Langdon and O'Connell also considered Daniel Day-Lewis, seeing him as a talented actor who could convincingly pull of an Ignatius.[8] Although Day-Lewis wasn't American, he had astonished O'Connell especially with his Oscar-winning performance as the Irishman Christy Brown in *My Left Foot,* a role which convinced everybody of his versatility. O'Connell was also quite interested in casting Penn Jillette, one half of the successful magic duo Penn & Teller, and who struck the producer as somebody of the right build to play Ignatius. She never discussed this idea with John Langdon, though.[9]

IV

O'Connell and Langdon didn't have any better luck than with Tim Burton. Next, through a mutual friend, they set up a meeting with writer-director Alexander Payne. Payne had just finished *The Passion of Martin,* a 50-minute film about a lonely photographer who falls in love. He would later enjoy a big success with his comedy *Election.* The director wasn't interested in *A Confederacy of Dunces.* He wanted to write his own material.[10]

The effort involved in trying to entice Joel and Ethan Coen—who had by this point made *Blood Simple, Raising Arizona, Miller's Crossing,* and *Barton Fink*—was also in vain, since they only worked from their own scripts and, as they informed O'Connell and Langdon, already had other projects on their minds.[11]

Baz Luhrmann, the Australian filmmaker who had just finished his feature film debut *Strictly Ballroom,* also passed.[12]

Veteran director Robert Altman, already a legend by that time thanks to films such as *M*A*S*H, Nashville* and *3 Women,* turned out to be the wrong choice for *A Confederacy of Dunces.* After Altman had read the book and given his opinion of it to Langdon and McConnell, the duo realized he didn't understand the character of Ignatius. Robert Altman did not like *A Confederacy of Dunces.*[13]

Michael Radford had a different reason for passing on the project. Although he had directed another well-known and famously difficult to adapt novel—George Orwell's *Nineteen Eighty-Four*—the British Radford felt *A Confederacy of Dunces* should be made by an American. He wished Langdon good luck—and passed.[14]

John Avildsen was also contacted, but he had been badly burnt by *Neighbors* in 1981, a comedy starring John Belushi. Screenwriter Larry Gelbart, who had penned the *Neighbors* script, never believed Avildsen could direct a comedy and had lobbied for the filmmaker's dismissal.[15] The producers had stuck by him but would soon regret it. Belushi was soon fed up with Avildsen's style of directing as the shoot turned into a nightmare of epic proportions. When the film finally premiered in 1982, it turned a profit but received only middling to negative reviews. Nevertheless, Avildsen was offered *A Confederacy of Dunces.* And passed.[16]

A filmmaker renowned for cerebral, surrealist satires declined, too: Terry Gilliam had just completed *The Fisher King,* starring Robin Williams. Williams had finally been approached directly about the adaptation of Toole's novel in the early '90s. By then, his wife Marsha acted as his personal assistant and producer and it was she who decided that her husband wouldn't play Ignatius at that point, but who kept a door slightly open by adding that the couple would consider the project if a screenplay met their approval.[17]

> *Any human action presupposes two things: will and ability. If either one of these is lacking, no one can do anything. Without the will, no man can begin any action, and without ability, the will is frustrated.*[18]

V

Although every director they had approached declined for one reason or another, Langdon and O'Connell still saw a chance in Penelope Spheeris.[19] Spheeris had made a name for herself by directing the documentary *The Decline of Western Civilization* about the Los Angeles punk scene (part one) and heavy metal scene (part two). More importantly, Spheeris had just finished what would be her biggest-grossing success: *Wayne's World*, a comedy about two slackers who get their own public access TV show. The film was so successful that the director was flooded with offers.

Despite being in very high demand, Spheeris took the time to hear out John Langdon and Susan O'Connell. She had read *A Confederacy of Dunces* and already pondered the idea of directing it some years before. She was especially attracted to the character of Ignatius and was enthralled by John Kennedy Toole's life. For Spheeris, both of them fell in the category of crazy geniuses.[20]

As the director explains, she had "always been extremely fascinated by the mentally unstable, probably because my mother was I believe bipolar, although never formally diagnosed. *Her* mother was in a mental institution and died there and was really, really crazy and did terrible things to my mother. It's probably genetic, although I think things out a bit. My boyfriend is a diagnosed schizophrenic and I have been with him for 20 years. My sister's girlfriend is bipolar and my brother is also attracted to crazy people, because they are just interesting. My boyfriend is so smart that it is astounding."[21]

Spheeris had met her boyfriend while working on *The Decline of Western Civilization*. He had been homeless for ten years, and as a schizophrenic, he even gave his girlfriend a possible key to unlocking *A Confederacy of Dunces*. She continues, "Many of [the schizophrenics] hear voices. It's conceivable that all those characters that were written about [in the novel] could have just been voices as opposed to real life people Ignatius met. My boyfriend describes these voices he hears. He is on medication, so it's calmed down. The characters in the book could have been imaginary characters. The complexity is a result of [Toole] having extremely intelligent mental capacities. He was so smart. Just like my boyfriend."[22]

Spheeris knew, though, that this interpretation alone wouldn't solve the problems that presented themselves when it came to developing a screenplay. The book was so complex that the director was at a loss when it came to considering an approach that would work. She knew that a lot of people had problems understanding Ignatius as a character. Plus, the book consisted of many "blanks" that were filled in by the reader's imagination.[23] How does one present that in a film?

VI

Spheeris always imagined Chris Farley as Ignatius. She had given the comedian a small role in *Wayne's World* and would work with him on *Black Sheep* in 1996:

> There's four years in between there but Chris would have been perfect for it. I know Belushi was up for the role. He was a friend of mine and he would have been perfect for it, too. Farley said to me one day when we were shooting he loved John Belushi so much that he wanted to live and die just like him. I laughed and thought he was joking. Obviously he wasn't. [Chris Farley died of a cocaine and morphine overdose in 1997. Like John Belushi when he died, Farley was 33 years old.] John Goodman I worked with on *Roseanne*, and John would have been a good choice [for Ignatius] although I wouldn't cast John because you would have to be a little bit crazy to play that crazy. John is pretty stable and level-headed.[24]

It never got as far as discussing a possible lead actor for the project. Spheeris wasn't willing to devote her energies to developing a script for Bumbershoot Productions, since she had learned that "if the film is not financed, don't go too far down the line with it because you are just wasting your time. At that point it fell into that category."[25]

VII

Indeed, Langdon still hadn't been able to find backers, and to make matters worse there was somebody else running around Hollywood trying to obtain financing for an adaptation of *A Confederacy of Dunces*. That somebody was Scott Kramer.

Following the debacle with Carson Productions, the young producer had spoken with various studio heads about getting the project off the ground. One such producer was Robert Shaye who, after his meeting with John Waters, now pondered the idea of discussing the project with director Jim Jarmusch, responsible for acclaimed independent features such as *Mystery Train* and *Stranger Than Paradise*. A deal with Jarmusch was never signed, though, primarily because there were questions as to who actually owned the rights to the intellectual property.[26]

Kramer claimed that the rights were his, that Wallace Wolf had simply whisked them away from him in an illegal transaction ten years prior. John Langdon had been well aware of Kramer's claim, but paid him no heed since he had paperwork to prove that no one other but himself held the motion picture rights.[27]

In 1992, Susan O'Connell was approached by Brendan Tartikoff, the former head of Paramount Pictures. Tartikoff had, like many others before him, fallen in love with the story of Ignatius J. Reilly and wanted to become involved in setting up a screen adaptation. It had come to his attention that Robert Shaye was in discussions with Scott Kramer. Feeling this could be his way in, Tartikoff told Susan O'Connell about it.[28] Unlike John Langdon, she didn't want to leave the situation unresolved. Certainly, O'Connell thought, Kramer couldn't simply be allowed to walk around claiming the rights were his when in fact they weren't. A few months after she had started working for Bumbershoot she attended the film festival in Cannes. Naturally, all the important producers from Hollywood were in town, giving her the perfect opportunity to clear up the matter once and for all.

By then, Scott Kramer had not only been able to convince Robert Shaye that the rights were his, but he had also attached Steven Soderbergh as a director for a feature film adaptation. O'Connell remembers: "I was in the bar at the Carlton. I saw Bob Shaye there. I had heard that Kramer had gotten involved with Soderbergh and they were acting like they owned the rights. So I just very boldly walked up to Bob and said, 'Hi, I hear you are talking to these other people. I represent the person who actually does own the rights,' and we spent some time together. When I got back from Cannes we connected with Soderbergh and Kramer and basically said, 'You can't do this. You are trying to sell something you don't own.'"[29] It was quite a mess.

Yours, Mine, Ours

*How Bumbershoot gets in a dispute with Scott Kramer et al., and Frank
Galati re-enters the stage after a ten-year break from Ignatius*

Soderbergh's and Kramer's plan was already well-advanced. Part of their team
would be John Hardy, a producer who had worked with Soderbergh on *sex, lies and
videotape*, and would continue to work with him throughout the 90s and early 2000s,
until and including *Ocean's Twelve*. Kramer had been in touch with Shaye for a while,
offering him a package: Soderbergh would be the director, Kramer and Hardy the
producers, Frank Galati the writer.

By this point, Soderbergh had already directed two hits: *sex, lies and videotape*,
and *King of the Hill* (while his *Kafka* project in 1991 turned out to be a financial and
critical failure). With the independent success *sex, lies and videotape* under his belt,
the young filmmaker was the darling of Hollywood and in the fortunate position to
choose his next endeavors. John Kennedy Toole's *A Confederacy of Dunces* was close
to his heart for several reasons. Soderbergh's father was the dean of education at Louisiana State University, while his mother worked as a psychic for a local TV station
in Baton Rouge, being well-known both for her show and interest in fine arts.[1] One of
her acquaintances was Joel Fletcher, who met Mary Ann Soderbergh when he ran an
art gallery in Louisiana. Mrs. Soderbergh, surrounded by "some very strange people"
at an opening in Baton Rouge, left her mark on Fletcher. "She was a very odd person,"
he remembers with a snicker.[2]

Steven Soderbergh attended LSU, read *A Confederacy of Dunces* and fell in love
with it. He even went to one of the performances of the stage musical which Frank
Galati had directed in the early '80s, and which had been met with great acclaim.[3]

II

Soderbergh's and Kramer's enthusiasm didn't change the fact that neither of
them owned any rights to *A Confederacy of Dunces*. Those were in the hands of an oil
man from Texas, who would therefore need to be involved. Bob Shaye then backed
out. He wasn't willing to pay Langdon $1 million for the rights in order to mount the
production at New Line with Soderbergh and Kramer.[4] Scott Rudin at Paramount,
though, still passionate about the novel and enthused to work with Soderbergh, was
open to negotiations.

Susan O'Connell then started receiving calls from Rudin at Paramount. He barraged her by ringing her up at four, five, sometimes six in the morning. O'Connell

didn't mind, as she recalls laughing: "It was delightful because it was the one time in my life in the film business when I had leverage."[5]

Langdon was open to selling the rights to Paramount, especially because the price of oil had gone down and some additional money would be welcome. Scott Kramer had lawyered up before and was now still insistent that he owned rights to the property, claiming that John Langdon had acted improperly by purchasing them and now trying to sell them to Paramount. Kramer was in a weak position, though, and everybody knew it, as O'Connell remembers with a wry smile: "Kramer had over the years been a thorn in Johnny's side because he would every once in a while come forward and claim that it was his. It wasn't. Clearly he missed that moment. Johnny had all the paperwork but Kramer kept acting like he was going to be part of it. The power of chutzpah.... It got him really far, it got him to Soderbergh. When that whole transfer of rights happened, Kramer was in there with his lawyer, trying to sue. Johnny was aware that Kramer thought he had the rights. Johnny didn't acknowledge them."[6]

The Texas businessman and Rudin negotiated a $1 million purchase for the rights.[7] Paramount would finance the film with Langdon as an executive producer and O'Connell as a co-producer. The duo would also have consultation rights, get paid per diem and have the right to be on set during shooting.[8] It was Susan O'Connell who was tasked with getting hold of all the contracts and papers stored in different places and sending them to the various lawyers involved.

Paramount also paid more than $1 million in upfront fees which would go towards paying the producers, the director, as well as to back-end agreements for creative talents such as the writer. By that point, Brandon Tartikoff, who had already spoken with Chris Farley as his favorite leading man, backed out to focus on other projects—his idea of casting Farley had not sat well with O'Connell and Langdon.[9] Tartikoff died four years later, in 1997, after a recurrence of Hodgkin's disease.

While it was not easy to find common ground when it came to a lead actor, there was no doubt that Paramount's choice to contract Steven Soderbergh as director was a sensible one. There were also no objections to hiring Frank Galati as writer. In July 1993, Soderbergh was officially announced as director of a *Confederacy* feature, with the production supposed to start filming next year. The budget would be $12 million.[10]

III

News of Paramount's recent acquisition opened up possibilities for John Hardy's then-wife, writer Deborah Sue Hardy—though the idea of writing a book about the making of a film of *A Confederacy of Dunces* only entered her mind when a friend suggested it.

Who else would be better? As John Hardy's wife, she had access to the production. Books about the making of movies were popular at the time, and, together with her friend and colleague René Pol Nevils, she suggested the project to LSU Press.

Hardy and Nevils's idea was met with great enthusiasm, and they were given the green light. Since the film project was now going well and his dream of producing an adaptation of *A Confederacy of Dunces* seemed to finally become a reality, Scott Kramer was only too happy to share information with Deborah Sue Hardy, particularly about his relationship with Thelma Toole.

One of his biggest regrets was that he hadn't been able to bring Ken's work to the screen before her passing. Hardy remembers: "Scott was wildly open to sharing information, and I put everything in the book that I could. He had great stories about Thelma. She thought he was a very promising young producer at the time. He was. She was already planning her Oscar debut and she didn't really comprehend how [the film business] worked. He had to constantly sew her feathers, but I think he was charming enough and had a good relationship with her. LSU Press on the other hand found her very difficult. In fact, at one point somebody said to me, 'You should count your blessing that she passed on, otherwise she would make it very challenging for you.'"[11]

Hardy and Nevils started working on their book in 1994, when Paramount were (still) determined to see the project through with Soderbergh, Kramer and John Hardy.

IV

Frank Galati, though, wouldn't stay involved for very long. He was by no means an unknown name in Hollywood. He had, after all, written an Academy Award-nominated script for *The Accidental Tourist* with William Hurt, a melodrama which Galati had originally developed for John Malkovich and his then-wife Glenne Headly, who had been supposed to play his love interest in the film.[12] Following their separation, the film was recast with Hurt and Kathleen Turner.

The Accidental Tourist was based on the novel of the same title by Anne Tyler, and tells the story of a middle-aged loner who, against all odds, falls in love with a quirky and sociable dog-obedience trainer. Both *The Accidental Tourist* and *A Confederacy of Dunces* are about an oddball who seems to have fallen out of time and who doesn't even try to fit into a rapidly changing society.

The parallels were obvious to Galati, who says: "Anne Tyler gains access to [the main character] Macon's interior life in the novel. That's one of the great successes of *A Confederacy of Dunces*. It's to do with the whole medieval Fortuna. The obsession with the philosophy in history of that period is in his interior life. That's what makes *A Confederacy of Dunces* hard to adapt, because you have to get the audience inside his head. It's not a place that you can dramatize easily."[13]

Galati, who had a few scripts floating around Hollywood, wanted to try. He took a meeting with Scott Kramer, Steven Soderbergh and John Langdon, whose Texan accent etched itself into Galati's memory. After delivering an outline which was lauded by the players involved, the writer was contracted.

V

Setting up *A Confederacy of Dunces* at Paramount was an especially big deal for one svengali behind the scenes. At that time, Pat Dollard was one of the most powerful agents in Hollywood, working for one of the most powerful agencies in town, William Morris. Dollard was the brother of Soderbergh's original agent, Ann, who had died in her early 30s—following a horseback riding accident—in the middle of pre-production for *sex, lies and videotape*.[14] Dollard also represented Scott Kramer, Frank Galati and Scott Rudin at the time.[15]

A Confederacy of Dunces was supposed to be one of Dollard's biggest scoops as an agent, or it was before he was fired from William Morris for continued absences, as well as for alcohol and substance abuse. He continued working for Soderbergh though, among other things, helping in 2001 to set up *Traffic*. Soon after this, Dollard would vanish from Hollywood.

Years later, *Vanity Fair* caught up with the former agent, giving him a profile several pages long: in 2004, Dollard's business was still in full swing, making the "coked-up, Armani-sheathed" agent wealthier by the minute.[16] But things took a turn for the worse, and instead of turning himself into a rehab facility—always a beloved meeting place for Hollywood celebrities—Dollard decided to go to Iraq, join the Marines and film a pro-war documentary, going on patrols with the Marines in Fallujah and Ramadi for seven months.[17]

VI

Before shooting, or even casting of *A Confederacy of Dunces* could begin, Galati needed to finish his script. Needless to say, it wasn't easy, and, like Beth Henley, he wasn't interested in taking great liberties with the book. After many years of directing adaptations of legendary novels for the stage, he had learned one lesson: don't tamper with the source material.

Galati explains: "My aesthetic is very conservative, I think. I have done *The Grapes of Wrath* and *Ragtime* and all kinds of adaptions of classical novels and contemporary works like Haruki Murakami, so I have been around stage adaptions a lot and I tend to be very faithful to the original material. Why mess with it? It needs to be given life, that's all. Let it live. Find out what it feels like when it's alive. Don't squeeze it into something else. Don't crush it. Let it breathe through living performance, not through manipulation of the text and transforming it into something that it isn't, even though it comes with the challenge of Boethius and the inner life of this crazy character."[18]

Although the initial meeting had gone well, Galati's approach to Toole's novel soon jarred with Soderbergh's.

INT. STEVEN SODERBERGH'S OFFICE. DAY.
FRANK and STEVEN sit next to each other,
deep into conversation.

STEVEN
Frank, I have an idea....

FRANK
What is it?

STEVEN
I want to start the film with Ignatius taking a bath!

FRANK
Wait a minute, that doesn't happen in the book!
What would be the purpose of that?[19]

"I wasn't on the same page in terms of my own imagination," Galati continues. "I was experiencing the novel alive and they were making a movie. That's great, that's what they do and God knows films are not really ever totally faithful to the original. Soderbergh had a set of ideas and Rudin had another set of ideas. I had my draft."[20]

VII

Not a man for big fights, Galati bowed to some of Soderbergh's suggestions, such as the one with Ignatius in the bathtub. "That Reilly kook" does take quite a few baths in Toole's novel, and clearly revels in it. Galati, under the instruction of Soderbergh, plays up the absurd picture of a gargantuan in an overflowing tub for comic purposes.

Lying in a bathtub, "Iggy" imagines himself standing on the stage in Carnegie Hall, giving an address by imploring the audience to accept that they need more medieval philosophy in their lives. Although Ignatius gives what he perceives a rousing speech, it remains unclear until much later in the screenplay what Ignatius's philosophy of life actually is.

The internal monologues are a conundrum for every screenwriter who labors over condensing this beast of a book, as are the letters and diary entries Ignatius and Myrna exchange. Reading the book, one understands what makes Ignatius tick largely due to his writings in his Big Chief tablets. In them, he captures his thoughts on philosophy, something which needed to be woven into a script in order to capture the spirit of Toole's work: "With the breakdown of the Medieval system, the gods of Chaos, lunacy, and Bad Taste gained ascendancy. After a period in which the western world had enjoyed order, tranquility, unity and oneness with its True God and Trinity, there appeared winds of change which spelled evil days ahead."[21]

Ignatius's writing also reveals his scathing critique of the sexual revolution which was beginning to blossom in the early '60s, as well as his heated exchanges with Myrna on the subjects of homosexuality and orgasms. Myrna, who wants to see herself as Ignatius's sexual savior, writes: "You know that ever since I first met you I have directed pointed questions at you in order to clarify your sexual inclinations. My only desire was to aid you in finding your true self-expression and contentment through satisfying, natural orgasm."[22]

Since Galati—much like other screenwriters who have tried their hands on an adaptation—wasn't keen on using voice-over to explicate what Ignatius writes in his Big Chief tablets, the scriptwriter found another way to explain the underlying philosophy of the main character. He does this by making Ignatius apply for a job at various venues—a brewery, a warehouse, a telephone company, a supermarket, a box factory, a shipping company, a mushroom farm and a candy company. (In the novel, the job interviews are notable for their absence. Following his mother's inquiry as to how one interview went, Ignatius replies curtly: "I would rather not discuss it."[23])

Of course, the job interviews don't go too well for Ignatius, for the precise reason that it's in his nature to direct long speeches at his potential future employer about Boethius and the meaning of life. His constant complaints during interviews about having to live with his mother don't win Ignatius any favors, either. In fact, in Galati's screenplay Ignatius is presented as an unhinged wackadoodle from the very beginning—and not as a likable one with whom the audience might have sympathies.

While Maidee Walker decided to have Irene explain Ignatius's state of mind fairly early on by recounting the tragic tale of her son's dead dog, Galati had no interest in doing so. Instead, he saves the backstory for the very end. It is Miss Annie who addresses the audience, explaining how Ignatius became the oddball he is while the end credits roll—and by that point, it is too late to make anyone sympathize with or even like the rotund main character who yells abuse at his mother and is incapable of holding a job, and who furiously spanks the monkey in his room while fantasizing over transforming society by implementing medieval philosophy into the daily routines of the Big Easy's citizens.

Miss Annie's speech is not the only instance in which the fourth wall is broken. Galati's script is surprisingly playful in this regard, considering his usual approach of sticking as closely to the source as possible. The camera, for example, is supposed to roam around Levy Pants from Ignatius's point of view, while the "Myrna problem" is solved even more creatively.

VIII

The exchanges between Iggy and his sometimes-best friend are tricky to translate cinematically and a large part of *A Confederacy of Dunces'* humor and charm is elicited through the elegance of Toole's prose. Some of this could be externalized via voice-overs, or by having Myrna read Ignatius's letters out loud, but most would be lost in translation into the medium of film. Toole's idiosyncratic language is key to the heart of his work, and to capturing *A Confederacy of Dunces'* spirit. While Ignatius's adventures are certainly "cinematic" in that they are described colorfully and with great wit and comic timing, *A Confederacy of Dunces* is highly literary in that the prose itself clearly sets the tone for the whole work: "Doris Day and Greyhound Scenicruisers, whenever they came to mind, created an even more rapid expansion of his central region."[24] As is obvious, a lot of the humor is in the narrative itself and in Toole's descriptions rather than in dialogue spoken by the colorful characters, for example: "Mr. and Mrs. Levy, who considered each other the only ungratifying objects in the house, sat before their television set."[25]

Although the free-spirited Jewess makes her appearance early on in Galati's screenplay, she only meets Ignatius at the very end, shortly before he is to be taken to the asylum—much like in the novel. She is, though, a constant presence before this. At the beginning, she is portrayed riding a subway through Brooklyn while explaining her world-view to Ignatius by reading his letters out loud, directly into the camera, and by commenting on them. Shortly afterwards, she sits in a small studio apartment, posing nude for a Kenyan sculptor in Greenwich Village. This occupation leaves her enough time to address the camera again. It also provides a perfect opportunity to inject some sensuality in the film.

Ongah, the exchange student from Kenya, displays a powerful body, caked with clay. Myrna, on the other hand, is nude, sitting on a kitchen table while sorting through her mail. The scene then introduces a visual joke which becomes a running gag—Myrna re-forms Ongah's portrait of her breasts into a huge penis, before fashioning the balls with wet clay. The phallus will appear again later.

There are sound gags as well, when, for example, Burma Jones can't help but call Lana Lee Scarla O'Horror, and Max Steiner's "Tara's Theme" from *Gone with the Wind* starts playing as a diegetic music cue. Galati has great fun with references to the screen actress who, in the '60s, was beloved by almost everyone but Ignatius: Doris Day. Her face is shown on magazine covers used as props and appears in Ignatius's nightmare; she is the star of a film that Santa suggests Irene should watch. Miss Trixie is even portrayed as wearing a Doris Day wig. She is a constant presence in the script, lurking everywhere. Whereas Dorian Greene's party was either cut from other screenplays altogether or shortened considerably, it is laid out carefully by Galati, who lets Ignatius be shamelessly insulted and humiliated.

On the other hand, the relationship between Ignatius and Myrna is underdeveloped, as is Claude Robichaux's courtship of Irene Reilly, while Dr. Talc is not mentioned once. The cutting of scenes that were carefully set up in the novel made it necessary for Galati to resort to various characters to explain parts of the plot to each other, and so to the audience. Ignatius's and his mother's escape to the bar at the beginning of the plot, is, for example, not shown. Instead, Irene resorts to reminding her moody son in an expository dialogue that they had only gone into the Night of Joy bar because they were being chased by the law. In another instance, it is Ignatius who has to explain that he is required to wear a ludicrous outfit while pushing his hot dog cart through New Orleans simply because the company's owner insists on it.

18

Don't Lose the Plot

How Scott Rudin enlists the help of a British writer, who decides to take an altogether different approach to John Kennedy Toole's novel than his predecessor

With his approach, Frank Galati drew from a rich palette. Present in his script are sound gags, visual gags and old-fashioned slapstick combining both, as well as dream sequences and moments that break the fourth wall. Unfortunately, "nobody liked it," as Susan O'Connell, associate producer of the film-to-be, confesses.[1]

Steven Soderbergh, especially, wasn't shy to express his dissatisfaction with parts of the script. As Galati remembers: "He wanted a completely different, much more radical approach. 'Don't bother about the book, these characters are not important.' I really admire Steven Soderbergh. He is an extraordinary artist. Of course this was early in his career, he was just out of *sex, lies and videotape*. He was a very hot property and of course he has matured into a very serious artist. He is a visionary, too. I am not a filmmaker. I am a writer, an adapter. So Steven Soderbergh had radical transformative ideas which had nothing to do with the novel in terms of specifics."[2]

Galati was reasonably perplexed by the reception his script received. The initial meeting had gone well—maybe a little too well, as the writer would ponder in hindsight. Kramer, Soderbergh and Langdon hadn't been very hands-on. Instead, they had given Galati free reign, which should have been a warning sign early on.

Concentrating on the satirical aspects of the novel seemed the only thing everybody involved could agree on—and there really wouldn't have been any other viable approach, as Galati explains. The depth of the novel comes out of the comic situations anyway:

[I didn't want] to force a kind of artificial silliness on something that really does have substance and depth, but rather to let the mode that it expresses itself in terms of narrative style have its playful life. When you are in the midst of the mayhem at the Night of Joy and the bird is flying around, you have the culmination of a comic pickle that is set up so beautifully from the very beginning that it's like Molière. You would be a fool to tamper with a comic mechanism when it's brilliantly constructed the way it works. Don't tamper with it, because you will squeeze the life out of it. Play it to the hilt honestly, don't make fun of it. See that there is psychological depth and three-dimensionality in these characters. They are not flat, they are not cartoons, they are breathing and living human beings, living in a world that is vividly real. If you believe it and you are disarmed by its comic triggers and you are laughing, you get the dark inside, you get there.[3]

123

II

There were also disagreements between Soderbergh and Rudin. While Soderbergh suggested letting Galati pen another draft, Rudin wanted to move on with another writer, and Galati soon felt like a "rag doll" between the two of them.[4] Rudin's proposal was especially jarring for Soderbergh since the producer had promised the director and Kramer creative control with no interference from the studio.[5] Nevertheless, as head of Paramount, Rudin naturally had the upper hand, and dismissed Galati's script.

The writer had no choice but to accept the decision—a decision of which he was, as is often the case in Hollywood, never officially informed: "I was new at this, too. I didn't have any balls or burning ambition. I just thought, 'Well, this is not the way they want to go. They want to go a different way.' That's always how they put it: 'We want to go a different way.' Fine. It had certainly happened before to me with other projects. I had done lots of screenplays and some of them that were not ever produced were still very much admired, but others were simply dropped because I didn't do what they wanted me to do."[6]

Galati worked on many screenplays which were never filmed. Among them are *The Living End*, which was based on a novel by Stanley Elkin and deemed too arty and strange for the average cinema goer; *The Quiet American*; *All the King's Men*; *Summer Gloves*, about a beauty pageant; *The Girls*, for Sally Field; and *Pigs in Heaven*, an adaptation of an Anne Tyler novel which was supposed to be a star vehicle for Jane Fonda.[7]

III

While Frank Galati has fond memories overall of his work on *A Confederacy of Dunces*, initial disagreements between Rudin and Soderbergh/Kramer would soon erupt volcanically and turn everything into ashes. But even putting these arguments aside, Paramount's attempts to bring *A Confederacy of Dunces* to the screen suffered a major blow early on.

While Galati had been working on the screenplay, John Candy was very much on everybody's mind for the title role, as he had been for over ten years when other companies had tried to set up production. "He seemed ideal," says Galati, "physically and in terms of his skills, his comic chops."[8] The writer turned in his fully-fledged screenplay in April 1994.[9] By then, John Candy had already been dead for a month—the actor had been shooting what would be his final film, *Wagons East*, in Mexico when he succumbed to a heart attack. A family history of heart attacks and the stressful production of *Wagons East* were reported to have led to Candy's early passing at the age of only 43.[10]

IV

Before the film could be cast, Paramount needed a satisfactory screenplay, and it was still a long way off from getting one. Scott Rudin had an idea, though.

While Galati was working on his draft, Rudin was producing *I.Q.*, an innocuous romantic comedy with Walter Matthau as Albert Einstein.

Cast in the role of James Moreland was an acquaintance of Rudin's named Stephen Fry. Rudin and Fry had worked together before the shooting of *I.Q.* started. The latter had already developed a screenplay for Paramount, titled *Long Island Iced Tea*, a romantic comedy which paid homage to the *Thin Man* series of the '30s and '40s. The lighthearted screwball film would see a divorced couple meeting at a wedding on Long Island and promptly fall in love with each other all over again.[11]

The script was never produced, but Rudin liked Fry and, while working on *I.Q.*, asked him whether he would be interested in writing a screenplay for *A Confederacy of Dunces*. Stephen Fry was an odd choice in one regard: he was English and had never set a foot in New Orleans.[12] For many producers and directors who had pondered the project over the years, it was indispensable that the writer be a Southerner, or at least somebody with a Southern sensibility. Fry was a national treasure in Britain, and a beloved funnyman as actor and writer, but the United Kingdom was far removed from the Mississippi River. Would the polymath actor-novelist-comedian-TV star with a middle-class background who had studied at Cambridge be up for the job?

V

Fry certainly loved the novel and was open to trying. He confessed to his love for Toole's work, explaining: "It's one of the great holy grails for some, one of the most extraordinary novels of the 20th century in America. It's written by a man, a boy really, called John Kennedy Toole, who at the age of 14–15 had written a novel called *The Neon Bible*, which Terence Davies made into a film, which was a satire on American churches. Then at a very young age he wrote his masterpiece, *A Confederacy of Dunces*, taken from a Jonathan Swift line. 'You may know a genius by this sign, that the dunces are all in confederacy against him.' It's splendidly paranoid. Unfortunately he produced the book and then committed suicide. It's just an extraordinary book and many, many people have wanted to set it for film."[13]

Stephen Fry had already read the novel in the '80s while he was working on a British comedy show with one of his closest friends, actor Robbie Coltrane. It was Coltrane who had suggested Fry read the book and even admitted that he would love to play Ignatius J. Reilly—an idea that Fry found "quite brilliant."[14]

Before committing to anything, Fry confessed to Paramount that he had never been to New Orleans. The studio's travel office swiftly organized a trip to the city, which Fry found enthralling from the minute his plane touched the ground.[15] For executive producer John Langdon and associate producer Susan O'Connell, the idea of commissioning Stephen Fry to write a screenplay was perfect, as O'Connell remembers fondly: "It was great because his writing is so similar to Toole's. It's almost seamless. 'That's a good idea,' was what we thought. Rudin brought everyone together, Soderbergh and his producing partner Scott Kramer. Johnny and I had meetings and we got to play, we got to be part of the thing."[16]

Langdon and O'Connell thought of Fry as the perfect choice for another reason: they had never perceived Ignatius J. Reilly as homosexual, contrary to the many readers' understanding of the character. Instead, they thought of him as asexual. Who could understand the character better than an asexual writer? O'Connell commences: "Stephen Fry is asexual—at least at that time he was saying he was—and that was another reason why we said, 'This guy is really going to understand Ignatius.'"[17] In fact, Fry was openly homosexual, but chose to live in celibacy for 15 years.[18]

VI

Following his trip to New Orleans, during the filming of *I.Q.*, Fry delivered a draft for *A Confederacy of Dunces*. The work had begun, and over the next few months both Rudin and Soderbergh would be heavily involved in the creative writing process when it came to further work on the draft. As Fry remembers:

> At the time, there was an understanding that Steven Soderbergh would come and work with me on the draft I had submitted to Scott Rudin, which the latter had liked but which we all agreed needed work. I was filming on *I.Q.* at the time, which was shooting in and around Princeton, New Jersey. I was staying at the weekends in Manhattan, and Steven Soderbergh came to my room at the St. Regis and we worked there and in a Paramount office on Columbus Circle—since demolished of course—over a number of days and weekends. Steven not only had the advantage of being a supreme filmmaker and assured writer, he was even from Louisiana, so had a lot to contribute as far as local color, character and detail were concerned.[19]

VII

The draft did need work and it wasn't well received by any of the producers involved. O'Connell and Langdon were especially shocked to find their high hopes in Fry dashed. As the former explains: "It started out with a takeoff from the scene from *All About Eve*. At the very beginning of the film there is a banquet dinner. One of the things Johnny was really adamant about—rightfully so—is Ignatius wasn't gay. He was, if anything, asexual. The campiness of starting out with *All About Eve*, a homage to the film, was just the wrong tone. It wasn't serious enough and it made it silly. It made him sound like he was going to be an icon, which is fine, but that's not what Johnny thought the story was about. I don't think what it's about either, except the creative genius who is dysfunctional and asocial and asexual."[20]

Fry took even more liberties with the source material. First of all, Fry's version of the story opens with Ignatius's death (not with the banquet as O'Connell suggests): Irene, Claude Robichaux, Santa Battaglia and Mancuso arrive at the Reilly house following an afternoon of bowling. In the kitchen, Irene discovers a letter which she duly opens and reads with increasing terror. The script then cuts to a search party at the Mississippi River, out of which Ignatius's infamous green cap is fished. There is no doubt in poor Irene's heart: her son committed suicide.

Obviously, this is not in the novel. But Fry had a good reason for making up this sequence, since his idea had always been to merge Ignatius's story with John Kennedy Toole's. The screenplay commences to show—skillfully, without any words spoken—how Santa discovers a manuscript under Ignatius's bed. It is titled *A Confederacy of*

Dunces. Mrs. Reilly decides to show it to an academic called Dr. Talc at Loyola University where Ignatius studied. Talc and a fellow professor, who examine the novel, take the place of Walker Percy who famously helped get Toole's book published. Ignatius's *Confederacy* gets published in the first few scenes of Fry's draft, after which it is awarded the Pulitzer Prize for fiction and the Mark Twain Award, which in turn leads to the aforementioned banquet scene to which O'Connell objected. Here, everybody Ignatius has encountered is brought together, assembled to celebrate the unique genius who caused them much sorrow when he was still alive. For Fry, there really was no other way than merging Ignatius with Toole and crafting a meta-moment in which *A Confederacy of Dunces* was written by Ignatius as his autobiography. The content of this autobiography is then presented by Fry in the course of the rest of the script.

VIII

How could one read the story of Ignatius and not draw comparisons to Toole's own troubled life? "I think it's enormously difficult to read *Confederacy* without linking the frustrating life and early death of John Kennedy Toole with the adventures of Ignatius," muses Fry.[21] "Inspired by the 'Sarah Siddons Awards' device that brackets *All About Eve*, I thought that perhaps a Mark Twain Award evening (especially aggravating for both Toole and Reilly, who abominated Twain [calling him a 'dreary fraud'[22]]) would give some shape to a notoriously shapeless novel. Well, I say shapeless, it's shapeless in the way that Ignatius's clothes are shapeless—they are shaped by Ignatius's body—the whole novel is Ignatius-shaped of course but studio movies—even those that are given a long 'artistic' leash—are expected to conform to some sort of structure. That was especially true in the 90s I think."

Fry's structure is an especially complex one. The writer uses the banquet to let all the attendees—the Levys, Mynkoffs, Mancusos and Joneses—tell Ignatius's story from their own points of view. The president of the Mark Twain Award praises Ignatius and his genius in one long speech, in the course of which he introduces the various acquaintances of our rotund hero. These attendees, in turn, remember their encounters with Ignatius through flashbacks, making Toole's story even more episodic than it already is. This structure results in a non-linear, non-chronological retelling of Ignatius's adventures, sometimes employing flashbacks within flashbacks.

The main story itself, for example, begins with Ignatius being bothered by Mancuso outside D.H. Holmes. It is an episode told by the police officer who remembers chasing Ignatius and his mother, but arresting Jones and Robichaux instead. Mancuso's memory commences with Ignatius and Irene coming out of the Night of Joy, ready to get in their car while being observed by the officer. Since Mancuso was neither with Ignatius nor his mother while they sipped their beers in the Night of Joy, this particular episode is missing from Mancuso's retelling of the story. Instead, it is told about 60 pages later by Myrna Minkoff. Although she was equally absent from the club, she remembers sitting in a coffee bar in Greenwich Village, reading one of Ignatius's letters. This leads her to envision her sometimes-friend sitting in the Night of Joy with his mother (a flashback within a flashback: the award ceremony as present time, Myrna's memory of sitting in a coffee bar as past, Ignatius's escape from the club as an occurrence preceding this flashback.)

Fry is consistent in this regard: he lets the individuals remember what they can remember. Certain episodes told in the novel are moved around or sometimes simply cut. Ignatius's demonstration at Levy Pants, for example, is told before his successful job interview is described. Much like Galati, Fry uses various job interviews to let Ignatius explain his philosophy to his potential future employers, and therefore to the audience.

In order to prominently feature Myrna—a problematic figure for any screenwriter for obvious reasons—Fry further developed Ignatius's backstory. Here, he uses another flashback within a flashback: Ignatius and Myrna meet for the first time in a class given by Dr. Talc, who continually misquotes philosophers and is always promptly corrected by Ignatius in his unmistakable manner. Ignatius's remarkable intelligence is noted by Myrna who strikes up a conversation with her fellow student, only to find him next to insufferable. However, they decide to play a trick on Dr. Talc to extract a long overdue revenge. In the evening, Myrna, Ignatius and his dog Rex assemble on campus. With weedkiller, Ignatius and Myrna write a message on the lawn of Tulane campus stating that their professor perverts his students in body and mind. It is signed: Zorro.

IX

Out of necessity, Fry simplifies the character of Myrna. In the novel, she is just as complex—as is indeed every minor character in the novel—as Ignatius. Stage director David Esbjornson summarizes:

> Myrna is a New York Jewish lefty with a myriad of social causes and opinions on almost everything, including her former boyfriend Ignatius. Myrna is a force of nature, very intelligent but like Ignatius, is full of paranoid and implausible fantasies. The role requires a highly spirited, no-nonsense, tough-love quality with a heart of gold.[23]

She claims to be sexually liberated, tolerant and open, while at the same time chastising Ignatius for what she perceives are homosexual urges: "Are you hanging around with some queers? [...] Your normal sexual outlets have been blocked for so long that now the sexual overflow is seeping out into the wrong channels." Myrna concludes by calling homosexuality a "sexual aberration."[24] Equally, while she presents herself a feminist, she adores the work of Norman Mailer, one of the prototypical alpha male macho writers of the 20th century.[25]

It is worth noting that politically, Ignatius is just as confused. Clearly left-wing, in that he desires to create better working conditions for the employees of Levy Pant's and in scoffing at the bourgeoisie,[26] he rejects communism and prefers a "good, strong monarchy with a tasteful and decent king who has some knowledge of theology and geometry and to cultivate a Rich Inner Life."[27] And while rejecting the ruthless corporatism displayed by Levy Pants toward its workers, Ignatius wears a Mickey Mouse watch[28] and appears to appreciate the movies produced by Walt Disney.[29] Similarly, he is appalled by Myrna's sexual adventures, by lesbians and the pleasures available at the Night of Joy, but wants to start lobbying for transvestites in the senate.[30] He's a complex character. "My being has many facets."[31]

X

In Fry's script, Rex is still alive at the time Ignatius attends university. While his beloved dog dies during his owner's childhood in the novel, in Fry's script he passes in 1962, when Ignatius is in his 20s. Therefore, Rex's passing doesn't explain Ignatius's irritating manner. He has obviously always been like this. His mother blames all the reading.

Exhausted by her son wreaking havoc in her life, Irene ponders sending him to "chariddy." But unlike in the novel, she discussed this idea openly with Ignatius, reassuring him he would always be able to write in his notebooks while kind people take care of him. Needless to say, Ignatius rejects this idea outright. But he soon runs out of options, and is, in the end, defeated: neither his fellow workers at Levy Pants nor Dorian Greene's friends appreciate him or his visions for a better society. Worse, they humiliate him.

Fry is ruthless in this regard: even after a painful episode at Dorian's house, three lesbians decide to follow the irritating Ignatius J. Reilly from a distance. His path leads them outside the Night of Joy, where "Iggy" collapses following an episode with a cockatoo. Already unconscious, he gets beaten and kicked by Dorian's enraged friends. (This episode is foreshadowed in Fry's script by showing Ignatius with a bandage around his head long before the reason for this injury is explained.) After this, Ignatius, it seems, has no choices left. He writes a tear-stained suicide note and leaves the house.

However, Fry has played a trick on the audience. After disrupting the Mark Twain Award ceremony for its hypocrisy, Myrna waits outside the building, followed by Burma Jones. It is Jones who tries to calm down the "minx" before a limousine stops in front of them. Inside sits Ignatius. He is very much alive and, with Jones's knowledge, just faked his suicide. His mother is still grieving. Ignatius has no intention of informing his next of kin about his still beating heart. Instead, he orders an incredulous Myrna to get in the limousine and drive with him to New York, where by all intents and purposes Ignatius wants to live with her in their own apartment.

Soderbergh, Langdon and O'Connell didn't appreciate any of this.

19

Grand Exit. Curtain.

How Stephen Fry nearly ends his life the way Toole had, and Steven
Soderbergh sees no other way than to burn his bridges.

The director and producers didn't even know where to begin to unpick Fry's
draft. The writer defends his finale, saying: "I was aware that the ending of the novel
needed some attention. It's hard not to agree that Ignatius was unfitted for the 20th
Century just as John Kennedy Toole seemed sadly to be unfitted. It struck me that
either one constructed a fantasy in which Ignatius and Myrna found a school/make
a fortune/strike it lucky in New York/marry and become tragically bourgeois/are
imprisoned, or one took inspiration from real life and gave Ignatius an even more
John Kennedy Toole-shaped destiny. No one can doubt the autobiographical nature
of his picaresque peregrinations after all.... I'm not saying it was the right idea for the
screenplay, but it was one idea."[1]

Developing a screenplay based on *A Confederacy of Dunces* was one of the tough-
est jobs Fry ever undertook. While still working on his draft in February 1995 at the
St. Regis hotel in New York, he already seemed exhausted: "I've been here a week
working on it. [...] It's a devil to do."[2] Shortly thereafter, his situation worsened considerably. Rudin, Soderbergh, Kramer, Langdon and O'Connell wanted a new draft
from Fry, but alas, he vanished.

Susan O'Connell remembers: "Fry disappeared and we thought he had committed suicide. Then he went into the hospital or an asylum for a little bit. It was very
dramatic. It's Hollywood."[3]

II

In late February 1995, Fry was scheduled to appear at the Albery Theatre in London in a production of Simon Gray's play *Cell Mates*, based on the true story of spy
George Blake and his cellmate Sean Bourke. Fry had finished shooting *I.Q.*, and was
furiously working on *A Confederacy of Dunces* while rehearsing the new play and toying with a variety of other projects. It was the busiest time of his life.

Cell Mates received unanimously negative reviews in the British press, and Fry's
performance was singled out, and not in a positive way. After only few performances
the actor pulled out and vanished. For several weeks, the headlines in all major British newspapers wondered about his whereabouts and mental state. Prior to his disappearance, he had written to colleagues about his perceived failure as an actor.

Everybody was worried. In a statement, Fry would later explain: "I'm afraid I suffered a dreadful attack of what golfers call the yips and actors call stage fright and I slunk away rather than cause a scene in public. [...] I can only offer cowardice, embarrassment and distress as excuses for such absurd behaviour. I'm a silly old fool and don't deserve this attention."[4]

> *As soon as I saw you with your tearstained face, I knew that you were suffering, and I understood that you had been banished. You have been banished from yourself, and one could even say that you are therefore the instrument of your own torments, for no one else could have done this to you.*[5]

For several days, there was no trace of Fry. He had even left a message on his answering machine which said, "I'm sorry, I'm so very sorry," which led some of his friends to believe he had committed suicide.[6]

As it would later turn out, Fry had boarded a ferry to France. Before that, he had indeed contemplated ending his life, as he later explained. He had even wanted to do so in the same way John Kennedy Toole had ended his existence: "I had my hand on the key and a duvet cover around the car door so the exhaust fumes would be kept in. [...] I was deeply, deeply unhappy and lonely."[7] He didn't go through with it: "I think the only thing that stopped me was the knowledge of the devastation it would cause to my family. It was the only bit of reason, the little voice in my head, which did not desert me."[8]

Days after his disappearance, Fry was admitted to Cromwell Hospital, a $625-a-night private hospital in London. Newspapers tried hard to find an explanation for Fry's state of mind, *The Guardian* even citing an arts psychologist named Andrew Evans, who mused: "Stephen Fry is a creative artist and he has been hit from two directions. He has simultaneously had bad reviews for *Cell Mates* and his TV show (*A Bit of Fry and Laurie*) and the combination of both is a shock, a double whammy."[9]

Fry had long suffered from cyclothymia, a particular variation of bipolar disorder, having tried to take his own life years earlier at the age of 16. He described his battling with two poles thus: "The one gives you hope and a vainglorious, grandiose belief in the future; the other convinces you of life's entire and eternal futility. The one gives you an urge to communicate by text, letter, phone call, Twitter and personal visit. The other casts one alone into a darkened room, refusing visitors and rolling away to turn one's back on those poor concerned ones who love you and want to speak to you."[10]

III

In Hollywood another storm was brewing. There were already tensions between Scott Rudin and Steven Soderbergh, which only escalated after Fry turned in a second draft following his hospitalization.

Although Rudin had promised Soderbergh creative control over *A Confederacy of Dunces*, the latter hadn't been involved in the discussions concerning Fry's new draft and was dumbstruck when Rudin informed him that Fry's script was the one that would be made into the movie. All of this went on without Fry's knowledge, as the scriptwriter explains: "I only became aware of all this later. Fortunately I am rarely party to or interested in the business, contractual and ownership side of things. I tiptoe away when it comes to that sort of issue. I sensed none of this. But then I'm the kind of person who, on a film set, for example, doesn't notice when members of the crew or cast pair off on location and have steamy affairs. I am notorious for my lack of curiosity and/or perception when it comes to matters like this."[11]

Fry thought he was still involved while Soderbergh had already decided that he wasn't going to turn his script into a film. He disliked it just as much as John Langdon did.[12] ("Good grief. Is this supposed to be a comedy?" Ignatius demanded in the darkness. "I have not laughed once. My eyes can hardly believe this highly discolored garbage. [...] Please! Someone with some decency get to the fuse box. Hundreds of people in this theater are being demoralized.")[13]

In December 1995, Fry turned in draft number three, which was met with radio silence from Soderbergh. This wasn't unusual for a writer who was about to be kicked off a project, as Fry explains: "One is rarely fired from a writing job, you just find out that someone else is doing a draft or that the project is in turnaround or held in a pride stand-off or lost in some kind of contractual black hole somewhere. Such is life. If a long lost project breaks surface again years later one's agents excitedly crawl over the revisions and new scripts to see if there's an imprint of their client's work remaining which might justify an application to the Writers Guild to claim nuggets of credit, but I have to confess I have no such fantasies."[14]

IV

Soderbergh and Kramer took matters into their own hands, with the director deciding to develop his own script. From these turbulent times, Susan O'Connell remembers: "It was the best script. It really adhered to the book a lot, but it was creative and not too different. It wasn't trying to put it in different times. Paramount and Rudin refused to read it because it was on spec. Nobody paid [Soderbergh] to do it. First he did the script and no one wanted to read it. This was part of the process of saying, 'This is not the project we signed up for and we are not allowed to work together.'"[15]

Soderbergh and Kramer claimed they had been shut out of the creative process and that Rudin had therefore violated the contract he had signed with Messrs. Soderbergh and Kramer. Worse, they claimed Paramount had secretly bought the rights in order to proceed with Fry's script.[16] The duo still wanted to make the movie, but not based on Stephen Fry's screenplay. Rudin didn't want to work with Soderbergh's script. Everybody had reached an impasse. To break the deadlock, Soderbergh and Kramer contemplated suing Paramount for interference. They wanted to set up their project someplace else—anyplace but Paramount, which had the duo under contract.

In summer of 1996, Soderbergh and Kramer tried (again) to entice Robert Shaye of New Line to take on *A Confederacy of Dunces* and let Soderbergh direct from his own script. It would then be Shaye's obligation to negotiate with Rudin and wrestle the project away from Paramount. At the same time, Soderbergh sent his script to Universal Pictures and began talks with Harvey Weinstein of Miramax, which had distributed *sex, lies and videotape* and *Kafka*.[17] For Soderbergh, all options were on the table except continuing to work with Paramount.

Rudin didn't react kindly to the news that "his" director had shown his script to other companies. Soderbergh, though, was convinced that since Paramount didn't own his script he had nothing to fear. In truth, the director shopping around his script in Hollywood started a year-long legal battle that would drain Soderbergh of all energy.

V

In mid–June 1996, Paramount sent Scott Kramer a letter of termination for tortuous interference.[18] It had come to their attention that Kramer and Soderbergh had begun talks with other studios, and Paramount's legal department also warned Soderbergh—through his agent Pat Dollard—that he would be fired as director if he was responsible for circulating the script in La La Land.

Soderbergh was outraged: "Thursday I got a fax from Scott Rudin. On Tuesday I had sent a brief note saying that I was in New York and we should sit down and see if we can sort this out one way or another. His response was that Paramount's lawyers had said it would be unwise for him to do so, until the legal situation is sorted out. What irks me is that they can't even be honorable. They want to get rid of me and not even pay me, *and* have a gag order on me."[19]

Since Soderbergh had received positive feedback for his script from New Line and Miramax, he found the situation especially galling. He had also sent his script to United Artists and alleges it found great acclaim in their offices. This might have been true for studio executive John Calley—who passed away in 2011—but it wouldn't have been accurate for United Artists' vice-president Jeff Kleeman, who confesses to "hating" the book. Although he doesn't remember a script ever hitting his desk, he "would have passed immediately."[20] But at least New Line and Miramax seemed to be willing to contract Soderbergh and let him make his version of the movie, if the costs were right. But this, of course, was impossible while Soderbergh was still under contract at Paramount and was supposed to develop *A Confederacy of Dunces* for them.

Steven Soderbergh and Scott Kramer then decided to hire Pierce O'Donnell, a highly experienced entertainment lawyer who had already won a high-profile case against Paramount which would become known as the Art Buchwald Case (and which concerned Paramount's production of *Coming to America*).[21] Materials had to be compiled and sent to O'Donnell, who in turn reviewed them and gave his opinion as to whether his clients had any chance of escaping Paramount's clutches. They had a strong case, O'Donnell assured them.

There was one problem, though: if Soderbergh and Kramer reached a settlement with Paramount, the money awarded to them wouldn't be enough for O'Donnell to take the case on contingency. It was a verifiable dilemma for Soderbergh and Kramer. They decided to let their lawyer take a few meetings with his counterparts at Paramount. "Then, once we've gotten the lay of the land, we'll figure out how to proceed," wrote Soderbergh. "Both Kramer and I are torn between getting money to walk away and fighting to make the movie. I just don't want this thing hanging over my head for too long, causing psychic distress. As much as I want to make it, if that is unlikely or liable to be hugely unpleasant, then I'd rather be bought off."[22]

By now, Rudin hated Soderbergh with a passion because he refused to work with

Fry's script. Soderbergh hated Rudin because of his creative interference. Kramer hated Rudin because the producer had fired him. Rudin hated Kramer because he was in cahoots with Soderbergh. O'Donnell hated Rudin because he was paid to.

Only a few days later, Soderbergh came to the realization that "the whole thing is a fucking mess and will take a long time to sort out."[23] Kramer expected Paramount to re-hire him in order to be able to fire Soderbergh for breach of contract, since the latter had refused to direct Stephen Fry's script. Paramount, though, wasn't keen on taking any more meetings with Pierce O'Donnell. Their goal was, or so Soderbergh thought, to slow the process down until Soderbergh and Kramer gave up. They weren't about to do that. At the same time, the director was finishing his new film, *Schizopolis*, and needed money to pay for additional cuts he wanted to make.[24] This was just one reason to settle the *Confederacy* dispute as soon as possible.

VI

It was a dispute which also had consequences for Deborah Sue Hardy and René Pol Nevils. They had wanted to compile a book about the making of the movie, and the chances of that movie actually happening were decreasing spectacularly quickly. Although they had transcribed Kraemer's reminiscences, these wasn't enough to fill a book, and what they had certainly didn't meet the criteria they had discussed with LSU Press. "I had to go to LSU Press and say, 'Look, there is no movie happening,'" explains Hardy, "and the publisher said, 'Well, why don't you write a biography then?' It was dropped into my lap."[25]

Their book about the making of *A Confederacy of Dunces* would instead become a book about John Kennedy Toole's short and tragic life. Still, Hardy and Nevils devoted a substantial number of pages to Kramer's early endeavors towards producing the film. The writing duo titled their manuscript *Ignatius Rising*.

VII

While Hardy and Nevils could "rescue" their book, it wasn't a good time for Soderbergh. During the time Stephen Fry had worked on his script for *A Confederacy of Dunces*, Soderbergh had opted to shoot a movie called *The Underneath*, which had under-performed at the box office, only received mixed reviews, and gave the director a most uneasy feeling: "I think it's a beautiful film to look at and I think the score is beautiful, but fifteen seconds in I know we're in trouble because of how *fucking* long it takes to get through those opening credits."[26]

Soderbergh had felt uncomfortable throughout the shooting and was dissatisfied with the film. In order to cleanse himself, he decided to make one of his most personal films to date: *Schizopolis*, which premiered in 1996 and starred Soderbergh as a worker for a company offering self-help to its clients. Shot on a budget of only a quarter of a million dollars, *Schizopolis* flopped. Had the formerly most-promising newcomer lost his magic touch?

He had already lost out on making *Quiz Show*, which Robert Redford then directed.[27] While embroiled in a fight with Paramount, Soderbergh desperately needed to find a new, commercially viable project in order to pay his lawyers. But all projects he worked on during the troubled months of 1996 would fall through: *Neurotica*—a sort-of sequel to *Schizopolis*—needed to be pushed back; a *Charlie Chan* mystery for Miramax was scrapped; *Human Nature* would later be directed by its writer, Charlie Kaufman; and *Toots and the Upside Down House*, which Soderbergh was developing with Henry Selick, didn't meet the expectations of Fox, which would have financed the production.[28] Steven Soderbergh needed a hit, and he hoped that *A Confederacy of Dunces* would be it, if he was allowed to direct the film after all. However, it became increasingly difficult for Soderbergh and Kramer to reach Scott Rudin or Sherry Lansing at the studio so as to settle their dispute without having to go to court. That, in turn, held up the above *Charlie Chan* project, since Soderbergh only wanted to be announced as director if the *A Confederacy of Dunces* case was resolved.

The Place Where
Dreams Go to Die

*How Steven Soderbergh and Scott Kramer celebrate a Pyrrhic victory in
their battle against Paramount, and find out that not too many Hollywood studios are willing to invest in their baby*

By October 1996, things were far from resolved, as Soderbergh wrote: "I'm still
trying to get a meeting with Sherry Lansing and/or Scott Rudin. Sherry Lansing has
been, well, weird. At one point, when I tried to explain what was happening, she
stopped me by saying, 'I don't know what's going on and I don't want to know.' That
about sums up her role in this scenario. Rudin, after receiving a fax from me requesting a meeting, has called, but we keep missing each other. I have no idea what the call,
should it take place, will be like."[1]

Ignatius J. Reilly even chased the director in his dreams. Soderbergh continued: "I literally dreamed about it all night last night, sequence after sequence, endless
variations on what might occur, from good to bad to inconclusive. The huge success
of *The First Wives Club* makes things harder for Kramer and me, we think. [Para-
mount would point out their approach to comedies had been successful.] After Mon-
day's *Toots* meetings and Paramount's stonewalling and lack of interest, it's pretty
clear I'm a very small fish in this particular pond nowadays. Of course my impulse is
to sit by the phone all day, but I can't do that. I need to carry on doing what I need to
do, which includes going to the Dodgers-Braves baseball game later this afternoon. I
mean, one has to prioritize."[2]

Going to court against Paramount would have bankrupted Soderbergh
and Kramer. Both were acutely aware of that. O'Donnell and his associate kindly
informed the duo that their combined fees for *A Confederacy of Dunces* would not
include costs for a trial, should they decide to go to court. The fees alone would total
close to half a million dollars. Court cases, especially in the field of entertainment,
have always been expensive.

Soderbergh and Kramer now decided to look for new, cheaper attorneys.
The problem with abandoning O'Donnell and his associate was that the former
had immeasurable experience, especially when it came to going to court against
Paramount.

Not knowing what to do next, Soderbergh and Kramer decided to involve the
Directors Guild of America to give them advice. They still couldn't wrap their heads
around Paramount's attitude: "Scott Rudin doesn't want to meet until the Kramer

situation is straightened out, but neither Kramer nor I can figure what Kramer's 'termination' and reinstatement have to do with my directing the film," Soderbergh wrote in early October 1996.[3] Since Paramount was "stalling," the director and his producing partner Scott Kramer eventually decided—in mid–November—to sue the studio simply to get things moving.

> *Wealth was supposed to make a man self-sufficient, but it actually makes him dependent on the help of others. And anyway, money doesn't prevent a person from wanting.*[4]

In their suit, Soderbergh and Kramer alleged the studio had intended to defraud them, as well as breached oral and written agreements. Soderbergh was livid and hoped that Rudin and his colleagues would be equally furious once they received O'Donnell's letter. By that point, of course, Soderbergh and Paramount were bitter enemies, and the director would later describe the studio as "the place where dreams go to die."[5] He had had enough, just like Ignatius at the hands of Dorian Greene's friends: "This is an outrage! [...] I have not only been ignored and vilified at this gathering. I have been viciously attacked within the walls of your cobweb of a home. I hope that you carry liability insurance. If not, you may well lose this flamboyant property once my legal advisers have attended to you."[6]

II

Soderbergh was giddy to find out that Paramount was indeed furious upon receiving the letter in question, though he and Kramer had speculated and hoped the studio wouldn't let the case go to trial. A few weeks later, they were less sure of that and became understandably anxious, since arguing the case in court would cost the duo an arm and a leg.

By December 1996, the walls were closing in on Soderbergh—he had received an invoice from O'Donnell for $20,000, only half of which he was able to pay at the time: "We need to come to an agreement about finances before they move any further. It's easy to imagine a scenario in which we have to drop our lawsuit because of lack of funds."[7]

Susan O'Connell and John Langdon watched the spectacle unfold from afar. Although they were also unhappy with Rudin's behavior, they would have never dared to sue. As O'Connell explains: "We were pretty amazed that Soderbergh was going to depose Sherry Lansing or Rudin. It was pretty bold."[8]

After filing the lawsuit against Paramount, Soderbergh decided to hire a new legal team for his and Kramer's case. In late January 1997 they met with their new partners in crime, and were pleasantly surprised by their attorneys' aggressiveness and confidence. They weren't much cheaper than their predecessors, though.

III

All the while, Soderbergh didn't appreciate being asked about the progress he was making with *A Confederacy of Dunces*. In March 1997, while giving a talk at the SXSW Film Festival in Austin, Texas, a member of the audience inquired about the still ongoing lawsuit against Paramount. Soderbergh snapped: "All I can say is that if this thing goes to court, I will humiliate them."[9] It was rare eruption, since only a few weeks earlier, Soderbergh had been more careful when speaking about Rudin and his "baby" in public: "It's a project that I feel very connected to. [...] Rudin is known for being a control freak. I'm a bit of a control freak. There's not room for two such people on a movie, I don't think. [...] I have zero clout on this level, with Paramount or with Rudin. Zero. I should have been smart enough to know that."[10]

IV

The case was settled out of court in Soderbergh's favor in May 1998. The litigation had taken two years of everybody's time, and although it never went to trial, it cost the director and his producer Kramer a lot of money. Paramount relented after Soderbergh and Kramer brought in their new attorneys, as Susan O'Connell remembers: "The threat made Paramount and Rudin say, 'Okay, you can have it for [three] years. You can take it away and try to get it set up.' That went on for a while. We were still somewhat involved and spoken to near at the end of the turnaround period."[11] Scott Rudin claimed he preferred to concentrate on several movies he was then producing, rather than spend his time sitting in court.[12]

A Confederacy of Dunces was now in turnaround with Soderbergh and Kramer. They had three years in which they could set up their production with a new studio.[13] By that point, though, Soderbergh had been involved with the project for five years, and he had become tired with the struggle. Instead of wasting any more time with an adaptation of Toole's novel, he decided to direct Out of Sight, which would be his big comeback as director.

Leaving Ignatius behind turned out to be the right decision. Years later, Soderbergh remembered: "We got the project back, and at that point—it was a good lesson to learn, actually, because I realized once we got it back that my enthusiasm had been beaten out of me. Now it was an obligation, as opposed to something that I wanted to do. I don't know what's happening with it. I think it's cursed. I'm not prone to superstition, but that project has got bad mojo on it."[14]

V

A Confederacy of Dunces moved to the back of Soderbergh's mind, as setting up the project with another studio following the lawsuit against Paramount proved to be a problem. There was no shortage of studios willing to speak with Soderbergh and Kramer, but by this point the costs had become an obstacle. A Confederacy of Dunces was by now heavily financially burdened, and whichever studio made the film would have to pay—the story of Ignatius J. Reilly now had a price tag of approximately $5 million on it, and that was only the development costs that had accrued.[15] For example, any studio would have to reimburse Paramount for spending $1 million on Langdon's rights and $400,000 for Frank Galati's script.[16]

O'Connell remembers that Scott Rudin had no intention of making life easy for Soderbergh, Kramer and the competition: "While we were developing A Confederacy *of Dunces* at Paramount, Rudin moved into new offices and charged the redecoration of new offices to this project. He was often flying on a Concorde to meet with Stephen Fry. All that stuff was charged to the project."[17]

Money was always an issue. Artisan Entertainment, United Artists and Universal weren't willing to pay the sums involved, and they didn't even include the budget for the actual film.[18]

Meanwhile Steven Soderbergh was out as director. This was unfortunate for Kramer since the filmmaker was no longer part of a package the producer could present to the studios. Instead, Soderbergh would work as producer on a possible *A Confederacy of Dunces* adaptation. Money and Steven Soderbergh's leave of absence as the director were only two reasons why Kramer had a hard time convincing studio heads to back his project.

Like a doctor examining a patient stricken with every imaginable illness, Michael Arata would soon find out what the true crux of the *A Confederacy of Dunces* problem was.

VI

Arata, born in 1966, is a native of New Orleans. A trained attorney, he was always passionate about films, television and the stage, and therefore tried to break into the movie business. As an actor, he has had bit parts in *Runaway Jury* and *Déjà Vu* (2006), among others—films which were partly shot in New Orleans.

In the early '90s, Arata met John "Spud" McConnell, another Louisiana native. Coincidentally, he had played a small part in one of Soderbergh's earliest films, *King of the Hill*. Born in Baton Rouge in 1958, Spud grew up in Gonzales, attended Louisiana State University and tried to make his living as a stand-up comedian in Louisiana's capital, before hitting the road for several years.[19] In 1994, he settled back in New Orleans and became a household name, not least for his portrayal of Bob in the popular sitcom *Roseanne*. The role that would make him famous locally, though, was Ignatius J. Reilly. Spud played Toole's obese anti-hero countless times on stage, and was rewarded not only with laudatory reviews but also with his own statue on Canal Street in New Orleans that depicted him as Ignatius.

He is a character who never ceases to fascinate McConnell: "He is so socially inept and yet so incredibly well-read. He's unparalleled; there's nobody to really compare him to. Some folks say he's kinda like this guy in Shakespeare or he's kinda like that guy in Molière, but the truth is: He is so unique that there is nothing to compare him to. I spent a lot of time developing this character and it was all hit-or-miss."[20]

One of Spud's dreams was to play Ignatius on the big screen. His problem early on was that he had no close connections to the film business and was at a loss as to how to set up an adaptation of *A Confederacy of Dunces*. Fortunately, Spud met Michael Arata and shortly thereafter, in the mid–June, mentioned the idea to him. Of course, his new friend was familiar with the novel and a great admirer of Toole's writing. "A light bulb went on in my head and I said, 'Well, why don't we try,'" recounts Arata.[21] As an attorney, he knew what steps to take in order to evaluate the property.

Fortune's Wheel spun in Arata's favor: coincidentally, Pat Dollard had just shown up in the Bayou State. Since Louisiana hadn't yet started giving tax breaks for film productions, the local community of filmmakers was still relatively small and close-knit. Everybody knew everybody. It didn't take long for Arata and Dollard to become friendly, as the former explains: "Patrick Dollard is an interesting character. He showed up in Louisiana in 1996 or 97. His third or fourth ex-wife and he had a child, and his ex-wife was from Louisiana. She was in the film business and moved back to Louisiana with her baby. Pat, in one of the rare moments of altruistic feelings in his life, moved back to Louisiana to be a good dad for the baby. That lasted for about four weeks until he met his next wife and got married. In the interim I met him. There weren't many film people in Louisiana to talk to."[22]

Dollard proved an immeasurable support. He introduced Arata to various filmmakers based in the state and had a surprise in store for him when, over the phone, the part-time actor mentioned *A Confederacy of Dunces*. Incredulous of the coincidence, Dollard divulged that his client, Steven Soderbergh, not only "held the rights to the book"[23] but had also just written his own screenplay.

Arata was over the moon. He was introduced to Kramer, John Hardy and Soderbergh, who all seemed open to the idea of teaming up with the aspiring producer. Soderbergh promised to send Arata and McConnell a copy of his script. Of course, they wouldn't hold any rights to it, but Soderbergh was interested to hear what they thought about his take on Toole's material.

Shortly afterwards, the script arrived. Arata remembers: "We thought the script was good. It wasn't perfect. It wasn't what Spud and I had expected. He sent it to me and it was enormously laden with what I would call inter-dialogue, inner monologue. There was very little action in the story, and it was very different from what Spud and I had anticipated. But at least we had a start."[24]

Arata and Spud couldn't believe their luck. They were small-time producers from Louisiana, operating solely in New Orleans, and suddenly a big hot-shot director from Hollywood had offered to sell them the rights to *A Confederacy of Dunces*! It all seemed so easy, it was all going so swell, especially considering the troubled history of the project. Could it be so simple? As if anything ever was.

21

Many Paths Lead to New Orleans

How a lawyer from the Big Easy can't believe his luck, but is soon confronted with a bitter reality

Michael Arata and Spud McConnell flew out to Los Angeles. They had set up a meeting with Scott Kramer. It was a curious, informal meeting that should have rung alarm bells, but Kramer was convincing, charming and a charismatic storyteller. He showed his colleagues from Louisiana around his library, causing Arata to think: "It was fascinating that this guy wanted to show me how erudite he was. I was captivated by that and thought, 'That's a very interesting way to introduce yourself by showing your guests a collection of your books.' Many of those books hadn't been opened. The book bindings were just pristine."[1]

Arata let this pass, though, and was soon captivated by Kramer's recollection of his encounters with John Belushi nearly 20 years before. The stories were fascinating and Arata and Spud listened attentively. At the same time, they were wondering why Scott Kramer, the Los Angeles–based producer who had met with Belushi and tried to get the project off the ground with Steven Soderbergh, was suddenly interested in striking a deal with an independent producer from Louisiana who did not represent any of the big studios. Arata waved these initial doubts away by flattering himself. Maybe, he thought, Kramer simply didn't have the right stuff to get it done. Maybe Arata did.

After he and Spud had bid Kramer and his wife, actress Cynthia Gibb, farewell, they reflected on their meeting and asked each other the same question: "'This was a nice song-and-dance, but why after going through all of this come to us?'"[2] Arata remembers: "[Kramer] had all these stories about everybody involved, and I thought to myself, 'You are *here*! You have Steven Soderbergh's name on a script.' Although it wasn't a perfect script, you are here. Steven was the hottest guy in show business at the time and still is."[3]

II

Despite their doubts, Arata and McConnell were willing to work with Kramer and see where the road would take them. While Spud would be responsible for finding the talent to put in front of the camera, Arata would take care of fundraising. The first part was easy. McConnell had long wanted to play Ignatius on the big screen, but was aware that his name didn't have the same weight the Hollywood big hitters who were equally suited to portraying Ignatius, and would make it easier for Arata to raise the necessary money.

For that reason, Spud approached his friend John Goodman, with whom he had appeared on *Roseanne*. Goodman, born in 1952, was a New Orleans resident as well and a beloved screen presence for his much-lauded performances in comedies such as *King Ralph, Barton Fink*, and *The Flintstones*. Arata was friendly with Goodman and liked the idea of casting the actor as Ignatius: "This showed Spud's real commitment from a producing standpoint to say, 'Listen, it may not be in the best interest of the project that I play Ignatius.' That's the top producer's call. 'Hey, you are my pal, but it's called show business.' Spud was willing to do that."

As the producer remembers, Goodman wasn't interested in *A Confederacy of Dunces*, though: "[He said to 'Spud,'] 'No, you should do it. Really, you are going to be fantastic! This is going to define who you are. People are talking about it, but I am too old.' He offered his support, though. We never got a chance to get back to him and say how he could help, but we had always envisioned to say to him, 'Look, we need this or that.' It never got back to that stage."[4]

III

McConnell was delighted by Goodman's support, by his confidence that Spud would be a brilliant Ignatius on screen. John McConnell it would be, then.

The money-raising part seemed equally easy at first, although Arata was slightly disconcerted by Scott Kramer's demands. Kramer wanted to stay involved as executive producer, which was fine with his Louisiana counterpart, and Arata would need to pay for Steven Soderbergh's script, but that was only logical. Although Soderbergh's draft wasn't perfect, Spud and Arata were sure they could work on it.

After several conversations over the phone, Kramer laid out his plans: he demanded $1 million from Arata for the rights to use Soderbergh's script, and an additional $2 million for Soderbergh and Kramer as producer and executive producer.[5] The duo would be content to wait for the money until the movie was fully funded and in pre-production. If Arata proved he had the funds necessary, a contract could be drafted.

All the while, the Louisiana-based producer wasn't even sure whether Soderbergh did indeed own the rights to the property. Kramer's demands did nothing but increase Arata's doubts about their possible co-venture: "Probably after my fifth or sixth conversation with Scott Kramer, I realized all Scott was asking us was to just give a few million dollars for us to get the rights that Steven owned so that we could produce Steven's version of the script. Steven wasn't interested in directing it but he would sell us the rights. He kept saying, 'If you can come up with a million now and then a million later that would be fine.'"[6]

Arata could show that he had the money. Instead of approaching big studios, he employed a tactic similar to that of John Langdon. He figured the easiest way to raise the money was to approach local equity groups in Louisiana. They were supportive of the film industry in the state and now had the chance to be associated with a famous local novel—in fact, *the* most famous local novel.

Arata didn't find it a hard sell. He knew his pitch: "You know the book we grew up with and that everybody knows and that is the most famous novel that has never been turned into a movie? Guess what, you now have a chance to change the ending of that story!"[7]

Although business people are by nature careful when it comes to investing in art, they were willing to support *A Confederacy of Dunces*. Arata had their backing. If he and Kramer signed a contract, the equity group would pay the money required to commence pre-production. It wouldn't be all that was needed to get the project off the ground, but it was another step in the right direction, another hurdle passed.

With the money in the bag, Arata could now phone Kramer and forward the good news to him. The former was smart enough to follow up his news with some relevant questions. Arata wanted to make sure that he, Spud and the equity group were safe, and so he demanded to see Kramer's hand—could he prove he had all the rights to the project and that he was a reliable business partner?

IV

The first email Arata received from Kramer was not unusual for the film industry—it simply laid out how the money would be divided into various entities. It was convoluted but decipherable. An email from Kramer's lawyer was another kettle of fish. Said lawyer had been instructed to verify that Kramer had the right to receive money from Arata. Did he own the rights?

Michael Arata couldn't believe his eyes when he opened the email in which a chain of title was included. The email listed who had to be paid off before filming could begin. The file ran several pages and included every person who had ever been associated with *A Confederacy of Dunces*. "That's the ultimate Rube Goldberg," marvels Arata.[8] "It's magnificent. From a lawyer's standpoint it's a Jackson Pollock. It is art at that level. It is so convoluted, it is an invitation to join a lawsuit. All you do is sign up for one expensive, hysterical undertaking that will eventually lead to an abyss."

Arata was presented with the Who's Who of Hollywood. Among the entities owed money were Johnny Carson's estate; Bumbershoot Productions; and even Walker Percy, who had helped get the novel published. Based on an estimate, it would cost Michael Arata and John "Spud" McConnell at least $15 million dollars to clear the historic legacy costs before filming could even begin. They were informed that the debts were likely to be closer to $30 million. Arata was stunned: "I am not that type of transaction lawyer, but I looked at it, showed it to Spud, and Spud and I were both, 'What do we do now?'"[9]

Pandora's box had been opened.

V

Michael Arata called Scott Kramer's lawyer, who had yet another surprise in store for him. Only in the course of the phone call did it become clear that Soderbergh and Kramer had filed a lawsuit against Paramount. Legally speaking, Soderbergh and Kramer didn't own the rights. They were still held by the studio. The nightmare wasn't over yet.

Arata was frustrated but not surprised that what he had been told by Kramer's team didn't appear to him to be the complete truth. The story of the production of *A Confederacy of Dunces* was even more convoluted than what Kramer had let on during his vivid storytelling. As Arata continues: "It came to pass that what rights they would have possessed were actually provided to them by Scott Rudin, and Scott was the one who actually held the rights. He hadn't even granted Soderbergh the rights to the movie yet. Soderbergh wrote the script on spec and had hoped to do the film himself. When he couldn't, he was looking to unload it on people."[10]

Only then did it become clear to Michael Arata and John McConnell that the project would never happen with them. Even if they were able to pay the legacy costs, at some point down the line they would have to negotiate with Scott Rudin and Paramount. Nobody could predict what the outcome of that would be. Arata felt the project was "snake-bit"[11] and eventually decided to pass. He had wasted 1.5 years on the project.

The Louisiana–based producer was bitter about the experience for several reasons: "As soon as we were able to verify that we could deliver on our part, [Soderbergh and Kramer] showed us their hands. When they showed us their hands we realized they were going to swap up their crazy issue to us which set off alarm bells to us. Every step I took to try to advance our own interest in getting the film made was just one more weird revelation. I hate to call it duplicity or deception, but it was always something that could have been easily disclosed or volunteered in a collegial way that never was. It seemed that everything about this project had some mysterious bent to it. Every time Spud and I would talk to someone we would be alerted to the presence of another unseen force that was really controlling what was happening."[12]

VI

It had become clear to Arata that nobody was really controlling *A Confederacy of Dunces* despite the fact that many people thought they did. The producer and his friend McConnell simply didn't want to mess with Scott Rudin, of whose reputation they were only too well aware.

In the course of their negotiations with Kramer, Pat Dollard had also introduced the duo to Sid Sheinberg and his sons. Sheinberg had been the president of Universal before devoting his time to his own company, The Bubble Factory, from 1995 onward. Sheinberg and his sons seemed interested in financing *A Confederacy with Dunces* as a co-venture with Arata, but they also struck him as experienced, aggressive Hollywood players. And surely, Scott Rudin would be ten times worse. Thanks, but no thanks.

> See the lust in their hearts, and observe their poisonous greed.
> Note their anger that scourges their minds like a mighty whirlwind
> lashing the waves of the sea. Their sorrows gnaw within them,
> and their boundless hopes torment them, helpless and wretched victims.[13]

Needless to say, Scott Kramer didn't take kindly to Arata's refusal to engage further with him before Kramer could prove he owned the rights, as he claimed he did. Tensions had already flared high after Arata had demanded more information from him.

Arata and Spud had consulted a lawyer who, in turn, had drafted a letter to Kramer, explaining his understanding of the rights.

Arata remembers: "He got very offended and said, 'I am not going to deal with you guys anymore unless you can prove you have funds,'"[14] in a variation of Ignatius's famous remark: "I am beginning to suspect that you people are not actually deserving of this cause. Apparently you are not prepared to make any of the ultimate sacrifices."[15]

Continues Arata: "When we did that, we took the initiative again and said, 'Now tell us how our interpretation is so wrong.' He gave us more documentation which led our lawyers to write another letter explaining our position, which he of course again got extremely agitated with."[16] Like Ignatius grew evermore irritated by his mother when waiting for her at the front of D.H. Holmes, Kramer was already "polishing a few carefully worded accusations designed to reduce [Arata] to repentance or, at least, confusion."[17]

Kramer's and Arata's last phone call was therefore short, but not sweet. After Kramer had insulted Arata by calling him names and saying he was through wasting time with him, he slammed the phone down.

VII

Michael Arata learned a lot from his experiences with Steven Soderbergh, Scott Kramer and Pat Dollard. For him, it was a story stranger than fiction: "It was really an eye-opening experience for us, getting involved more and more as the details started to reveal themselves and as we started to understand that what we were being told was really the opposite of what it really was. We weren't naive, just excited and ambitious. I had produced films before, but that was the first film where I said, 'This is the underbelly that people talk about,' the tough aspect of show business that we hadn't been privy to. That was real hard knuckle, no-holds-barred fight, this is ruthless money-getting. That's all this is really about."[18]

His friendship with Pat Dollard didn't suffer, though, and even Steven Soderbergh seemed to harbor no ill will against Arata and McConnell. Arata's view of Scott Kramer is much different, describing him as a "Jekyll/Hyde" character, as somebody who is funny and charming right before he has one drink too many, then "turns into this vicious brawler, a rough-around-the-edges kind of guy."[19] Scott Kramer declined to comment.

Soderbergh and Dollard stayed close for several years after this episode, as did Arata and Dollard. The powerful agent would meet with the actor-producer in Los Angeles, drive him around in his sports car and then announce he had to pick up Kiefer Sutherland before Marisa Tomei joined them for lunch.

It was a lifestyle vastly different from Arata's, and although the latter was impressed and star-struck, he quickly realized it wasn't a way of life he would want to lead. Pat Dollard was a character straight out of Bret Easton Ellis's novel *Less than Zero*, and he slowly unraveled in front of his friends. Arata couldn't help but feel sorry for Dollard's fourth wife, who he had married at the Royal Sonesta Hotel in New Orleans. It was a marriage performed by a voodoo priestess who had a large white python draped on her shoulders, and it was apparent to Arata that Dollard's wife had no idea about what she was getting into.[20] Steven Soderbergh was present, too.

After Dollard and his wife separated, his drug consumption escalated. He moved back to Los Angeles and sent his friends and acquaintances an email one night. It consisted of one word: "Later."[21] Around 350 people—none of them in blind copy—received the mail, most of them big Hollywood stars. Arata and his colleagues were convinced "Later" meant "Farewell, I am no more."

After had received several replies urging him to hold on—that he was loved by everybody—Dollard decided to clarify matters: "You pussies don't understand. I am on my way to Iraq to see what's really going on."[22] He was injured a few months later while he was filming troops for a documentary he was making in Ramadi, where he "learned the joys of killing."[23]

When a Humvee in which he was riding was struck by a bomb, two Marines were killed. Dollard, thrown from the Humvee, was lucky in that he emerged with only a two-inch cut on his right leg. Michael Arata saw him a few years after that, when Dollard came back to New Orleans for a short while: "He was really scarred. He wasn't the same person I had seen years before, and he never was. It was a very weird short meeting, and then I just lost touch with him. Then I saw this radical hard-right stuff,"[24] such as Dollard writing "if there is even one more act of Muslim terrorism, it is then time for Americans to start slaughtering Muslims in the streets, all of them."[25]

22

A Cautionary Tale

How Harvey Weinstein presents himself as the savior of a cursed project,
and Scott Kramer pens his own draft of Ignatius's adventures

In the hope of repackaging his project, Scott Kramer went hunting for directors. In 1999, he discussed the project with Spike Jonze, a celebrated director of music videos who had just finished his feature debut, *Being John Malkovich*, a film which would soon become a modern cult classic.[1]

Through Creative Arts Agency the Soderbergh-penned script also reached Doug Liman the same year. At that point, Liman was not yet famous for his hard-hitting, fast-paced action films, but for three successful comedies: *Getting In*, *Swingers*, and *Go*, which had found considerable critical acclaim and made Kramer believe Liman might be his man. Luckily for Kramer, the director was interested in the project.[2]

In 2000, the script also found its way to up-and-coming Brazilian director Fernando Meirelles, who would later film such prestigious projects as *City of God* and *The Constant Gardener*. Meirelles's Hollywood agent John Lesher had always been an admirer of Toole's novel and remembers forwarding the script to his client.[3] Meirelles loved it: "I thought about Philip Seymour Hoffman [for "Dunces"]. [...] I read the script thinking about him. But then I realized I wouldn't know how to do it. You have to be born [in America] to understand [it]."[4]

Also considered was Paul Thomas Anderson who, following his successes with *Boogie Nights* and *Magnolia*, had become one of the most acclaimed directors of his generation.[5] The Bumbershoot camp favored Anderson, particularly for his collaboration with actor John C. Reilly, who they considered perfect for the part of Ignatius J. Reilly. However, a studio still had to be found to finance the venture.

II

While their attempts to set up *A Confederacy of Dunces* with Michael Arata and John "Spud" McConnell had resulted in nothing but bitterness, Scott Kramer and Steven Soderbergh seemed to hit the jackpot a short while later when Harvey Weinstein at Miramax decided to take on the project, attempting to wrest it away from Scott Rudin.[6] Drew Barrymore and her business partner Nancy Juvonen were attached as co-producers with their company Flower Films, a film studio which had already co-financed Barrymore's *Never Been Kissed*, *Charlie's Angels*, and *Donnie Darko*.

Along with his brother Bob, Harvey Weinstein had founded Miramax in the late '70s, to distribute independent films. It would be almost a decade until Miramax took flight, their truly groundbreaking success coming with Soderbergh's *sex, lies and videotape*, which premiered in August 1989 and went on to make $25 million (against a budget of just $1.2 million) at the domestic box office alone.[7] Oscar-winning hits such as *The English Patient* and *Shakespeare in Love* followed, and Miramax became infamous in the industry for its aggressive marketing—much as Harvey was infamous for his temper tantrums and for taking films away from their creators and re-cutting them, a practice that earned him the nickname Harvey Scissorhands.[8]

In Scott Rudin, the volatile Weinstein had met his match—Rudin's reputation was, at that time, equally bad. (Former) assistants had leaked some of their boss's temper tantrums to the press, which gobbled up Rudin's comments such as: "My silence is high praise," "This is a new level of stupid" and "[You're] Valium with skin."[9] There was also the tale of the legally blind assistant who had to keep ordering cabs and sending them away again as Rudin fired and rehired him several times in the course of one day.[10] In short, Rudin and Weinstein were made for each other.

> *Think, too, how, if those offices and their powers had anything inherently good in them, they would never be possessed by wicked men, for in nature opposites do not attract one another. And since there can be no doubt that offices are often held by evil men, then it follows that they are not in themselves good.*[11]

III

In May 2001 Weinstein sent Rudin a check for $1.5 million, which the latter freely admitted at the time he would rather burn than cash: "I fully intend to make that movie. [...] It was a great project at its inception, and it's still a great property. There are a handful of projects that are timeless, and this is one of them."[12]

Rudin had devised a cunning plan: Soderbergh and Kramer had three years to set up "their" project with a studio other than Paramount. That period expired on May 17, 2001. Harvey Weinstein had sent his check to Paramount on May 15, 2001. On May 18, Rudin hadn't yet cashed it. Soderbergh's and Kramer's period had run out.

Naturally, Scott Kramer was furious—the project had been with Paramount long enough, and the result had been nothing but blood, sweat and tears. The producer vented: "I don't know why this has to be contentious, because part of that agreement is that we have the ability to buy Paramount out. [...] This isn't a turnaround deal and so a change of elements doesn't apply."[13]

Rudin saw the situation differently: Soderbergh and Kramer (and therefore Miramax, which the duo had attached to the project) were in no position to buy the intellectual property because the terms as laid down in the contract signed between Paramount and Soderbergh/Kramer had changed. For example, Soderbergh was no longer the director. The script had not been approved—or even seen—by Paramount, and with Drew Barrymore and Nancy Juvonen, new producers were now attached.

IV

In 2001, Paramount and Miramax co-financed *Iris*, the biographical story of writer Iris Murdoch—played by Judi Dench—who starts experiencing symptoms of Alzheimer's disease. In their tug of war over *A Confederacy of Dunces*, *Iris* would serve as a rag doll between Weinstein and Rudin. The rights to Toole's novel were now with Paramount, and if its head got his wish, his adversaries Steven Soderbergh and Scott Kramer would never again get their hands on the property.

Since a traditional negotiation proved fruitless, Weinstein reverted to an old tactic: threatening his nemeses. He tried to intimidate Scott Rudin.

INT. SCOTT RUDIN'S OFFICE AT PARAMOUNT. DAY.
SCOTT RUDIN is on the phone.

<u>HARVEY (V.O.)</u>
If you don't sell me *Dunces*,
I'm going to put *Iris* on the shelf.

<u>SCOTT</u>
Do what you want. I've made the movie, I've delivered it, I don't care what you do.
You don't want to release this movie, I'll give you Judi Dench's number, you call
her up and tell her you're gonna shelve it!
'Cause I'm not gonna be the guy delivering that message.
Hope you have a nice phone call.[14]

The last thing Weinstein wanted to do was phone up Judi Dench and be the bearer of bad news he himself had created. Only two years before Dench had won the Academy Award for Best Supporting Actress for her portrayal of Queen Elizabeth in Miramax's *Shakespeare in Love*. Instead, the volatile New Yorker would continue to try to intimidate Rudin, who went on record saying: "After a year of torture, threats, blackmail, and after holding *Iris* hostage, he finally agreed to pay me. It was probably the single most painful and unpleasant thing I have ever been through in the movie business. Solely at the hands of Harvey."[15]

In mid–2001, Miramax and Paramount finally closed the deal when Weinstein's company paid $1.5 million for *A Confederacy of Dunces*.[16] The rest of the costs which had accumulated over the decades would have to be paid as soon as the film went into production.

Meanwhile, Weinstein and Rudin would continue to fight. They had agreed to co-finance *The Hours*, based on Michael Cunningham's Pulitzer Prize–winning novel, and their power play lasted for a few more months. Steven Soderbergh, watching the spectacle unfold from the sidelines, wryly commented: "It's as simple as, there can only be one control freak on a movie."[17]

V

In 2001, LSU Press published Hardy and Nevil's *Ignatius Rising*, the first biography of John Kennedy Toole. It didn't take long for the movie rights to be optioned—by Paramount, no less.[18] Needless to say, Hardy was thrilled. A deal was negotiated, and Rudin could now adapt Toole's life for the big screen. He did nothing.

As the years went by, the key figures surrounding *Ignatius Rising* started to suspect the powerful Hollywood producer only wanted to keep the project off the market—which would not be an unusual move in Hollywood. Screenwriter Jeffrey Hatcher is familiar with such tactics, explaining: "The funny thing about film studios is they set up a property—it's terrible to call those things property, it turns everything into real estate—and sit on it for years and not do anything because it's dangerous. A movie like that would cost a few million dollars just to get up and start talking about it. They don't want to release the rights either because they don't want to think that somebody else has the idea that they don't have. They would kick themselves for the rest of their lives."[19] Hardy and Nevils never heard anything from Scott Rudin.

VI

At Miramax, *A Confederacy of Dunces* would be executively produced by Rudin, Kramer, John Hardy and Soderbergh. Furthermore, everybody who over the years had tried to produce the adaptation would receive credit; among them John Langdon, Maidee Walker, Susan O'Connell, even Sandy Ignon.

Weinstein was aware of how burdened the project was and he didn't seem enthusiastic about starting production, as Jonathan Gordon, who was vice president of production at Miramax at the time, recalls: "I love that book! I do remember having some conversations with Scott Kramer back then, however no memory of the substance of them. I think my lack of recollection about the project stems from the fact that Harvey Weinstein never had any intention of actually making it. I don't remember any conversations with him about making it, leading me to believe it wasn't a priority for him."[20]

Mark Gill shares this view. Gill had started working for Miramax in 1994 as marketing expert. He didn't have the best time of his life at the company, as he remembered: "You got an overlord who lived by the most vicious methods possible in order to instill fear. [...] I've ducked from a couple of ashtrays being thrown at me, one of them that probably weighted five pounds, made out of marble. [...] Miramax broke a ton of people. Harvey broke a ton of people."[21]

In 1997 Gill was promoted to president of the company's Los Angeles office. As head of production, he oversaw films such as *Frida* before exiting Miramax in 2002. While *Frida* was a priority for Weinstein, *A Confederacy of Dunces* was not. Mark Gill remembers Steven Soderbergh passionately pitching his baby to Miramax and attending a few subsequent meetings, but no further engagements with Weinstein. *A Confederacy of Dunces* was put on the back burner.[22]

Following the tumultuous collaboration on *Iris*, it would appear that Weinstein had made it his mission to wrestle *A Confederacy of Dunces* away from Rudin out of spite and as a favor to Steven Soderbergh, and that once he had purchased the title, he lost interest in producing the film. Naturally, Harvey Weinstein disagrees, with his publicist Judah Engelmayer saying: "Not doing this was among the biggest disappointments in Harvey's career. He thinks Steven Soderbergh and Scott Kramer did a great job with it and they deserve accolades."[23]

This claim certainly is in line with Weinstein's statement given to the press in 2002: "*Confederacy* is one of those incredibly unique projects that Miramax has traditionally embraced. We are really impressed with Scott's commitment to developing this story and are excited to be working with Steven again."[24]

VII

Like he had always done, Scott Kramer took matters in his own hands—already, in July 2000, he had written his own adaptation of the novel. Soderbergh's screenplay—which had been written while the director was still under contract with Paramount and which had made the rounds in Hollywood—was no longer to be used. Assembling a new script was safer legally than taking Soderbergh's script to Miramax and risking a new battle with Paramount.

Although it was Kramer's script, he did incorporate a few of Soderbergh's ideas, primarily among these that Ignatius take many a bath. As in Soderbergh's version, "Iggy" never gives the impression of being anything but asexual, even muttering at one point: "You know how I feel about touching other people." Although it was hard for everybody involved to agree on anything when it came to an adaptation of *A Confederacy of Dunces*, it was a consensus that Ignatius had to be portrayed as asexual. As O'Connell comments: "In the best scripts Ignatius is asexual. If you go one way or the other, if you make him too gay or too straight where his relationship with Myrna is actually something, it doesn't work. That's what really worked about Soderbergh's script. What didn't work with Stephen Fry was presenting the opening scene like *All About Eve*. It was too arch. You should just leave the structure of the story alone."[25]

The beginning of Kramer's script closely resembles Stephen Geller's approach, with the tragic hero sitting in a dark movie theater, commenting on the spectacle unfolding on the screen. While the credits for Miramax's *A Confederacy of Dunces* adaptation appear, Ignatius can't help but spout his vitriol at the names that pop up. His comments regarding Miramax as the production company would prove prophetic only a few years later: insulted by what his eyes have to witness, Ignatius asks himself out loud why this company is still in business and hasn't been shut down by the "League of Decency."

Kramer did agree with O'Connell that the structure of the story should best be left alone and his adaptation is largely faithful to the novel. Doris Day, for example, pops up several times—once in a film Ignatius is watching and in another instance when Miss Trixie is spotted wearing a wig that closely resembles Day's haircut in the '60s. This is an idea Kramer shares with Frank Galati's adaptation.

However, there are also elements that differ from the source material. Most are minor changes, as when Miss Annie explains Ignatius's state of mind by recounting Rex's death while Super 8 footage is shown of a younger Ignatius playing with his beloved dog. Dr. Talc is omitted altogether. Robichaux and Irene's relationship is hardly given any screen time and is, as a result, underdeveloped—although they do fall in love, they only share a few short scenes together.

Also cut is arguably one of the funniest and most disturbing parts of the novel: Ignatius's desperate attempt to convince Dorian Greene's party guests of the value of his radical social concepts. Although Ignatius is shown entering Greene's apartment, Kramer then cuts to him being violently thrown out shortly thereafter, with what happened during the ill-fated party being left to the imagination of the viewer. Ignatius's job interview at Levy's Pants is gone. Instead, various other job interviews are shown: at a brewery, a telephone company, a supermarket, a chicken processing plant.

Maidee Walker would be pleased that Kramer decided to cut most of the slapstick elements in the book. Miss Trixie, for example, is spared the mayhem which ensues in the novel following Ignatius's decoration of his office. Also cut is the brawl during the demonstration at the factory.

As in the novel, Kramer lets Ignatius bring all the major characters together at the end. Unlike in other screenplays, Ignatius doesn't appear to change his mind about moving to New York with his Myrna, the free-spirited communist.

Toole's coda—showing how every character finds a new perspective on life—was an essential aspect for every screenwriter, including Kramer. The greatest irony in the novel is that, after all, it is the troubled character of Ignatius who brings everybody together. Ignatius turns out to be Fortune who, in the end, brings luck to his colleagues, nemeses and what, for lack of a better word, can be called friends. It is Ignatius J. Reilly who improves their lives: Irene is finally in a relationship with somebody who respects and clearly loves her; Mancuso gets promoted and no longer has to sit in a restroom cubicle in a ridiculous costume; Miss Trixie is finally allowed to retire after Ignatius convinces Mr. Levy that it was she who had written the infamously insulting letter to Abelman; and Mr. Levy finally has high hopes again for his struggling factory, deciding to produce Bermuda shorts, as opposed to his outdated product line which nobody was willing to buy anymore.

Ignatius, of course, receives no thanks for any of this. As the tragic hero he gets severely injured and has to flee his home after his own mother called the "chariddy." As to whether he will be able to find a better life in New York: who knows? Sadistically, and unlike Scott Kramer, John Kennedy Toole creates an ambiguous ending, while letting the story end on a gentle note: "Taking [Myrna's] pigtail in one of his paws, he pressed it warmly to his wet moustache."[26]

VIII

Another problem Kramer faced was how to grant Myrna as much screen time as possible in order to establish what could, with great generosity, be described as a love story. He decided to follow Frank Galati's approach. At the beginning, for example, Myrna can be seen riding in a subway car through Brooklyn, looking fiercely into the camera, thus breaking the fourth wall, but addressing Ignatius. At another point, Myrna's monologue accompanies a montage which shows the essence of what she is saying to Ignatius, and therefore to the audience as well.

Only a few scenes are completely made up by Kramer, most surprising of which is a short interlude of Ignatius preparing to leave the house to attend several job interviews. It is early morning; Gothic music is playing; and "Iggy," seemingly in good spirits and motivated to engage with potential employers, is handed a lunch bag by Irene. His usual attire is gone. Instead of his infamous cap with ear flaps, his hair is combed back. As out of character as this is for Ignatius, his flatulence remains a constant.

Indeed, throughout the screenplay Ignatius farts in abundance—fruity farts blast through the cinema, bubbles rise between his legs in the bathtub, gaseous emissions are released when he is in his room. Such moments satisfy fans of flatulent humor, popular in American comedies from the '90s onward, and they also illustrate how skillfully John Kennedy Toole combined gross-out humor and intellectual elements in his novel.

Kramer goes to great lengths to elaborately set up the various plot points. George and Lana Lee's plan to distribute pornography—hardly a concern in the California of the 2000s—is carefully explained in a dialogue between the two. In fact, very little is left to the audience's imagination. Where Toole left blanks, Kramer elaborates. It is the need to constantly explain what happened, what is happening and what is likely going to happen that distinguishes Kramer's adaptation from the previous scripts. It is as if, after a decades-long battle to see his dream realized, decades of misunderstandings and disagreements, Kramer wants to make sure everybody understands his take on *A Confederacy of Dunces*. As a result, his screenplay—re-written in September 2002 after a director had been cast and again in December 2003 after the project had fallen apart once more—doesn't have the exuberant playfulness of Galati's, the exhaustive originality of Fry's or the crass outrageousness of Geller's.

23

Damaged Goods

How David Gordon Green can't wait to direct the stars of the hour in Kramer's adaptation, while Miramax drives the car with one foot firmly on the brakes

With a script in place and an initial transfer of $1.5 million, *A Confederacy of Dunces* was slated to go in front of cameras in the fall of 2002. Steven Soderbergh was out of the picture as director. Who would helm the adaptation for Miramax?

David Gordon Green was the star of the hour, a young filmmaker who had wowed audiences with his feature film debut *George Washington*, a heart-wrenching independent film which came out in 2000. There was no doubt that critic's darling Green was an intelligent filmmaker who would understand *A Confederacy of Dunces*.

Green was, of course, familiar with the novel, saying: "I've been obsessed with this book since an English teacher of mine gave it to me when I was a kid. [...] It really captures human emotions and the way they relate to each other, but not in a carica-tured way. It's an ambitious step forward."[1]

He would go on to say: "I've had two goals as far as movies are concerned for-ever that I can remember. One of them was to [make] *Dunces*, and [then] more than anything in the whole world, I really wanna do *Fat Albert*."[2] Neither of Green's goals would come to fruition. *A Confederacy of Dunces* would soon be abandoned, and *Fat Albert* would be directed by Joel Zwick in 2004. If it was any consolation, the comedy, featuring *Saturday Night Live* star Kenan Thompson, received devastating reviews and tanked at the box office.

Not everybody was convinced that Gordon Green was the perfect choice for *A Confederacy of Dunces*, as Susan O'Connell admits. She didn't find Green's feature film debut, which was about the aftermath of the accidental death of a child, funny enough: "I remember Scott talking to us about David Gordon Green because then I went and watched his picture. I thought, 'This guy has no sense of humor! What are you doing?' He is a real cineaste, he understands cinema. But what a mistake that might have been! [Weinstein's] confidence in David Gordon Green as a director was not very high."[3] Gordon Green was, after all, only a newcomer with two shorts and one feature film under his belt. He certainly wasn't everybody's first choice. He would have been Michael Arata's, though.

The two had hit it off a few years before when Arata was still enthralled by the possibility of producing *A Confederacy of Dunces*. Gordon Green had then been an unknown director who had shot two short films in North Carolina, *Pleasant Grove* and *Physical Pinball*. When his feature debut, *George Washington*, premiered, Arata

154

was certain that a young genius had burst onto the scene. However, when Gordon Green was finally announced as the man who would helm *A Confederacy of Dunces*, Arata felt that Miramax didn't share his enthusiasm for the upcoming talent: "Steven [Soderbergh] liked him but I just don't think the larger higher ups were willing to sign on to that."[4]

In fact, Gordon Green had lobbied hard to get the job. Previously, co-producers Drew Barrymore and Nancy Juvonen had tried to talk Miramax into hiring Dean Parisot, their first choice as director.[5] Parisot had worked with Barrymore in 1998 on the romantic comedy *Home Fries*. Gordon Green, though, still saw himself as the best candidate for the job, as he confessed in 2003: "I heard who they'd been talking to and I got angry and just tried to campaign for it. I mean, I've got no business making movies that cost more than $5 by Hollywood standards, but [I wanted it]."[6] Green's brash approach was successful. He got the job.

II

Weinstein gave the green light, and a director for *A Confederacy of Dunces* was announced in the trade papers. Then Kramer, Green and Weinstein started to assemble a cast. Deciding on an actor for the role of Ignatius had always been a problem, but one rising star caught the trio's attention: while Jack Black had been considered for the part, first choice was Philip Seymour Hoffman.[7] The New York native had made his screen debut in *Triple Bogey on a Par Five Hole* in 1991 and had made memorable appearances in *The Talented Mr. Ripley*, a Miramax co-venture; in Paul Thomas Anderson's *Magnolia* and *Punch Drunk Love*; Todd Solondz's controversial, nihilistic satire *Happiness*; and in Cameron Crowe's success *Almost Famous*. For Susan O'Connell, Hoffman was a dream, a pitch-perfect choice for the role of Ignatius because of a "tortured nature" which closely resembled that of Ignatius: "He was not well known at that time. Oh boy, my God. That would have been amazing."[8]

III

Other actors who were contacted for *A Confederacy of Dunces* were of no less repute: Lily Tomlin as Irene Reilly, Mos Def as Burma Jones, Olympia Dukakis as Santa Battaglia, and Drew Barrymore as Darlene.[9]

Scott Kramer was ecstatic, proclaiming after the deal with Miramax and Flower Films was finally signed and the differences with Paramount settled: "This is a satisfying and just conclusion to many years of hard and often frustrating work. [...] I am pleased to be continuing my association with Steven Soderbergh and Miramax Films and to forge a new relationship with Nancy, Drew and Flower Films. I am deeply indebted to Harvey Weinstein who read the script, immediately saw its potential, and through great effort and expense rescued it from impending oblivion."[10]

It was as if Kramer had just devoured the most delicious hot dog of his life, marveling: "I cannot recently remember having been so totally satisfied. I was fortunate to find this place."[11]

Soderbergh concurred: "Scott's [Kramer] unflagging passion for this project should be a lesson for anyone attempting to bring challenging and outrageous material to the screen. Should I mention that I am a salaried executive producer on the film?"[12]

Happiness is a good thing, surely, but it is a mood and no matter how pleasant it may be, one cannot prevent its passing when it will, as moods do.[13]

With the addition of Barrymore and her business partner Nancy Juvonen, the list of co-producers on *A Confederacy of Dunces* was ready to burst: Scott Kramer, Steven Soderbergh, Scott Rudin, Harvey Weinstein, Nancy Juvonen, Drew Barrymore, John Langdon, Maidee Walker, Susan O'Connell, and Sandy Ignon would all receive a credit. O'Connell and Langdon were also granted consultation rights. David Gordon Green would soon find out how difficult it is to steer a ship with ten captains safely into a harbor.

IV

The director embarked on location scouting in New Orleans. While doing so, he fell in love with the city in general and with one house in particular. He couldn't help but buy it. At least one good thing would come out of David Gordon Green's involvement in *A Confederacy of Dunces*: his first home of his own, a "1919 shotgun doublewide" house that the director fixed up and made his home, having up to that point lived out of suitcases and slept on couches following his success with *George Washington*.[14]

The director had a very clear approach in mind for his version of the story. To him, it was essential to make New Orleans a major character in itself, to let the audience smell the city and drink it in: "We're rooting it in reality. [...] This is not a cartoon. It's going to bring an authenticity to the time and the place. It's a New Orleans movie. This is not Tim Burton necessarily. We're trying to find that time and place and those people. And they are funny, and they're also sad."[15]

Miramax, meanwhile, had submitted the necessary application for a tax credit to the Louisiana Film Commission which would make it possible to properly scout for locations with a guide, choose areas to film in and commence shooting with the tax incentives the state offered—an essential process for any studio which is keen on filming in Louisiana or similar states which offer such incentives.

Alex Schott was the state film commissioner at the time and remembers receiving the initial application: "That first application is a pre-qualification which means you would meet the requirements to receive the credits. Anybody would qualify that entered the information and was spending the amount of money that was the minimum amount. It was more for record keeping, in terms of how many movies were scheduled to come. We pre-certified many more films than ever got made simply because films fall through. That's just the first step, to get the conversation going."[16]

Schott was delighted about the project. However, he became slightly concerned when the studio failed to include a shooting script with its application, since both usually go hand in hand: "Personally I was excited because I was curious to see the direction they would take it. I was a fan of the director and I figured with the talent behind it it would be something interesting, more so than everything else given the story and the uniqueness of the New Orleans area and Louisiana in general. I knew there would be a lot of interest around it."[17]

Although the studio never pulled the application, the Louisiana State Commission would never hear from it again.

There were issues.

V

Without enthusiasm on the part of Harvey Weinstein to pay off all debtors and finally let the cameras roll, excitement needed to be drummed up. An opportunity presented itself to Scott Kramer while he was attending the Sundance Film Festival in January 2003. He met Mystelle Brabbee, head of the Nantucket Film Festival which takes place every year on the island of Nantucket off the coast of Massachusetts. Brabbee and Kramer started talking, and it didn't take long for the latter to mention his pet project.

Brabbee remembers:

> I spoke about the unique things the Nantucket Festival does, one of which is a reading of un-produced screenplays. We have been doing those readings since the inception of the festival, often with a high profile cast attached. Scott said, "I might have a script for you." We have had successes with Kenneth Lonergan and various writers over the years, but it's always a tough road to hose. When Scott said he might have a script for me, I asked what it was and he said *A Confederacy of Dunces*. He mentioned David Gordon Green who was attached at the time. David Gordon Green was pretty hot at the time as a director, and Scott was passionate about the project. It was clear it was win-win. When we worked on the casting for it, it was an unbelievable few months of people saying yes left and right.[18]

Mystelle Brabbee and Scott Kramer agreed to organize a stage reading of the script. The plan was to get every actor attached to the film on stage and read their dialogue to the audience. However, a couple of actors weren't available, among them Drew Barrymore and Philip Seymour Hoffman. Needless to say, the Nantucket Film Festival needed an Ignatius. Who to book? Brabbee and her colleague Jill Burkhart were heartbroken to learn that Hoffman wouldn't be able to make it.

The founder of the Nantucket Film Festival had another idea, and swiftly placed a call to Will Ferrell's agent. A short while later, Brabbee received the news that Ferrell was indeed interested in becoming Ignatius J. Reilly for an afternoon in June 2003. She was over the moon, as were Scott Kramer and David Gordon Green. Brabbee recalls: "It was the easiest project to book talent to. I think actors wanted to participate in it. They wanted to participate in the reading of a script based on a beloved book."[19]

Will Ferrell was all game for the stage reading, although, as he would later admit, slightly intimidated by the prospect of possibly appearing in a film version of *A Confederacy of Dunces*: "That was a heavy thing, though; I thought 'Wow, if this happens, this is like a big one to bite off.' The book is so talked-about that its fans are either going to be like 'They blew it,' or 'Wow, great job!' So I was like, 'Be careful what you wish for on this one.'"[20]

Olympia Dukakis and Mos Def, who were already attached to the film, were available and made their way to Nantucket for the stage reading. Brabbee and Kramer relied on stars who had already been to the film festival before as replacements for actors who weren't available. Thus, a magnificent cast could be assembled for the stage reading: Will Ferrell as Ignatius Reilly; Anne Meara as Mrs. Reilly; Paul Rudd as Officer Mancuso; Alan Cumming as Dorian Green; Mos Def as Burma Jones; Rosie Perez as Darlene; Olympia Dukakis as Santa Battaglia and Miss Trixie; Natasha Lyonne as Myrna; Kristen Johnston as Lana Lee; Jesse Eisenberg as George; John Shea as Gonzales; Celia Weston as Mrs. Levy, Miss Annie and Miss Inez; John Conlon as Robichaux and Mr. Clyde; Jace Alexander as Bartender Ben; and Dan Hedaya as Mr. Levy.[21] John Shea, Anne Meara, Paul Rudd, Rosie Perez, and Alan Cumming had all been to the festival before. The stage reading would become the success Kramer could only have wished for the film that never was.

24

Stunned, Still

How a stage reading in which Will Ferrell surpasses himself becomes a
crowd-pleasing success, and the film dies a slow death at Miramax

The 800-seat auditorium quickly sold out. It turned out to be an experience Mystelle Brabbee would never forget: "When the [actors] come we don't over-rehearse,
deliberately because we want to hear the actor's first or second impulse. We read it
once or twice before. It was fully magical. The actors were great and spontaneous.
Will Ferrell jumped off the stage and was walking the aisles. It was not a dull stage
reading by any stretch."[1]

Michael Arata and John "Spud" McConnell were in the audience. Arata had been
invited by his friend David Gordon Green. It was a sublime event which washed away
all the bitterness the producer had still felt about his time with Kramer and company.
As Arata says: "After going through that experience it was cathartic. Having gone
through it and seeing what's behind the curtain on all this stuff and then watching
the play.... David Gordon Green did a nice job as dramaturg, but when Will Ferrell
walked into that audience the place was electrified. For an hour and 40 minutes that
we were there it was magical and captivating. Mos Def was magnificent. I got back
from that and said to Spud, '[Kramer] couldn't make it,' but this kind of crazy train
was a fantastic experience. [The stage reading] was a showcase that it could be done,
that it had real viability."[2]

For the role of the narrator, Brabbee and Burkhart contracted their friend Garret Savage, who remembers his experience with great fondness: "I worked in various
capacities at the festival in the late '90s and early 2000s. In addition to being a filmmaker, I was, at the time of the reading, doing some acting. I was just getting my feet
wet in the acting world, so it was a thrill to work such a star studded cast."[3]

With a new cast, the start of the script had to be changed. In Kramer's adaptation, Ignatius can't help but comment on every credit that appears on the screen
before him. After some necessary revisions, the lights were dimmed and the show
began:

A CONFEDERACY OF DUNCES

DIRECTED BY	IGNATIUS (OFF)
David Gordon Green	Hack extraordinaire!
PRODUCED BY	IGNATIUS (OFF)
Scott Kramer	That's not a good sign.
Drew Barrymore	
Nancy Juvonen	

A STEVEN SODERBERGH Production

READ BY	IGNATIUS (OFF)
Anne Meara	Who?
Paul Rudd	I've never!
Kristen Johnson	Blecch!
Mos Def	Oh, my, no!
Rosie Perez	Awful!
Olympia Dukakis	Overpaid!
Alan Cumming	Terrible!
and Will Ferrell	That c***s***er!
FADE-IN, INTERIOR ROOM	Oh, this is even worse
	than I dared imagine![4]

II

Although Brabbee and her colleagues were disappointed that producer Steven Soderbergh hadn't made his way to the festival, they were glad to see that several members of the audience had traveled to the island specifically to attend the stage reading of *A Confederacy of Dunces* as directed by David Gordon Green. Brabbee was struck by the director: "He was a new, young, fresh talent with an original voice. Scott found that intriguing and thought he had a very bright future and that he would be able to give it a very distinct feeling."[5]

But, as always, tensions were bubbling under the surface. Shooting, which had been supposed to start in the autumn of 2002, was now delayed while the legal department at Miramax sorted through the chain of title in order to determine who would have to be paid off once filming began. It would be no small sum, Weinstein knew.

III

This delay gave David Gordon Green the chance to work on *All the Pretty Girls*, which came out in 2003, and *Undertow* which was released the following year. By that time, he was already frustrated by the lack of movement regarding *A Confederacy of Dunces*, and he wasn't shy to voice his disappointment to the press, in 2004 saying: "There were too many cooks involved, too many producers, the egos of a lot of people. [...] It had a lot of financial baggage [that] was propelling the budget to a place where you would have to make compromises in casting and the narrative by the time you started paying off all these jackasses."[6]

It should hardly have been a surprise that moving the project into production would, (a) be ridiculously expensive, since writers and producers needed to be paid off, and (b) a diplomatic masterclass in how to navigate around a multitude of voices who all wanted to have their say. What would have been Green's Hollywood debut had turned into a nightmare, and it wouldn't get any better.

Around the time Miramax and Scott Kramer tried to find a way forward for *A Confederacy of Dunces*, Green was also planning to realize several other projects he had in mind. *Shockproof Sydney Skate* was another adaptation of a successful novel which would never be made into a film: Steve Kloves had written several drafts for Cameron Crowe to direct before Green changed the screenplay and, in 2003, started talks with Sydney Pollack to direct and Fox 2000 Pictures to produce.[7]

Green also dreamed of realizing *Nerd Camp*, a script he had written about a summer camp. However, after the script had been written in 2006, Universal took the film away from Green and his creative partner Danny McBride and brought in a new writer to rework the draft.[8]

In the early 2000s a demolition derby film, to be entitled *The Precious Few*, was written by Green and McBride, but no studio was willing to finance the project.[9] After Warner Independent had agreed to pick up Green's *Snow Angels*, he was enlisted to write an adaptation of John Grisham's non-fiction work *The Innocent Man*, but the project collapsed for legal reasons.[10] All this happened in just a few years around the time Green was trying to get *A Confederacy of Dunces* off the ground. He would later have to abandon multiple other projects, such as a remake of the '60s espionage thriller *Ice Station Zebra*.[11]

IV

Soon, the director understood what was going on behind the scenes, explaining a few years later:

> *Dunces* was burdened by the financial and political paperwork that ultimately shelved it creatively. It was at a standstill between so many people that had their hand in the project, and the financial baggage that accumulated over the last 20 years. We assembled what I thought was an extraordinary cast, and had what I thought was a wonderful adaptation of the novel written by Steven Soderbergh and Scott Kramer, but it was a circumstance where every move needed to be approved and calculated and re-approved and the financial circumstances needed to be reconsidered and baggage kept getting bigger and bigger, so it wasn't an ideal circumstance under which to make the creative movie that it should have been—so who knows if that will ever happen, I hear different things, I don't think anyone can make it until someone gets paid off or dies [laughs].[12]

There had always been suspicions that Harvey Weinstein wasn't enthusiastic about bringing the project to the screen. These doubts were not only shared by Mark Gill and Jonathan Gordon, who worked at Miramax, but also by Will Ferrell, who was astonished to find his name in the trade papers as a replacement for Philip Seymour Hoffman. As he later confessed:

> We really just did a read-through at the Nantucket Film Festival of the script, and I was asked as a guest to do it, and that's what kind of generated a wave of "I'm attached." I don't even know how real it was for a studio ever to make it. I think it might have been leaks and trade paper momentum and things like that. It never got to that place of where I started thinking of it. Because I learned enough to know that stuff was talked about all the time, and then it just disappears. So I don't get that in-the-mode with anything until I know for sure that it is happening.[13]

For Green, carrying the weight of the project wasn't creatively healthy, and now, after shooting had already been postponed in 2002, the film was again put on hold in late 2004. The director was by this time very aware of how differently the various producers saw and understood Toole's work. In short, *A Confederacy of Dunces* was not commercially viable enough for Miramax, as the director explained in 2005:

> To the disappointment of many of us, *Dunces* was put on hold last year. We had assembled the cast of my dreams (Will Ferrell, Lily Tomlin, Mos Def, Drew Barrymore, Olympia

Dukakis, etc.), and I adopted New Orleans as my new home, but politics over the property rights—torn between Miramax, Paramount and various camps of producers—put a weight on the property that wasn't creatively healthy to work within. The draft of the script by Scott Kramer and Steven Soderbergh did the novel justice, and also provided a healthy cinematic spotlight for these eccentric characters, but it didn't cater to a lot of the cliches or conditioning of contemporary American studio sensibilities.[14]

By now, Green had encountered the same problem every writer had, starting with Maidee Walker 20 years before: how much of the story was comedy, how much was tragedy? How much emphasis should be put on the slapstick elements of the book? The director had zero interest in making Toole's work a straightforward comedy for the masses. Rather, he was intrigued by the shades of gray the novel displays. It was this determination to make the film his own way which made him clash with Weinstein, as Gordon Green continued: "I have yet to develop a project within the studio system that has been made, for whatever stubborn resistance to compromise on my part with the machine."

By late 2004, with the project on hold again, it was clear that Miramax was not going to pursue *A Confederacy of Dunces* any further. The future looked grim, but neither Kramer, Soderbergh nor Green were willing to give up without a fight. Instead, they looked for a different way of making their vision come true before the rights expired and reverted back to Paramount.

A new studio had to be found. And quickly.

V

In a company called Warner Independent Pictures, a studio which had been formed in 2003, Messrs. Kramer, Soderbergh and Green saw one more chance. Coincidentally, they encountered a familiar face from Miramax: Mark Gill.

The producer had left Miramax in 2002 to form Warner Independent Pictures and serve as its president. His powers of decision-making were, however, limited; the authority to greenlight a production remaining with the head of the film division at Warner Bros., a company which celebrated its fruitful relationship with Steven Soderbergh. Along with George Clooney and John Wells, the director had in 2000 formed Section Eight, a Warner Bros.-based company which was responsible for the immensely successful *Oceans* movies.

Rather than producing *A Confederacy of Dunces* with Section Eight, Soderbergh approached Gill at Warner Independent, who was at once flabbergasted about how diligently the filmmaker and his colleagues had prepared their pitch: "Effectively Steven came in with the script and they had a whole lot of cast attached to it. Seven or eight actors. They had done a very good job of filling the roles. Usually what happens is you get a script and a producer. If you are lucky there is a director, which was David Gordon Green. If you are really lucky you get one or two actors. They had seven or eight. The budget was fairly reasonable, $11 or $12 million. It was very much a labor of love. It was not that everybody was getting paid a fortune to do it."[15]

Soderbergh presented Kramer's script, which had been written for Miramax and used for the stage reading in Nantucket. Gill loved the adaptation and felt it did the novel justice. The producer had read Toole's work many years before and admired it greatly. If it had been up to him, the film would have gone ahead—*A Confederacy of Dunces* was the right kind of project for Warner Independent.

Over the next few days, several discussions were carried out between the parties, mostly via email. Soderbergh and Kramer were, again, well prepared and sent everything—such as a detailed budget—quickly and without any hiccups. Mark Gill loved the cast Soderbergh and Kramer had suggested and which consisted mostly of the actors who had taken part in the Nantucket reading a year prior: Will Ferrell was supposed to play Ignatius; Drew Barrymore, Olympia Dukakis, Natasha Lyonne, Paul Rudd and Mos Def would all also be involved. "The cast was amazing. It wasn't actors that only insiders in Hollywood had heard of," marvels Gill.[16]

The cast met his approval, the script passed his judgment, the budget was realistic—what could possibly go wrong? Even the accumulated legacy costs didn't deter the producer, who admits: "There was quite a bit of money against it that was a sort of sunken cost. That's always fun. But it wouldn't be the first time in the history of Hollywood. So what do you do? You decide if you want to make the movie or not. If you want to make it, you have to pay it."[17] Gill decided he wanted to do it and quickly approached his bosses at Warner Bros., Alan Horn and Jeff Robinov, and asked for their assessment of the project.

Unfortunately, by now *A Confederacy of Dunces* had gained a reputation among producers, and it wasn't a good one. Trying to sell it to Warner was like asking Goldman Sachs to hire a sack of rotten eggs as a financial adviser for one of its most prestigious clients. Making matters worse, Horn and Robinov were decidedly less impressed with the script than Gill had been.

The producer explains:

> We just couldn't get them to say "Okay." They didn't love the script. I had read the novel a long time earlier, not when it first came out but many years before I ever got anywhere near the prospect of possibly being able to produce a film based on it. I always loved the novel and thought this could be a really interesting independent film. But for whatever reason the people I was working for didn't love the script and weren't prepared to proceed. It wasn't the case that [they said], "Well, we like the script but there are a few things we would like to see changed or if you can fix this, we would consider it." It was just a "no."[18]

Was it just the script, or did the legacy costs play a part? According to Gill, this wasn't the case, as he explains:

> The money was fairly easy. I suppose you can always say it's the money, because when you are asking people to make the movie you are asking them to take a risk and make some sort of judgment on whether they actually have a decent chance of making the money back. So in a way it's always about the money, but it wasn't the usual Hollywood problem which is a shortage of cash to make the movie. That was never the issue. It wasn't like the budget of $40 million and everybody said, "Can you get it down to $12 million?" It was all very well put together and reasonably calibrated. But half the time we see things even now—which is a more sane era than that was—where the economic expectations are completely out of whack. This was not. They had really put it together well and done a good budget and cast it well and had a good director and had a good script also. But that's what makes some opinions. People can disagree.[19]

It was a painful but quick experience for Kramer and his colleagues. Overall, Warner Independent Pictures didn't spend more than two weeks pondering an adaptation of *A Confederacy of Dunces*—a surprisingly quick process made possible by

Soderbergh's and Kramer's meticulous planning. Since actors and a director had already been approached and a script had been written, it enabled Gill, Horn and Robinov to come to a decision immediately. Also, Gill prides himself in wasting no time when it comes to potential new projects, as he says: "You try to get the 'no' out of the way. 'Let's just try to decide, please.' The reason we were able to decide quickly is because we had all the information. They had already build a full house and you could see what it was and how much it cost and see that it worked. You just had to decide if you wanted to buy it or not. You didn't have to say, 'Let's see if they can put a roof on it.'"[20]

25

It's Not Dead,
It Just Smells Funny

How John Langdon and Scott Kramer try everything to breathe life into
A Confederacy of Dunces, *but find their hands bound*

A Confederacy of Dunces had died a slow death at Miramax, New Line had passed, and Warner Independent Pictures had to accept Horn's and Robinov's decision not to pursue the project—which meant that Warner Bros. as a whole had no interest in the property. Yet again, options were running out for Soderbergh and Kramer. It seemed that by now the filmmakers, but most especially Kramer, had become akin to Ignatius, stumbling through a melting pot of a city, trying to convince others of their creativity and willpower without much success, but meanwhile encountering many shrewd characters along the way; with Kramer himself maybe being the shrewdest of them all.

Among many others, he had made the acquaintance of Thelma Toole, the overbearing, theatrical and eccentric grand dame of New Orleans; John Belushi, the supremely talented yet drug-addicted star of the early '80s, who always failed to recognize Kramer and remember their appointments; John Langdon, the Texas millionaire and cattle-rancher who desperately wanted to break into movies; Stephen Fry, the British polymath who was courted by Scott Rudin and suffered a nervous breakdown while wrestling with Toole's source novel; and Harvey Weinstein, the notorious Hollywood mogul whose fights with Rudin escalated over the rights to *A Confederacy of Dunces*. Kramer saw himself caught up in the universe of John Kennedy Toole, albeit in a different way than he had originally hoped. The pursuit of *A Confederacy of Dunces* had become a comedy of errors.

II

By 2005, the rights to *A Confederacy of Dunces* reverted to Paramount. While Soderbergh and Kramer might understandably have felt frustrated by now, this turn of events could have led to some unexpected good news for Stephen Fry—his script was still owned by Paramount.

Early that year, Rudin gave his British friend a surprise call: the already legendary Spanish director Pedro Almodóvar had gotten his hands on Fry's script and liked it. Moreover, Almodóvar had mentioned to Rudin that he was interested in helming the adaptation at Paramount, thus making the project his English-language debut.[1] A few years prior, Almodóvar had entered negotiations with Miramax to direct an adaptation of Toole's novel but, as was reported in 2002, they ended abruptly and Gordon Green took over.[2]

As luck would have it, Almodóvar would soon be in London to attend the annual BAFTA Awards, as his movie *La Mala Educación* was nominated for Best Film Not in the English Language. Coincidentally, Fry would serve as host of the evening, which was on the 12th of February.

Although Almodóvar's film lost to *The Motorcycle Diaries*, he and Fry had the chance to exchange a few pleasantries, among which was the director's confirmation that he had indeed read the writer's script and was eager to work with him and Scott Rudin on it.[3] Would a film version of John Kennedy Toole's literary classic finally become a reality?

Fry was still hopeful—after all, *A Confederacy of Dunces* would always be relevant, no matter how much time passed:

> Many might think that a character like Ignatius railing against TV, pop music and contemporary culture is sorely needed to countervail the infantilism that has washed over us all since the book's publication. One lone, loud, roaring, erupting voice against the tsunami of comic book heroes and "live action" movies may not do anything to stem the tide, as indeed Ignatius and Toole didn't in their own time, but it would be a noble endeavor. It may be that longer form TV is the only way to cope with the structural problems that have obviated a traditional feature film version.[4]

The bad news for anyone who wanted to see the project on the big screen was that Scott Rudin, a champion of the book, was leaving Paramount. In April 2005, he accepted Disney's first look-offer, which was to last five years and enabled him to produce films under Disney's brands of Touchstone, Walt Disney, Hollywood Pictures, and—in an ironic development after Harvey and Bob Weinstein's departure—Miramax. Rudin's job change was a rupture which saw the chances of getting the film made in the foreseeable future decrease substantially. With Scott Rudin gone, *A Confederacy of Dunces* lost its loudest and strongest supporter at Paramount.

For Scott Kramer, John Hardy and Steven Soderbergh, it was good news, of course. Their "baby" was still at Paramount while Rudin, their arch-nemesis, was not. But because Rudin had brought *A Confederacy of Dunces* to Paramount in the first place, he would retain a credit as producer and could push the property since his name still carried weight. Obviously, he still had countless contacts at the company.

Meanwhile, Rudin was replaced by Brad Grey as CEO, a former talent manager who had started his career as assistant to Harvey and Bob Weinstein.[5] It's a small world.

III

It proved equally tough for David Gordon Green and his colleagues to breathe life back into the project at Paramount, regardless of Scott Rudin. Throughout the decades, there has always been one matter where everybody connected to a possible *A Confederacy of Dunces* adaptation was in accord. While there were differences about approaches to the work itself, it was clear to everybody that the film would have to be shot, at least partly, in New Orleans. Letting the cameras roll in any other city would be sacrilegious. Toole's work was, after all, the quintessential New Orleans novel and inseparably connected to the Big Easy.

However, any hopes of assembling cast and crew at the Bayou soon were shattered on the morning of August 29, 2005. Hurricane Katrina had arrived. It didn't take long for the hurricane to overwhelm the city's drainage canals, and only a few hours later, nearly 80 percent of the city was flooded.[6]

The Superdome housed 15,000 people who had to flee their homes. Many more thousands were left desperate for food, water and shelter. In total, Hurricane Katrina killed about 2,000 people and left a trail of devastation not only in New Orleans but also along much of the Gulf Coast of the United States. New Orleans would never be the same again. Indeed, for many years the city would be used by filmmakers who wanted to showcase a place of desolation as a backdrop for their stories (see Werner Herzog's 2009 film *Bad Lieutenant: Port of Call New Orleans*), but the soul of the city as portrayed in John Kennedy Toole's novel was no more.

With the reshuffle under Brad Grey at Paramount and the effects of Hurricane Katrina, it dawned on David Gordon Green that no feature film version of Ignatius J. Reilly's adventures would be forthcoming soon, if at all. In 2008 the director would sigh: "It's just caught up right now in a bunch of either legal or ego problems. [...] I think it's resting on the side of the road, taking a nap."[7]

IV

Stephen Geller has correctly pointed out that, for various reasons, many projects acquired by the former head of a studio are shelved when a new head takes over.

However, along with Johnny Langdon at Bumbershoot, Messrs. Gordon Green, Soderbergh, Hardy and Kramer kept pushing on, and in April 2006 when Gordon Green happily proclaimed in the papers that the project was in development again at Paramount, it seemed their efforts were to be rewarded. Talks with the various parties were ongoing, though many hurdles regarding the paperwork were still to be cleared, and Gordon Green was by now busy with another project: "I'm editing a film I just shot and hoping to begin putting more energy toward the potential of what I believe a proper production of that book might be. We'll see."[8]

If Paramount was to go through with the project, a new screenplay would have to be written—Scott Kramer's script was now copyrighted by Miramax. In May 2006, Gordon Green already sounded less hopeful than he had just one month before, despite the fact that he and his colleagues had reason to celebrate:

> Many of the rights issues have since expired, and from what I am told, Paramount holds all consideration on their own shoulders. That at least simplifies the objective. I am hopeful, with the new names and faces over there under Brad Grey, that Kramer, Soderbergh and I can again arm wrestle some enthusiasm. Scott Kramer is the die hard producer who has been with the project since before the book's publication. The history of the book and various efforts for a filmed version make an epic of their own. [...] My hope is that we get our paws on the flick and Kramer writes his memoirs of the whole deal.[9]

V

The wheels at Paramount were turning slowly, and David Gordon Green wasn't the only one who was growing impatient. Several hundred miles away, John Langdon got antsy. The novel was still dear to his heart, and he had spent many years and a lot of money trying to turn it into a film. Since he still held consultation rights, the entrepreneur from Texas was eager to see the project become a reality. He was not content to sit at the sidelines and twirl his thumbs.

He had his own problems at Bumbershoot, though. In 1995, his confidante and trusted colleague Susan O'Connell had moved to the San Francisco Zen Center, and was ordained as a Zen priest in 1999.[10] While she had always been busy at the center, her schedule from 2006 onward made it impossible for her to devote as much time to Bumbershoot as she had done before, as that year she was made vice president of the Zen Center before taking on the role of president. John Langdon needed a new sidekick and supporter who knew their way around the film industry. Luckily, while he continued working irregularly with O'Connell when the need arose, he was able to find just such a person.

In 2007 Langdon co-founded and financed the Lone Star Film Festival in Fort Worth, and it quickly became a prestigious place for filmmakers and fans to exchange views, learn from each other and watch the newest motion pictures on the big festival screen. In its second year, Langdon and his colleagues awarded the Pioneer Award to producer Carolyn Pfeiffer for her achievements in film. After working as Claudia Cardinale's assistant in Europe, Pfeiffer had co-founded Island Alive, a company which, before it folded in 1985, would distribute films such as *Koyaanisqatsi*. Under the banner of Alive Films, Pfeiffer continued producing features such as Alan Rudolph's *Trouble in Mind* and Lindsay Anderson's *The Whales of August*.[11]

Since Hollywood is a village, Pfeiffer had already gotten to know Susan O'Connell—back when Pfeiffer was still working for Island Alive, the now-Zen priestess had pitched several projects to the company, none of which were ever made. When Pfeiffer accepted the Pioneer Award she had just moved to Marfa, Texas, having fallen in love with the artsy town while scouting locations for a film (which also would never be made).[12] Since the prize winner and O'Connell got on well, the latter recommended Pfeiffer as a consultant to John Langdon. He was only too happy to work with the experienced producer to try to set up film productions at Bumbershoot, while still pushing to get *A Confederacy of Dunces* made at Paramount.

Pfeiffer remembers: "He was attached as executive producer and Susan was attached as associate producer if the film was made. They wanted to have good faith involvements. But in reality they had no legal involvement. There was nothing Johnny could do other than ask where things were going. Paramount owned it."[13]

However, Langdon and Pfeiffer had a few tricks up their sleeves to try and drum up interest in the project despite its complicated and frustrating history. Pfeiffer, for example, set up a meeting with Brad Pitt's production company, Plan B Entertainment, as a potential investor which—coincidentally—had been co-founded by Brad Grey. It was now run by Dede Gardner.

As an executive producer, albeit one without any legal involvement, Langdon found it easy to attract initial interest in *A Confederacy of Dunces*. He just needed to be straightforward about his role and the fact that he no longer owned the property, as Carolyn Pfeiffer explains:

> Nothing was done in a duplicitous way. In every meeting we took Johnny was very open about what his position was. He had enough history with the project that people were interested in talking to him. His lawyer and he were in touch with Paramount and we were given the occasional update if anything was happening. Everyone was extremely careful not to do anything untoward, but what Johnny was trying to do was keep the project alive and get it made. To that end he just kept breathing life into it.[14]

As frequently as every six weeks, Pfeiffer and Langdon would fly to Los Angeles to hold meetings and introduce "their" projects, *A Confederacy of Dunces* among them. Pitt's studio decided not to pursue the project, since it was "encumbered by that point," as Pfeiffer admits.[15] A few more polite emails were exchanged, and Plan B vanished from Bumbershoot's radar.

VI

The plan to involve a co-production company to help advance *A Confederacy of Dunces* at Paramount had failed. The polite exchanges with Scott Kramer and Paramount's lawyers didn't yield any results either, simply because "nothing much was happening," as both Pfeiffer and O'Connell remark, with the former elaborating: "I was mostly emailing with Scott Rudin. I saw the correspondence between Scott and Johnny and I saw the correspondence between Scott and me. It was always cordial after so many years of nothing happening. I suspect Paramount was really not particularly interested in the project. Scott was more interested in the project than Paramount was because they doubted its commercial viability, although the book was a success."[16]

John Langdon kept inquiring about the project at Paramount, exchanging emails with production president Marc Evans.[17] He also continued conversations with some old friends of his who had expressed an interest in the project at one time or another. Among them was Shirley MacLaine. Her interest in the role of Irene Reilly had never wavered. MacLaine's calls erupted like small earthquakes in the office of Bumbershoot Productions, as Langdon's assistant Lisa Arent remembers fondly:

> He would visit her at her ranch in New Mexico. He spoke to Shirley. He had other films and scripts that he had people working on for her. She was all in. He would still talk to her on the phone, and she would share ideas. She was very much like she is in the movies. Very curt and get to the point. No-nonsense. People would ask him about her brother. He would go to her house and ask her all sorts of questions. He was very open as to what he knew about her. We felt we knew her although we didn't. I was surprised by that relationship between those two because they were an odd couple of sorts although they were both into arts.[18]

Over the years, Bumbershoot had pondered various actresses for the role of Ignatius's mother, among them Florence Henderson, Bette Midler and Sally Field, but Shirley MacLaine would always remain the clear frontrunner.[19] Many lists were filled with casting possibilities for other roles; comedy legend Carol Burnett would be a brilliant Miss Trixie, Langdon was sure—a clear favorite. Should she have been unavailable, Jean Stapleton—well-known for her role in the classic series *All in the*

Family—would have been an alternative. Stapleton died in 2013. *Ishtar* director Elaine May was considered for the role.[20]

Lana Lee was a fierce character and thus needed an actress known and celebrated for portraying strong, charismatic, tough women. John Langdon hadn't forgotten Sharon Stone and was still open to casting her should the film ever be made. However, Sigourney Weaver had become his favorite, and she had already been approached by Scott Kramer and expressed an interest in the role. Other viable candidates, according to Langdon, were Jamie Lee Curtis, Catherine O'Hara and even Madonna. They would all bring a fierceness to the role that was indispensable for the part of Lana Lee.[21]

Finding a Myrna Minkoff would be much more difficult. Natasha Lyonne had read her part at the Nantucket Film Festival, while Scott Kramer had also approached Gina Gershon and Amanda Peet.[22] Gershon's career had peaked in the '90s with her much lauded performance in Lana and Lilly Wachowski's *Bound*. Unfortunately, she had also been in Paul Verhoeven's *Showgirls*, and her career had suffered from its commercial and critical failure, despite the praise for *Bound* a year later. Similarly, Amanda Peet was an exciting new star in the mid–'90s, starring in films such as *One Fine Day* alongside George Clooney and Michelle Pfeiffer. She was later cast next to John Cusack in Roland Emmerich's *2012* and would increasingly work in well-known television shows such as *The Good Wife*.

Over the years, there have been a few contenders for the role of Mancuso, not least Edward James Olmos and Sean Penn. While Paul Rudd had read as the police officer in Nantucket, none other than Johnny Depp had emerged as the clear favorite at Bumbershoot.[23]

While Lily Tomlin preferred to play Irene Reilly, she was open to the role of Mrs. Levy, as she assured Langdon.[24] If the multi-millionaire got his wish, her husband would then be played by Larry David, co-creator of *Seinfeld* and creator of HBO's *Curb Your Enthusiasm*, a show not a million miles removed from *A Confederacy of Dunces*. If David turned out to be unavailable, Kevin Kline or Gene Wilder would do.[25] Dabney Coleman had already been approached for the role in the mid–'80s but had requested a screenplay—which he was never given.[26] On the other hand, Bumbershoot took the liberty to send a copy of Steven Soderbergh's script to Bill Murray as a possible candidate for the role. The actor never replied.[27] There was, though, no shortage of actors. There never had been. The problem was always with the studio.

Part III

Certainly the End of Something or Other, One Would Sort of Have to Think[1]

It was the worst of times, it was the worst of times. Again. That's the thing about things. They fall apart, always have, always will, it's in their nature.

—*Ali Smith*, Autumn

As the Scholar says, blame the individual, and the problem persists; analyze the system, and you're already one step closer to finding a solution.

—*John Burnside*, Havergey

171

26

Irreverent and Quirky
and Fascinating

How John Hardy assembles the team of his dreams to finally celebrate a
success with a project that had caused him so many headaches

Although many years of work had yielded nothing but frustration, producer John Hardy wasn't yet ready to give up on *A Confederacy of Dunces*. While his associate and close friend Steven Soderbergh considered the project cursed and had long since backed away from it, Hardy couldn't stop thinking about Ignatius J. Reilly and the endless possibilities his misadventures in New Orleans presented for a creative filmmaker. The movie rights were with Paramount, but that didn't mean the source couldn't be exploited in other ways.

John Hardy had an idea, and in 2009 he approached his friend Robert Guza. They had become fast friends when studying at the London Film School decades prior. While none of the projects they subsequently developed together were made, their friendship had remained as strong as ever. In fact, it had been Guza who introduced John Hardy and his then-wife Deborah Sue to *A Confederacy of Dunces*. Guza had read the novel when it first came out and become an instant fan. He was so floored by Toole's prose that he couldn't help but read the book three times in a row. This was comedy gold, and Guza had fallen in love.

So when his old friend John Hardy broached the subject of producing a version of *A Confederacy of Dunces* with him, he was, of course, all ears. "John and I were talking about how weird it was this thing had never been made," explains Guza, "and how weird all the attempts to make it had been. We started saying, 'It's not going to be made as a film or mini-series but what if we looked into the theater rights?' I had been involved in some theater stuff before so we just contacted LSU Press. They couldn't have been sweeter."[1]

II

As it happened, since Paramount had never optioned them, the stage rights were available. This surprised Guza and Hardy, but they weren't about to complain. Paramount had, though, first right of refusal for a limited period of time after an offer was made. Dutifully, the two producers contacted Paramount and were met with silence. For the first time, John Hardy was grateful for that silence. It meant they could proceed with their vision of staging a theater production of John Kennedy Toole's work.

Guza and Hardy were under no illusion they needed proficient help if they wanted to mount a stage version of the novel. Hence, they approached Paradigm, the talent agency which represented Guza. Looking for pointers, the duo was intrigued when director David Esbjornson was suggested to them. Esbjornson was also represented by Paradigm and had directed several theater productions that both Hardy and Guza had seen and been impressed by.

Esbjornson had made a name for himself with countless Shakespeare adaptations, as well as the revival of Larry Kramer's *The Normal Heart*, F. Scott Fitzgerald's *The Great Gatsby* and several works by Henrik Ibsen. In addition, Esbjornson was no stranger to the novel: "I found the whole thing irreverent and quirky and fascinating, especially the characters. Toole has drawn such unique characters, you just don't forget them."[2]

For many other reasons, the director seemed a great choice from the start, as Guza explains: "He is very, very good at moving people around on stage, and getting character performances out of people who maybe don't have a whole lot to do in the course of the show. He was great at it."[3]

This was important, because—even if some actors played multiple parts—there would be many characters on stage. That much was clear from the beginning.

Less clear was if Guza and Hardy could raise the money for a theater production as expensive as *A Confederacy of Dunces* would inevitably be—although the book was a beloved modern classic, there was no guarantee they would be able to successfully attract investors. The theater scene in the U.S. had changed drastically in the previous decades, and by now it was increasingly difficult to find funding for productions which were not musicals, as Guza found out: "When John and I were first looking for the rights and we talked to people in New York, lawyers and such, across the board people said, 'Christ, it's going to be a musical, that's wonderful!' Everybody said that, and we said, 'No, we want to do that as a straight play.' You are more likely to get a major investor for a musical than you are for a play. Musicals are recouping, plays do not always."[4]

III

Eventually they did get the money from investors willing to take a risk, but as always with *A Confederacy of Dunces*, that was only one of many challenges. With Esbjornson on board, Guza and Hardy still needed a playwright. Because of his work with Steven Soderbergh, Hardy had become friendly with Scott Kramer. Would he be a good choice?

Certainly, the producing duo admired Kramer's film script, but after a brief deliberation decided to hire an experienced playwright, which Kramer was not. David Esbjornson's first suggestion was Jeffrey Hatcher, a prolific playwright and screenwriter with whom he had worked before. For the director, there was no better choice: "I didn't have any problem convincing them that Jeffrey should do it. As soon as they met him was clear Jeff was a really good choice. He is sort of Orson Welles–like. He has this big beard, he is extremely funny and very smart. He has the ability to be rich and deep but he can do a kind of lightheartedness, too. He can do quips and he is funny. He is a funny person to be around. It struck me he was the perfect person for this."[5]

Hatcher and Esbjornson had worked together before. The writer was also a client at Paradigm. It was an easy deal for the team. Without hesitation, Guza and Hardy signed Hatcher. The fact that until then he hadn't read the book seemed unimportant.

IV

"I knew about it, I heard about it, but I had never read it," confesses Hatcher.[6] "It was a very crowded, antique graphic design, and I remember thinking, 'This looks too wacky to me, too busy.'" So the writer had judged the book by its cover and never previously been tempted to open a copy. Hatcher says: "It seemed a bit too big and crazy. I remember reading the title and seeing the name of the main character and thinking, 'Ignatius J. Reilly sounds like the kind of wacky character name that someone makes up for a book,' and that was a bit too broad for my taste."

Would his prejudices be confirmed? Jeffrey Hatcher read the book while in Japan in 2010. Indeed, he did find elements of it over the top, seeing Toole's approach as "baroque," like a "Hieronymus Bosch painting."[7] Turning it into a play would be no small feat.

V

Initially, Hardy and Guza had toyed with the idea of staging *A Confederacy of Dunces* as a one-man-show, with Ignatius talking as Irene, Claude Robichaux and Myrna. This idea was quickly discarded, since Toole's characters were found too rich to have their dialogue all spoken by the same actor.

Also, the duo wanted to capture the flavor of the Big Easy, Hardy having grown up in Baton Rouge and being well-acquainted with New Orleans. Guza knew the city fairly well, and for him there was no question that Ken's work was the quintessential New Orleans novel: "What is so New Orleans about this book? Forget the setting, the characters and the dialogue. You can almost feel the humidity. Everything is a little off-kilter. Everything is much slower."[8]

In order to capture that particular New Orleans flavor, Hardy, Guza, Esbjornson and Hatcher traveled to the city, a crew in tow whose job it was to shoot New Orleans imagery which would be projected throughout the play. Involving the community in Louisiana was essential, as Guza explains: "We all needed to get there, shoot the pictures, immerse ourselves in the atmosphere, talk to the people and then start getting some of the creative community together. It was important to them, especially after Katrina. After Katrina so many felt written off. People didn't care about them. It became huge for them. This book brings people together."[9]

VI

While the team was thinking about staging the production of *A Confederacy of Dunces* in New Orleans, Jeffrey Hatcher was working furiously on the play. During the course of a second reading of the novel he decided what to focus on, as he explains: "There are lots of adaptations of that work for the stage. Most of them tended to put almost the whole book on stage. We didn't want to do that. The narrative that's in the book, that's especially strong was Ignatius's attempt to get the job and please his mother while showing his mother's desire to pull away and have her own life."[10]

For Hatcher and Esbjornson, *A Confederacy of Dunces* was a work with a wounded heart at the center. Certainly, it was very funny, but it also had a lot of pain and anger in it. All this needed to be captured, and Hatcher and Esbjornson decided to do so by focusing on Ignatius's relationship with his mother. The director explains: "We were trying to present a child whose issues with abandonment were very clear, with his father and with his dog Rex. The moment where [Irene] gets rid of Rex is like a turning point in his life. It's a trauma that he has not been able to get through. To some extent we have to link Rex to his father. That psychology is what keeps him outcast and keeps him from his ability to engage in the world in a conventional way."[11]

There were other challenges; the character of Myrna, for example. Initially, Hatcher perceived the minx as a guardian angel for Ignatius, as somebody who haunts the streets of New Orleans. Worried about her old friend, she would always be close to him, appearing as different characters throughout—as a waitress, bartender or passerby. Hence she would immediately be at his side when he eventually needs to escape. The downside to this idea was that seeing Myrna in different disguises could be unnecessarily confusing for the audience. It was therefore discarded. Instead, the stage lights would highlight Myrna whenever Ignatius opened a letter from her, and the New York hippie would read her thoughts directly to the audience. It was much more straightforward. Simplicity was needed.

Burma Jones was another challenge. The times had changed, and in 2010 there was heightened awareness of political correctness, or the lack thereof. Says Guza: "We went back and forth because Burma Jones is a pivotal character. He is very funny. People have argued he is a stereotype. Ken Toole would argue he is sending up stereotypes. That's a dicey line to run. The book was set in the early 60s, a very different time. How much do you violate that time?"[12]

It was felt that *A Confederacy of Dunces* was New Orleans in the early '60s and should remain so. Nobody was interested in changing the time or setting, unlike the way Stephen Geller had done in the late '80s. Neither did the new team want to change John Kennedy Toole's characters. They could only hope that audiences would understand the frame of reference, the fact that the work was by now 50 years old.

In a pitch to the Huntington Theater in Boston, David Esbjornson would later reassure the managers:

> What I believe makes the story work are the very things that may disturb others. The story is irreverent, it leaves no one untouched (including the protagonist) and it spins subjects like intellectualism, sex and race into a dizzy orbit of contradiction and humor. [...] This story pre-dates the Kennedys, civil rights, the feminist movement and Watergate and yet the naïve roots of these unformed ideas existed in New Orleans, one of the true melting pots in America. *Confederacy* holds a significant and meaningful place in the Louisiana culture, but it may also be a microcosm of an America attempting to define itself in a new way.[13]

VII

In his script Jeffrey Hatcher makes Burma Jones into a character as important as Ignatius J. Reilly. Both drift through various scenes, holding the threads together. Whenever Ignatius is absent, it is Burma who never tires of pointing out other people's flaws to them. His favorite object of ridicule is, of course, Lana Lee. As critics of society, Burma and Ignatius appear as brothers in spirit.

While John Kennedy Toole had already sketched Burma's character that way in the novel, Jeffrey Hatcher accentuates it. Similarly, he emphasizes Ignatius's phraseology, making it next to impossible for a common man such as Mancuso to understand the meaning of the convoluted, Dickensian sentences that have just been inflicted upon him. Hatcher achieves this without quoting Toole directly. Instead, he mimics his style, staying true to the idiom and general approach. This allows him to be playful with language without deviating too far from the source material.

Hatcher's main achievement, though, is to repeatedly and with considerable skill combine several scenes into one. For example, in Mancuso's second encounter with Irene and Ignatius—following his confrontation with the main character in front of D.H. Holmes—the policeman has already been ordered to work undercover. He is provided a copy of *The Consolation of Philosophy* by Ignatius and bears witness to Irene's suggestion that Ignatius get a job immediately.

In another scene, Irene stumbles across a job advertisement from Levy Pants and explains her son's complicated relationship with Myrna Minkoff to Mancuso before volunteering the information that Ignatius is clearly asexual. This approach enables Hatcher and Esbjornsson to keep the action in one location for extended periods.

In a logistically clever decision, since Ignatius's fight with the cockatoo commences immediately after his humiliation on the hands of Dorian's lesbian friends, the setting of Dorian Green's infamous party is changed to the Night of Joy.

Aware that a large number of people in the audience will either be fans of the book, or at least have read it, Hatcher dispenses with quoting Ignatius's letter to Abelman. It had by now become well-known as one of the most delicious treats in the novel, so not quoting it, for a change, would be even more amusing than laying out every sentence. Instead, Hatcher simply lets Ignatius spell out the first line of what he is drafting. The rest no longer needs to be stated.

VIII

Hatcher's adaptation is, in some respects, much fiercer than the original novel. Miss Trixie is used to elicit laughs through her constant confusion and foul mouth. The playwright also allows Irene Reilly to be angrier than in the book. In one scene, she lashes out at her son—finally tired of the fact that Ignatius always finds a way to blame others for the chaos he produces, Irene goes on a verbal rampage, humiliating her son in front of Santa and Claude. Ironically, it is the hapless mother who constantly finds ways to deflect attention from her own shortcomings and is quick to find culprits with any other name than Irene Reilly: she blames Claude Robichaux for the hullabaloo in front of D.H. Holmes, and Ignatius for the car accident. She also implies it was Miss Annie who poisoned Rex, an act which in turn led to Igna-tius's downfall.

IX

Guza, himself an experienced writer, loved what his colleague delivered. The play was at once sharp, funny and tragic. The challenges that the book presented were cleverly overcome by Hatcher's inventiveness. Although few lines were quoted directly from the novel and several characters were left out, the adaptation captured the spirit of Toole's work.

Guza marvels: "That fan base is hawk-eyed and rabid. You change anything and somebody is going to be on your tail. Pulling something out makes it collapse but it also can irritate this rabid fan base. Jeffrey had done a lot of adaptations. He had a real flair for multiple characters in a scene, how to move them around, how to give them equal attention. He has this droll sense of humor. From what I've seen, Ken Toole had that kind of humor. Jeff just got it from the get-go."[14]

Even with characters such as Dr. Talc left out and with multiple scenes com-bined the play would still be two-and-a-half hours long and require many actors. The initial trip to New Orleans had been helpful, but naturally the play was still a form-less piece of clay, a work in progress.

An initial table read was organized in Minneapolis with actors from the renowned Guthrie Theater, a company with which David Esbjornson had a particu-larly close relationship since he had been guest director there.

There was another reading in New Orleans and a third in New York, and Hardy, Guza and Esbjornson were especially in awe of how quickly Hatcher worked, furi-ously jabbing at his keyboard, changing scenes on the spot. By the time Esbjornson was running a scene, it was already being rewritten. By the second time the scene was run, the actors were looking at the fresh pages. Possibly for the first time in the his-tory of *A Confederacy of Dunces* adaptations, everything was working seamlessly, and bit by bit, a concept for the play emerged.

Esbjornson decided to have objects that would normally be props expressed through mime, though not for financial reasons, as he emphasizes: "When I'm given a situation I try to create a piece that makes sense for those circumstances. If you are doing a tour of a play there are things you can't do. It has to be essential. It has to move easily. There was something very practical about it, but I thought there would be fun in it."[15]

The possibility of organizing a tour of the play was on everybody's mind, though the best scenario would be to have it performed in a theater all year round, prefera-bly in New Orleans. Similarly attractive was the possibility of licensing the play after a successful initial run, allowing other companies to stage their own productions of the script. The quartet would then turn a profit from licensing.

Nevertheless, the idea of organizing a tour influenced their creative approach. Having props represented through mime also meant a real cockatoo wouldn't be needed for the infamous scene in the Night of Joy. Instead, the actor portraying Igna-tius would partly mime it, while images of a real cockatoo would be projected onto the stage. When Ignatius strangles the bird and falls off a chair, feathers would fly up in the air. The approach would be comparatively easy to execute while potentially being very funny.

X

The team behind the stage adaptation was still eager to receive feedback from the locals, dreaming of staging their show in the Big Easy. Says Esbjornson: "It's really important when you are doing a piece about somebody that's important to a particular culture that that culture embrace what you are doing. I would find it very hard to move forward without that."[16]

For the New Orleans reading, the team found an actor who by then had long since made a name for himself as the quintessential Ignatius J. Reilly: John "Spud" McConnell. He had gathered great experience in the role, and regardless of his advanced age—"Spud" was already over 50 years old—everybody loved his performance and his charm. The people of New Orleans were excited, as were Hardy, Guza, Esbjornson and Hatcher, with the latter explaining: "We thought that doing this very New Orleansian show in New Orleans would be a good thing for us and for New Orleans. A lot of the theaters that had been ruined by the floods had been renovated. But they didn't have any product to put in the theaters. The flood had sent a lot of actors away from New Orleans, and as we put together this workshop it was hard to put it together because a lot of actors had left for New York or Los Angeles. The flood had made it untenable. Then as we got closer to the workshop more actors would show up. We were aware that the diaspora was now returning. We thought this could be great."[17]

XI

The team had not yet decided on a venue, and it was clear that a big name was needed for the actual run—an actor in the role of Ignatius who could draw in big numbers of people. It was an expensive production and nobody wanted to count on die-hard fans of the novel alone as the whole audience. However, the number of people who could play Ignatius, who would be available for a theater production and who could attract a large audience was limited.

It didn't help that Ignatius had a very particular look that had been shaped over decades, as Hatcher wryly observes: "Ignatius Reilly is haunted not only by one's own reading experience but also by the book covers. In a way, the minute someone in a book puts Ignatius on the jacket design you can't shake the drawing. Most of the jackets I have seen are the same, but sometimes he is grotesque in an unpleasant way, sometimes he is fat and jolly like Santa Claus. It does affect the way you think in terms of casting."[18]

For his work on the play, Jeffrey Hatcher researched John Kennedy Toole's life and, in a similar way to Stephen Fry, found comparisons between the author and his main character: "It seemed to me Toole was disguising himself under mounds of fat, but inside all of that was a character like Claude Rains, George Sanders or Clifton Webb—a beautifully dressed, witty, likely gay, mid-century cosmopolitan wit, the kind of person you see in movies like *Laura* and *All About Eve*. Part of the tragedy was that in no physical way did Ignatius match his aspirations. He had made himself even more grotesque, because if you see yourself as that kind of New York cartoon, a fellow in a dinner jacket with a cigarette holder, and you haven't achieved that, part of you says, 'Why not become fatter and grosser and more reprehensible?'"[19] (To drive home that point, Hatcher has Ignatius say to Clyde, the hot dog vendor: "Do you mind terribly if I select my own [hot dog]? I'd like to pretend I'm in a smart seafood restaurant and this is the lobster pond.")

Hence, an actor needed to be found who was by nature precise, wry, and overweight yet had a certain sense of elegance buried deep within him. Hatcher, Esbjornson, Hardy and Guza considered Nick Offerman of *Parks & Recreation* fame; Josh Gad, who had already been in films such as *Love & Other Drugs* as well as several television productions; and James Corden, who was British but certainly had the right physical stature. However, Corden was not available, and the quartet quickly decided on Nick Offerman, who brought very special qualities to the production. As Hatcher continues: "Nick Offerman has a very precise, wry, one eyebrow raised way of performing. It's a distant, ironic kind of performance although he did a few moments of gargantuan, big blunderbuss acting. Rabelaisian. Inside it there was always a man who was happier."[20]

XII

With Nick Offerman, the crew staged an additional reading in New York City in 2014. The play was still changing, because every actor brought something new and special to the table, but also because Jeffrey Hatcher was still working on both small as well as larger revisions, such as combining several scenes from the novel into one for the stage.

Steven Soderbergh was invited to the reading, and was delighted not only with the script but also with Esbjornson's decision to have the actors mime rather than use stage props. Immediately after the performance, he called up John Hardy:

INT. NEW YORK LOFT. DAY.

STEVEN
(speaking into his telephone)
Come to my place tomorrow. I want to talk!

CUT. NEW YORK LOFT. THE NEXT DAY.
ROBERT and JOHN sit in STEVEN's loft.

STEVEN
(animated) Oh, you cracked it, you found a way
to do it that I couldn't! That material is better
suited to the stage than the screen.

ROBERT
(skeptical) Really? Why?

STEVEN
The screen is so very literal. Necessarily so. If you put up the Night
of Joy that's it. That's exactly how it looks. There's the bar, there's

the cockatoo, there's Lana. They are specific. What that does is it
cuts back on the audience's imagination if it doesn't eliminate it outright. The
people who read it all know what Ignatius's bedroom looks like. They have very
specific ideas. The more literal you make it the less figuratively it becomes
and the less the audience has the chance to impose their own vision on it.[21]

"That made us feel terrific," Hatcher admits.[22] Steven Soderbergh's compliments were high praise indeed. John Hardy and Robert Guza also decided to bring the director onboard as co-executive producer.

XIII

Efforts to stage the play in New Orleans, though, amounted to nothing. The problem was that, after an extensive investigation, no theater in the area was available. La Petite, for example, could only host an audience of 250 people. The production was simply too expensive for such a small theater—the investment would never be returned.

Another theater in New Orleans was already fully booked. The team looked in other areas: The Geffen Playhouse in Los Angeles, though renowned, was too small a venue for a production such as *A Confederacy of Dunces*. After unsuccessfully approaching several other theaters in the country, David Esbjornson decided to pitch the project to the Huntington Theater in Boston, with which he already had a relationship. At the same time, Esbjornson wanted to produce *Guess Who's Coming to Dinner* at the Huntington, which was only too happy to pick up both offers: they would stage *Guess Who's Coming to Dinner* first, since it was easier to plan, and then jump right in with *A Confederacy of Dunces*. The Huntington Theater seemed ideal, as Esbjornson saw it: "It's an intelligent community. They are well-read, and I thought maybe a lot of people read this book. There is Boston University as well."[23]

The Huntington is a regional theater. As a not-for-profit company, it put up half the money while the producers put up the other half. Robert Guza and John Hardy knew they wouldn't make a profit from the production, but that was acceptable since their production at the Huntington was only supposed to be the beginning of a decade-long nationwide success for the play. In order to maximize their longer-term profits, Hardy and Guza—as owners of the theatrical rights—decided to bar other major stage productions of *A Confederacy of Dunces*. However, smaller endeavors weren't a concern for the producers, as Guza explains: "Once we signed the rights with LSU Press we had authority for any theatrical production in the world. We could shut down anything we felt was threatening but we could also say, 'Of course, go with it,' for something we thought might help us. In the course of all those years we let some things happen."[24]

XIV

For *A Confederacy of Dunces*, the Huntington Theatre Company splashed out, giving the play its highest budget for a non-musical production. And it would make its money back quickly. The first night was on 11 November 2015.

The theater was packed, and it soon became clear that the popularity of Esbjornson's and Hatcher's production would warrant additional performances and *A Confederacy of Dunces* ran until 20 December. In the end the company earned more than $2 million from 45 performances,[25] resulting in the highest-grossing show for the company.

Along with Nick Offerman as Ignatius J. Reilly, the producers had assembled a stellar cast that had many years of experience in the theater: Phillip James Brannon as Burma Jones; Arnie Burton as Dorian Greene and Mr. Gonzalez; Stephanie DiMaggio as Lana Lee and Myrna Minkoff; Lonnie Farmer as Mr. Watson and Mr. Clyde; Anita Gillette as Irene Reilly; Julie Halston as Miss Trixie; Paul Melendy as Mancuso; Talene Monahon as Darlene; Ed Peed as Claude Robichaux; Steve Rosen as Gus Levy; Lusia Strus as Santa Battaglia; and Stacey Yen as George and Mrs. Levy.[26]

XV

Unfortunately for David Esbjornson, the director had to leave for Shanghai shortly after opening the show. "I did see one [performance] at the end," remembers Esbjornson, "but it's hard to analyze something when you are in the middle of working on it. I was looking forward to having another crack at it,"[27] because the fact was, while the audience was by and large enthusiastic about the production—laughing on a moment-to-moment basis—the reviews were mixed. *The New York Times*, for example, judged: "Perhaps inevitably, in clambering from the pages of Toole's capacious book onto the Huntington stage, where the rigors of dramatic form can pinch, Ignatius and company seem to have lost some of their seedy, vicious charm, and Ignatius himself some of his unforgettable comic girth."[28] The review also criticized the minimalist set design, thereby finding fault with exactly what Steven Soderbergh had lauded.

Variety was hardly more complimentary, suggesting the play should be further slimmed down: "Playwright Jeffrey Hatcher has already done an impressive job of editing and shaping the story for the stage, retaining its essence as well as some of its dandiest dialogue. But more work still needs to be done to keep new audiences beguiled by the adventures of this proud and mammoth misfit, trapped by the extravagance of his own imagination. [...] It's quite a crowd, and at times the gumbo of a production turns to goo as the performances rely on cheap laughs and the staging swerves out of control."[29]

At the box office the reviews hardly seemed to matter, though they did to Esbjornson, Hatcher, Hardy and Guza, since the quartet had future plans for their production. Explains Esbjornson: "We did a pretty good job of holding the threads. That's not easy to do. After that you have to find a way in which the production keeps it off-balance and a little crazy because you can't get ahead of it. If there was anything I would look at now is whether there was any moment in which the audience was ahead of the play in any way. That would have helped if I could have analyzed it a little more."[30]

Jeffrey Hatcher decided to take another look at his adaptation following the middling reviews: "We thought, 'If we are going to do this show again we have to work on the production, maybe recast it.' At that point putting it all back together again seemed untenable."[31]

XVI

Originally, the quartet had dreamt of taking the play to Broadway in the spring of 2016. But, according to the playwright, "people with money prefer a review that's so positive that the negative aspects are mere nibbling. That didn't seem to be in the cards."[32] In other words, the reviews simply weren't good enough to attract investors for a performance on Broadway. The idea of staging the production in the West End in London was also discarded.

For a long time, nobody seemed to know what the next step should be. A proposed five-city tour which would have seen Nick Offerman as Ignatius traveling through major cities such as Houston and Seattle, performing in big theaters usually reserved for musicals, also never happened. Following the tour, the show was supposed to end up in New York City, although there were no guarantees, and Offerman didn't like the prospect of being separated from his wife for many months. He wanted to be sure that the whole endeavor would be worth everybody's time, and a definite agreement to play New York would prove that worth.

The problem was that staging the production in commercial venues would be horrendously expensive and if audiences stayed away could be financially disastrous for everybody involved. The costs would also be staggering at non-profit venues, but the chances of disaster would be cushioned by the fact that a non-profit production was not entirely dependent on ticket sales. However, simply bringing *A Confederacy of Dunces* to non-profit venues would mean the producers would never recoup their investment.

XVII

Jeffrey Hatcher and David Esbjornson are still eager to see more performances of their work. They have continued discussing their approach and revising the play further as a result of the Huntington performances, with the director commenting: "We realized the ramping up took a little too long for our taste. It wasn't bad but maybe there was a way of combining a few things. We wanted to stage a scene in the bowling alley where a whole lot of information got disseminated because people without knowing each other were in close proximity. That was an exciting epiphany of a place that we could go if we were given another production. We weren't given that extra production. It's an expensive production. People are very shy of doing expensive plays here that don't involve music. There is also a slight controversy about the material that gives people pause. I feel we have something special."[33]

27

Bits and Pieces

How Paramount decides to give A Confederacy of Dunces *one more go, John Kennedy Toole's life continues to inspire storytellers, and how everybody in this sorry tale moves on to other things*

Eventually, Paramount decided to take yet another stab at a feature film version of *A Confederacy of Dunces*, and in May 2012, it was announced that James Bobin was in negotiations to helm an adaptation of Toole's novel.[1] The British director had just finished *The Muppets* for Walt Disney Pictures, which had turned out a big financial and critical success.

Bobin would direct from a script penned by Phil Johnston, also a celebrated newcomer who had written the screenplay for *Cedar Rapids* with Ed Helms and John C. Reilly. Johnston at the time was working diligently on *Wreck-It Ralph*, which would become his biggest success to date. The scribe had been approached by Scott Rudin, who encouraged Johnston to try and slay this beast of a novel. Rudin was "so good at making me a better and a smarter writer," Johnston later remembered.[2]

He continued:

> The way I initially approached it was that I transcribed the entire book into Final Draft so I could learn the rhythms of Toole's writing style. I had a 551 page Final Draft script—a transcript of the book, basically. From that then I just winnowed it down to the bits that I thought would be relevant to the plot that I needed from the book. Then I threw all that out and started from scratch, using pieces of the book and biographical things from John Kennedy Toole's life, working those into the Ignatius-Irene relationship. If nothing else, it made me a much better writer and I'm extraordinarily proud of the script that exists. Again, whether it gets made or not, I don't know. I hope it gets made.

The last time John Langdon, Carolyn Pfeiffer and Susan O'Connell would hear from Paramount was regarding their choice for the leading man. It would be one Pfeiffer had also considered: Zach Galifianakis.[3] With the success of *The Hangover* in 2009, the American actor had become famous internationally, since then cementing his image as a grumpy bear-like persona that suited Ignatius J. Reilly well. Although Galifianakis was by then already in his 40s, Paramount and Rudin were sure audiences would have no problem picturing him as the obese medievalist. Even Phil Johnston was happy, announcing: "For one thing, Zach Galifianakis is more Ignatius Reilly than anyone who has ever lived, probably. He is the best way into it."[4]

The script was written, the director signed, the main actor announced in the trade papers. But, again, *A Confederacy of Dunces* would not be made. Producer Robert Guza did not understand why a studio would just sit on the rights like an overly protective goose on a golden egg: "I will go to my grave trying to figure out the thinking at that studio when it comes to this novel. You assume people act in their best interests. How is it possibly in Paramount's best interest to let this major brand lie sour for so long?"[5]

II

A renewed interest in *A Confederacy of Dunces* in the early 2010s led to the development of various other projects. In 2012, Cory MacLauchlin published *Butterfly in the Typewriter* with DaCapo Press, his autobiography of John Kennedy Toole. In the book, MacLauchlin disputes George and Nevil's claim in *Ignatius Rising* that Ken was a closeted homosexual. One review, for example, noted: "MacLauchlin grants that Toole had a complicated relationship with his often-overprotective mother, but without psychobabble or gobbledygook he lays out the case that Toole suffered from paranoid schizophrenia; in fact, his condition perhaps made his talent too fragile for the bruising requirements of revising a work for publication."[6]

The positive reviews were a great joy to MacLauchlin, but he was surprised when the film rights were sold, and not even to Paramount. In September 2014, filmmaker David DuBos announced he had snatched up the rights and intended to write the screenplay for the film himself.[7] DuBos is a writer and director based in New Orleans who first found a foothold in the film business penning the scripts for such low-budget '90s genre fare as *Future Shock* in 1994, *Leprechaun 3* in 1995, and *Playback* in 1996. In 2015 his documentary, *Delta Justice: The Islenos Trappers War*, won him the Audience Award at the New Orleans Film Festival.

DuBos was to write the screenplay for *Butterfly in the Typewriter*, and, like Michael J. Nathanson and Stephen Fry before him, he didn't simply want to tell the story of either Ignatius J. Reilly or John Kennedy Toole, but to combine the two. As he explained:

> People who have read *Confederacy* are really going to appreciate the film, because I did weave in elements […]. If you've read *Confederacy*, you're going to see bits and pieces— but if you've not read *Confederacy*, you'll still appreciate the story. […] There's a character, Bobby Byrne, who was a teacher at Lafayette, where Toole taught for a year. […] Bobby was the inspiration for Ignatius. He's being played by Nick Offerman, who played Ignatius in the stage version. You're going to see the hot dog vendor. You're going to see the Myrna character he met in New York. This is, again, all based on Corey's book and research I did.[8]

The story of John Kennedy Toole and the publication of his major work would be an easy sell to any studio, DuBos was sure:

> How about this for a pitch? An elderly lady, destitute and living with her brother, finds her dead son's unpublished manuscript, one that he toiled on for years, put his heart and soul into it, only to see it get soundly rejected by a famous literary editor and publishing house. Already suffering from schizophrenia, he descends into madness and commits suicide at a young age (32). Years later, his mother, after discovering the novel, gets it into the hands of a famous writer who champions it to publication and then it wins the Pulitzer Prize for fiction. I mean, you couldn't script a more bittersweet ending to that story than that.[9]

In order to attract investors, DuBos announced the cast as he saw it: Nick Offerman as Ignatius, Diane Kruger as Patricia Rickels, Susan Sarandon as Thelma Toole, Brad Dourif as Arthur Ducoing, and Thomas Mann as John Kennedy Toole. With a stellar cast such as this in mind, DuBos went into negotiations with Spectre-Vision, Elijah Wood's production company, which was making a name for itself by specializing in horror films, such as director Ana Lily Amirpour's *A Girl Walks Home Alone at Night*. The company would later finance Panos Cosmatos' *Mandy*, Richard Stanley's *Color Out of Space*, and *Daniel Isn't Real*. However, financing has not been secured yet. While hoping to attract investors for his passion project, David DuBos directed *Bayou Tales*, a horror anthology, as well as the documentary *In a Good Place Now*, about the music of Bobby Charles. *Butterfly in the Typewriter* is still waiting to go into production.

III

There is competition: following the publication of *Ignatius Rising*, Deborah Sue George penned a screenplay entitled *New Orleans Son*. It "captures the tragic life of Pulitzer Prize-winning novelist, John Kennedy Toole, author of *A Confederacy of Dunces*. Set in the eccentric culture of New Orleans, the dark, bizarre, albeit amazing, life of Ken Toole is revealed. Erudite professor by day and back-street blues devotee at night Ken attempts to extricate himself from the clutches of his overbearing, fascinating and irritatingly brilliant mother. Ultimately, Ken believes his only escape to freedom is to take his own life. Ken's death sends his grief stricken mother on a crusade to get his novel published. Her persistent efforts pay off when *A Confederacy of Dunces* wins the Pulitzer."[10]

After several years, Deborah Sue George found a production company for her story: in 2019, she was approached by a studio which wanted to buy the rights and turn her version of John Kennedy Toole's life into a motion picture.[11] It has not been made yet.

IV

In 2015, Andrew Farotte wrote a spec script entitled *A Confederacy of Thelma*. It tells the same story Deborah Sue George and David DuBos wanted to tell with their respective screenplays: "With author John Kennedy Toole committing suicide a decade before his Pulitzer Prize-winning novel—*A Confederacy of Dunces*—is discovered, his aging, guilt-ridden mother, Thelma, dedicates her final years to find a publisher in the hopes of redeeming herself and her son."[12]

Farotte, who worked as a producer in non-scripted television, had his script optioned by Filmula, a Los Angeles–based production company which had financed *Hesher* in 2010 and *Another Happy Day* a year after that. Although *A Confederacy of Thelma* made the annual Black List of the most liked yet still unproduced screenplays, his film about Thelma Toole's special quest has not been made. A cast was never announced.

V

Without actively pursuing *A Confederacy of Dunces*, which was in limbo at Paramount Pictures, John Langdon had more time on his hands for other projects—the adaptation of Toole's novel was by no means the only film he wanted to get off the ground, although it was the one closest to his heart. There were numerous other projects Langdon dabbled with until his death: one was a biopic of Clay Allison, one of Langdon's ancestors, and also a well-known 19th-century gunfighter whose gravestone displays the memorable inscription: He never killed a man that did not need killing.[13]

A script was written by Mike Shropshire, a Fort Worth–based sportswriter, but the Clay Allison biopic would never see the light of day.[14] Funding for *Empire Man* by Roderick Taylor would also never be secured. Other projects Langdon worked on were *The Pro*, *The Shareholder* and *The Hidden Agenda*—all without success. They would never reach the screen.

VI

Langdon's passion for *A Confederacy of Dunces* was a constant, however, and although he grew frustrated with the lack of progress, John Kennedy Toole's work remained close to his heart. The entrepreneur from Texas was so passionate about the novel that it was a requirement for every member of his staff to read it, as his assistant Lisa Arent remembers: "We would buy many copies throughout the years. He would send copies of that book to people just so they could read it. He would give copies to people he met on the plane. When we ran out, we had to buy more copies. He always kept them in the office."[15]

As frustrated as Langdon became, simply giving up on his passion project was never an option. It just wasn't in his nature, as Arent continues: "He was still excited about it. One thing about John is that he always believed that he would see all that stuff take off. It didn't matter it had taken 30 years for any of his ventures. He always felt that he would see it and that it would happen soon. He never gave up on anything. I would hear him express frustration though, saying, 'I wish I could get this going.'"[16]

Regularly, Analisa Garcia, as secretary for Bumbershoot Productions, would reach out to Scott Rudin to ask about any developments at Paramount, always to no avail: "We tried to keep communications open more than anything, but there wasn't much happening."[17]

Although Langdon never lost his passion for making films, and although he would never produce a motion picture that would see the light of day, he stayed involved in the industry. In 1998, he volunteered at the Fort Worth Film Festival, and in 2007 he co-founded the Lone Star Film Festival, an event which would become one of the most cherished American independent film festivals. As a part of the festival, the Johnny Langdon Film Initiative devoted itself to supporting creative minds, setting up a film camp where students can shoot their work and see it projected on the big screen.

That same year, 2007, Langdon found new happiness when he married his third wife, Anne Livet, whom he had known for many decades—Livet had been a friend of Langdon's sister Jane, who had been killed in 1963. They fell in love around the time of the funeral of Livet's brother, who had lost his life in a vehicle accident at his ranch.[18]

After suffering from diabetes for many years, Langdon developed balance problems. His diet didn't help, as his assistant Lisa Arent explains: "He would go into shock sometimes. You would then have to give him juice or candy. He wasn't the most healthy person. He would drink wine when he wasn't supposed to. We never could control him. It got worse in his later years. He would stumble or lose his balance. It kind of affected him mentally."[19]

"I had already checked in for the flight going over to John's house," John Langdon's friend Roderick Taylor remembers.[20] "I got a call then from a friend who said, 'Did you hear John Langdon just died?'" Stumbling out of bed in the middle of the night, John Langdon had fallen and bumped his head against the wall. Disoriented, and with a serious wound to his head, he went back to bed. He died on Saturday, 4 November 2017, as a result of his injury.

Shortly after John Langdon's passing Bumbershoot Productions was shut down. His children did not share their father's passion for producing movies and, above all, found his bottomless expenditure on various potential motion picture ventures disagreeable.

It seems to me that wealth is more splendid in the spending of it than in the getting of it. Avarice is not admirable, but liberality is generally praised. So money is precious not when you have it but when it passes on from you to somebody else, in which case you don't have it anymore.[21]

VII

After a stint in New York City, Maidee Walker moved back to Fort Worth, where she continued writing novels and drafting poems. Among the works she produced is an unpublished children's book, consisting of poems and short stories involving talking insects that live on a spacious estate. The book was illustrated by Walker's husband.

Following Walker and Langdon's bitter dispute and eventual reconciliation, Walker stayed in touch with Langdon until his passing. Severe mobility problems didn't deter the writer from making plans with her old friend to adapt her children's book into a movie.[22] Langdon was keen on producing a feature film adaptation, and Walker and her husband had already prepared drawings for shoes and other merchandise. But the project would never be made. As Langdon's assistant Analisa Garcia explains: "I think he was so idealistic that things never reached the point of perfection for him. He worked tirelessly to perfect things. His hand was in so much that it took a long time to get the right attention to every project. Other than that, it might just have been bad luck."[23]

VIII

Following the legal dispute with Paramount and the frustrating period at Miramax, there was little else Scott Kramer could do with *A Confederacy of Dunces*.

Although bitter about his experiences, Kramer continues to write scripts in the hope they will eventually be made.

In 1999, he produced *The Limey* for Steven Soderbergh, a well-received thriller starring Terence Stamp, before working again with Soderbergh in 2002 on the financial and critical flop *Full Frontal*. Today Kramer lives in Los Angeles, refusing to participate in any projects about the failure to make *A Confederacy of Dunces*.

IX

Although Susan O'Connell continued to support her friend and business partner John Langdon long after he had sold the rights in his quest to get *A Confederacy of Dunces* made, she left the film business and instead fully committed to her work at the San Francisco Zen Center. "Zesho" Susan O'Connell was ordained as a Zen priest in 1999 and received her Dharma Transmission in 2016, a ritual in Zen Buddhism in which a student is given the permission to continue the lineage tradition of Zen. From 2006 to 2016, O'Connell worked as vice-president and then president of the San Francisco Zen Center. She is now the spiritual director of the Senior Living Community Project and in this role oversees the development of Enso Village, a zen-inspired continuing care retirement community in northern California.[24]

X

Harold Ramis would land his biggest success as a director after he had given up on *A Confederacy of Dunces*: in 1993, he helmed *Groundhog Day* with Bill Murray, a smash hit that would quickly become a cult classic. While his next two films, *Stuart Saves His Family* with Al Franken, and *Multiplicity* with Michael Keaton, proved to be box-office disappointments, Ramis celebrated another hit with *Analyze This* starring Billy Crystal and Robert De Niro. In 2010, the director contracted vasculitis, an inflammation of the blood vessels that causes tissue damage. Ramis died in 2014, at the age of 69.[25] Two years later, the Harold Ramis Film School was founded by The Second City. It is the first film school to focus exclusively on comedy.

XI

Stephen Geller's career in Hollywood ended with him as a plaintiff against the industry's power brokers. In the late '90s, agents in Hollywood were accused of "graylisting." Writers in their 40s and 50s alleged that they weren't receiving any more work, leading the Writers Guild to file a class action lawsuit against every major studio and television agency, as well as talent agencies and networks. Geller was the lead plaintiff.[26] Most agencies settled with the Writers Guild, but Geller would never work in Hollywood again.

Geller and his fellow writers were shut out of Tinseltown: "I was okay in the sense that I was in my mid–50s when that happened. It started with most of the people in their early 40s. It was horrible."[27] Stephen Geller continues to write novels and now is a general education professor at the Savannah College of Art and Design in Georgia.

XII

Beth Henley has continued to write for the stage and screen. She met director Jonathan Demme in the '80s, leading to a fruitful friendship that lasted until Demme's death. Among the many screenplays Henley wrote that would never get a green light was *The Stopwatch Gang*, the thriller about Canadian bank robbers that Henley and Demme wanted to realize in the mid–'90s, with Daniel Day-Lewis in one of the leading roles.[28] In 2000, the director brought her play *Family Week* to the stage. Among her other plays are *Control Freaks*, *The Jacksonian*, and *Abundance*. She is now President's Professor of Theatre Arts at the College of Communication and Fine Arts, part of Loyola Marymount University in Los Angeles.

XIII

Steven Soderbergh continued to have a difficult relationship with the film industry. Although he celebrated some of the biggest hits of his career following his dispute with Paramount (*Traffic*, *Contagion*, *Magic Mike*), the director grew increasingly frustrated with the power big studios wielded over him as he struggled to fulfill his creative vision. He hinted at retiring at the age of 50, but only a few weeks later (at age 50), he started working on the television series *The Knick*. He subsequently shot several films which he produced himself, backed only by distribution companies. His desire for complete creative control resulted in films such as *Logan Lucky*, *Unsane*, *High Flying Bird*, *The Laundromat*, and *Let Them All Talk*.

XIV

Although he enjoyed his work on screenplays, Frank Galati has always seen himself as a man of the stage. He continued to work on celebrated adaptations of classic works as well as writing original plays and appearing as an actor. From 1986 to 2008 Galati was associate director of the Goodman Theatre, where he produced, among other productions, *Cry, the Beloved Country* to great acclaim. He had already won two Tony Awards (for *The Grapes of Wrath*) in 1990 and was nominated for a third in 1998 for his production of E.L. Doctorow's Pulitzer Prize-winning classic *Ragtime*. From 1970 to 2005, Frank Galati was a full-time faculty member in the Department of Performance Studies at Northwestern University. He now lives in Sarasota, Florida, where he is associate artist at the Asolo Repertory Theatre.

XV

Stephen Fry got back on his feet following his suicide attempt while working on *A Confederacy of Dunces*. The multifaceted entertainer, jack of all trades and, in his native England, national treasure, continued to write books, host TV shows and awards shows, work on screenplays, and appear as an actor. Fry remained open about his mental health struggles both in television shows and in his writing. After his relationship with Daniel Cohen had ended in 2010, he married his partner Elliott Spencer in 2015. In 2018, Fry announced that he had recently undergone a successful surgery for prostate cancer. His non-fiction books, *Mythos* and *Heroes*, retellings of Greek mythology, quickly became international bestsellers.

XVI

Harvey Weinstein and his brother Bob left their own company, Miramax, in 2005 to form The Weinstein Company. There their slow decline as producers began, punctuated by occasional hits from the likes of Quentin Tarantino. Then in October 2017 the *New York Times* published an extensive story which would have international ramifications far beyond the film industry: several women, among them actresses Ashley Judd and Rose McGowan, accused the producer of sexual harassment.[29]

For over three decades, Harvey Weinstein was alleged to have raped or sexually assaulted actresses, force women to massage him, and watch him walk around naked. Shortly after the allegations surfaced publicly he was sacked by the board of his company.[30] His wife, designer Georgina Chapman, left him.

Along with several investigations into the producer's alleged crimes, the international #MeToo movement was born. In February 2020, Harvey Weinstein was found guilty of criminal sexual assault in the first degree and one count of rape in the third degree. He was sentenced to 23 years in prison.[31] As of March 2020, over 80 women had come forward to accuse Weinstein of sexual misconduct.

Summary

It comes as no surprise that John Kennedy Toole's *A Confederacy of Dunces* has never been successfully adapted for the screen. Although the novel has been astonishingly popular and was awarded the Pulitzer Prize, it simply is too complex in its structure and characters to make a financially successful Hollywood movie. After all, the hero of the story is an obese, flatulent bachelor who lives with his mother and masturbates frequently—hardly an easy sell to any studio. Without a love story per se, but with its irreverent, snarky, acid satire on hypocrisy and establishment folly, Toole's work resides outside the realm of commercially promising ventures. It is no wonder it took decades to find a publisher for the book itself. *A Confederacy of Dunces* insults everybody, and nobody wishes to be insulted.

There have been books which were thought of as similarly difficult to adapt. Doubters were proven right, when, for example, David Lynch's *Dune* reached the screens, or Joseph Strick's *Ulysses*, or David Cronenberg's *Crash*, which to this day is controversial, to say the least, and could only receive funding independently.

Too many things went wrong. Screenwriters and producers couldn't

It comes as a huge surprise that John Kennedy Toole's *A Confederacy of Dunces* has never been successfully adapted for the screen. After all, the novel has been astonishingly popular, even being awarded the Pulitzer Prize. The complexity of its structure and characters might not be a blueprint for a blockbuster success, but countless screenwriters, producers and directors have been attracted to Toole's story for a reason. Certainly, the hero is an obese, flatulent bachelor who lives with his mother and masturbates frequently—not an easy sell to any studio, but which great work of art is?

To this day, *A Confederacy of Dunces* is a breath of fresh air with its irreverent, snarky, acid satire on hypocrisy and establishment folly. Toole takes no prisoners, which is what every good satire both on the page and screen has done—consider *Network* or *Wag the Dog* as obvious examples.

There have been books which were thought of as difficult to adapt. But doubters were proven wrong when John Huston's *Moby Dick* reached the screens, or Terry Gilliam's *Fear and Loathing in Las Vegas*, or David Cronenberg's *Naked Lunch*—all of which weren't universally appreciated but have been financially successful and achieved cult status.

In stories such as this, no individual is to blame. Every great work of agree on a common approach, and people became greedy, as they are wont to do. *A Confederacy of Dunces* would be, or so its producers hoped, a prestige project. It was a valuable one. "Wally" Wolf snatched the rights from Carson Productions and Scott Kramer, and, to enrich himself, sold them to an entrepreneur from Texas who knew nothing about the film business but would neither listen to advice from experts nor part with his possession. Hapless and inept, he flailed around with *A Confederacy of Dunces* until the momentum was lost, only then to sell it to a large studio which, after many disputes with their director, indulged in a devious act of double-cross.

art inspires conversations, leads people to exchange points of view. Every great work of art is understood differently by different people since everybody brings their own experience to the work. *A Confederacy of Dunces* is, of course, no exception, and so it happened that screenwriters and producers could never agree on what this complex, intricate masterpiece was actually about and how it could possibly be condensed for the screen. What everybody shared, though, was a great love for Ignatius, who, as in the novel, inspired and changed lives in reality: an entrepreneur from Texas decided to venture into the film business, and a writer who had tried to commit suicide received the help he urgently needed for his mental well-being.

There have been enough adaptations of novels that were considered unfilmable to squash any claim that *A Confederacy of Dunces* simply can't be put on screen. If there is a will, there is a way. One only has to look at the list of works that have reached the screen: James Joyce's *Ulysses*, Hermann Hesse's *Steppenwolf*, Joseph Heller's *Catch-22*, William S. Burroughs's *Naked Lunch*, Frank Herbert's *Dune*, Hunter S. Thompson's *Fear and Loathing in Las Vegas*, Jack Kerouac's *On the Road*, Kurt Vonnegut's *Slaughterhouse-Five*, Miguel de Cervantes's *Don Quixote*, Herman Melville's *Moby Dick*, F. Scott Fitzgerald's *The Great Gatsby*, Anthony Burgess's *A Clockwork Orange*, Don DeLillo's *Cosmopolis*, David Mitchell's *Cloud Atlas*, Joseph Conrad's *Nostromo*, Alan Moore and Dave Gibbons's *Watchmen*, or William Faulkner's *As I Lay Dying*.

A list of well-known novels which haven't yet been adapted doesn't prove it can't be done, even if that list includes beloved classics such as Gabriel Garcia Marquez's *One Hundred Years of Solitude*, David Foster Wallace's *Infinite Jest*, J.D. Salinger's *The Catcher in the Rye*, Thomas Pynchon's *Gravity's Rainbow*, John Milton's *Paradise Lost*, or Budd Schulberg's *What Makes Sammy Run?*

More than anything, *A Confederacy of Dunces* has had the misfortune of suffering from a severe case of bad luck. Scott Kramer, way in over his head at age 23, failed to find the right writer in order to entice Fox; the rights were then taken by Wally Wolf as part of his severance pay following a bitter dispute caused by *A Confederacy of Dunces*; Kramer saw the rights being snatched up by an entrepreneur from Texas who knew nothing about the film business and, as a perfectionist, was never happy with any approach taken with his beloved book. Options and legal battles with studios and executives further complicated setting up any adaptation, while the chain of title became increasingly long and the project therefore more and more expensive.

In short, the 40-year failure to make a film of *A Confederacy of Dunces* is the perfect story of transcendent competence, boundless greed, creative interference, and bitter legal feuds. In a nutshell, no story seems better suited to describe Hollywood.

> *But riches have very often harmed those who possess them, because every man turns envious and greedy and supposes that he has a better right to the loot and wants all the gold and jewels for himself. So there you are, with your stuff, and you find yourself fearful about being waylaid or even murdered for your possessions.*[1]

The story of how *A Confederacy of Dunces* has never been successfully adapted for the screen is not over. Fortune's wheel keeps spinning and, doubtlessly, more writers will try their luck and turn John Kennedy Toole's complex kaleidoscope of a novel into a script. But their success doesn't solely lie in Fortune's hands. As laid out in the course of this book, *A Confederacy of Dunces* presents severe challenges to any screenwriter. These challenges still need to be overcome.

Toole filled his novel with a multitude of elements to which every reader gives different weight. The perceived sadness of the story serves as a case in point. Already Walker Percy wrote in his introduction: "I hesitate to use the word comedy—though comedy it is—because that implies simply a funny book, and this novel is a great deal more than that. A great rumbling farce of Falstaffian dimensions would better describe it; commedia would be closer to it. It is also sad. One never quite knows where the sadness comes from—from the tragedy at the heart of Ignatius's great gaseous rages and lunatic adventures or the tragedy attending the book itself."[2]

It would indeed be misleading to pitch an adaptation of *A Confederacy of Dunces* as a straightforward comedy, and various writers have struggled with that very issue.

While John Langdon, for example, wanted to approach his version as a farcical romp in the style of the popular *Saturday Night Live* skits of the '80s, Maidee Walker had a very different view, one which she made abundantly clear.

Frank Galati saw the story as a satire of Shakespearean proportions, as the struggle of a pariah in a crazy, sick society: "That inversion is the matter and manner of satire. It is a critique of the general society and the buffoon is the King Lear."[3]

When he opened the pages of Toole's book, and later tried to adapt it, Stephen Geller was convinced he was reading a novel about paranoia: "It was dark. It's a black comedy. You are watching a man come unglued in a society that is in a different way already unglued."[4] And so it goes.

Stripping *A Confederacy of Dunces* of some of its many elements, which are all interwoven in one way or another, would leave the audience with a shaky skeleton of what can only with great generosity be called a plot. But what plot would that be? *A Confederacy of Dunces* is a sprawling tableau of characters worthy of Dickens, a rambling collection of episodes which are eventually woven together with great mastery. Characters drift in and out of the story, making their entrances by way of mere coincidence. Claude Robichaux, for example, crosses Ignatius and his mother several times in unlikely circumstances before he becomes a fixture in their lives. He and Irene develop what could be described as the only love story in this novel—certainly there is no classic love story which binds everything together. There is no classic three-act structure. And it is no wonder that everybody understands the book

differently simply because the novel consists of so many complex, diverse elements
that flow together so effortlessly.

In a 120-page script, how to do justice to those carefully developed characters?
Portraying Ignatius, his mother, and the various minor characters in all their complexity is another stumbling block for any writer tasked with adapting Toole's work
for the screen. John Kennedy Toole's novel gives not only minor characters (such as
Mrs. Levy) a rich inner life and background but even characters who don't appear
in the flesh but only through the descriptions given by other people (Mr. and Mrs.
Levy's two daughters serve as an example).

People who choose to believe in the supernatural will never be convinced that *A
Confederacy of Dunces* wasn't cursed. However, when a project is in development for
several decades, it is inevitable for things to go wrong—how can one expect smooth
sailing over the course of many years, especially in the film industry? Or, as Max von
Sydow put it, when he was asked about the claim that William Friedkin's *The Exorcist*
was cursed: "It's very simple: If you have a production which lasts two or three weeks
nothing happens. But if you have a production which lasts a year or nine months, a lot
of things have to happen; accidents one way or the other. [...] It makes for good publicity, but if you don't believe in the devil, you don't believe in curses. It's simple."[5]

It remains to be seen whether a film with a chain of title as long and complicated
as *A Confederacy of Dunces* will eventually be made. The rights lie with Paramount
still, but—as many parties involved have pointed out—it seems today that the story
behind the project is by now more interesting than an adaptation of the source could
possibly ever be. Or perhaps you disagree?

> I think we tell this story to remind ourselves of our own vulnerabilities, foibles and dan-
> gerous stupidity. We all believe we see the world clearly and that other people are the
> problem. It will always be necessary to find the balance between our personal motivations
> and those of others and if we get it right once in awhile then we can thank Fortuna (David
> Esbjornson about *A Confederacy of Dunces*).[6]

List of Writers, Directors,
and Actors Considered

Writers

Roy Blount, Jr., Kit Carson, Stephen Fry, Frank Galati, Stephen Geller, Beth Henley, Buck Henry, Phil Johnston, Scott Kramer, Alan Ormsby, Steven Soderbergh, Roderick Taylor, Maidee Walker

Directors

Pedro Almodóvar, Robert Altman, Paul Thomas Anderson, Michael Apted, John Avildsen, James Bobin, Tim Burton, Joel and Ethan Coen, Miloš Forman, Terry Gilliam, David Gordon Green, Ron Howard, John Hughes, John Huston, Jim Jarmusch, Spike Jonze, Doug Liman, Baz Luhrmann, Shirley MacLaine, Mike Nichols, Alan Parker, Alexander Payne, Arthur Penn, Michael Radford, Harold Ramis, George Roy Hill, Steven Soderbergh, Penelope Spheeris, John Waters, Robert Wise, Robert Zemeckis

Actors (for the role of Ignatius J. Reilly)

Louie Anderson, Warren Beatty, John Belushi, Jack Black, Victor Buono, John Candy, John Coltrane, Daniel Day-Lewis, Dom DeLuise, Chris Farley, Will Ferrell, Zach Galifianakis, John Goodman, Richard Harris, Philip Seymour Hoffman, Penn Jillette, John Lithgow, John McConnell, Ian McNeice, Josh Mostel, Stuart Pankin, John C. Reilly, Glenn Shadix, Bruce Vilanch, Robin Williams, Jonathan Winters

Chapter Notes

The Consolation of a Preface

1. Boethius. *The Consolation of Philosophy.* Cambridge, MA: Harvard University Press 2008. Page 30.

Chapter 1

1. digitallibrary.tulane.edu/islandora/object/tulane%3A48821.
2. MacLauchlin, Cory. *Butterfly in the Type-writer.* Boston: Da Capo Press, 2012. Page 3.
3. Fletcher, Joel L. *Ken & Thelma: The Story of* A Confederacy of Dunces. Gretna, LA: Pelican Publishing Company, Inc., 2005. Page 72.
4. MacLauchlin, Cory. *Butterfly in the Type-writer.* Boston: Da Capo Press, 2012. Page 57.
5. Sipchen, B. (1989, March 13). Dead Men Do Tell Tales. *The Times-Picayune/The States-Item.*
6. Pol Nevils, René; Hardy, Deborah George. *Ignatius Rising.* Baton Rouge: Louisiana State University Press, 2001. Page 52.
7. MacLauchlin, Cory. *Butterfly in the Type-writer.* Boston: Da Capo Press, 2012. Page 28.
8. Fletcher, Joel L. *Ken & Thelma: The Story of* A Confederacy of Dunces. Gretna, LA: Pelican Publishing Company, Inc., 2005. Page 16.
9. MacLauchlin, Cory. *Butterfly in the Type-writer.* Boston: Da Capo Press, 2012. Page 99.
10. Pol Nevils, René; Hardy, Deborah George. *Ignatius Rising.* Baton Rouge: Louisiana State University Press, 2001. Page 78f.
11. www.digitallibrary.tulane.edu/islandora/object/tulane%3A17193.
12. www.digitallibrary.tulane.edu/islandora/object/tulane%3A17123.
13. www.digitallibrary.tulane.edu/islandora/object/tulane%3A17114.
14. MacLauchlin, Cory. *Butterfly in the Type-writer.* Boston: Da Capo Press, 2012. Page 169.
15. Fletcher, Joel L. *Ken & Thelma: The Story of* A Confederacy of Dunces. Gretna, LA: Pelican Publishing Company, Inc., 2005. Page 78.
16. MacLauchlin, Cory. *Butterfly in the Type-writer.* Boston: Da Capo Press, 2012. Page 177.
17. MacLauchlin, Cory. *Butterfly in the Type-writer.* Boston: Da Capo Press, 2012. Page 191.

18. Vespa, M. (1980, September 22). "A Much Rejected Novel Creates a Literary Sensation Thanks to an Indomitable Mother." *People Magazine.*
19. www.youtube.com/watch?v=WruYhMvFw2w.
20. Fletcher, Joel L. *Ken & Thelma: The Story of* A Confederacy of Dunces. Gretna, LA: Pelican Publishing Company, Inc., 2005. Page 76.
21. Pol Nevils, René, and Deborah George Hardy. *Ignatius Rising.* Baton Rouge: Louisiana State University Press, 2001. Page 170.
22. MacLauchlin, Cory. *Butterfly in the Typewriter.* Boston: Da Capo Press, 2012. Page 177.
23. Rubin, S. (1980, June 5). "The Posthumous Triumph of John Kennedy Toole." *Newsday.*
24. Eco, Umberto. *The Name of the Rose.* Introduction by David Loge. London, UK: Everyman's Library, 2006. Page xxf.
25. Fletcher, Joel L. *Ken & Thelma: The Story of* A Confederacy of Dunces. Gretna, LA: Pelican Publishing Company, Inc., 2005. Page 80.
26. www.youtube.com/watch?v=AQNsNC9fIE4.
27. MacLauchlin, Cory. *Butterfly in the Typewriter.* Boston: Da Capo Press, 2012. Page 228.
28. Pol Nevils, René, and Deborah George Hardy. *Ignatius Rising.* Baton Rouge: Louisiana State University Press, 2001. Page 208.
29. MacLauchlin, Cory. *Butterfly in the Typewriter.* Boston: Da Capo Press, 2012. Page 235.
30. Fletcher, Joel L. *Ken & Thelma: The Story of* A Confederacy of Dunces. Gretna, LA: Pelican Publishing Company, Inc., 2005. Page 103.
31. *The Tomorrow Show,* April 22, 1981, NBC.
32. Fletcher, Joel L. *Ken & Thelma: The Story of* A Confederacy of Dunces. Gretna, LA: Pelican Publishing Company, Inc., 2005. Page 171.
33. Feeney, S. (1984, September 7). "Don't publish book, Toole will asks." *The Times-Picayune/The States-Item.*
34. www.youtube.com/watch?v=AQNsNC9fIE4.
35. Joel L. Fletcher, author interview, November 27, 2018.

36. Maidee Walker, author interview, September 4, 2018.

37. Joel L. Fletcher, author interview, November 27, 2018.

Chapter 2

1. Michael J. Nathanson, author interview, November 1, 2018.

2. Michael J. Nathanson, author interview, November 1, 2018.

3. Michael J. Nathanson, author interview, November 1, 2018.

4. Michael J. Nathanson, author interview, November 1, 2018.

5. Fletcher, Joel L. *Ken & Thelma: The Story of A Confederacy of Dunces*. Gretna, LA: Pelican Publishing Company, Inc., 2005. Page 143.

6. Michael J. Nathanson, author interview, November 1, 2018.

7. Joel L. Fletcher, author interview, November 27, 2018.

8. Michael J. Nathanson, author interview, November 1, 2018.

9. Fletcher, Joel L. *Ken & Thelma: The Story of A Confederacy of Dunces*. Gretna, LA: Pelican Publishing Company, Inc., 2005. Page 145.

10. Michael J. Nathanson, author interview, November 1, 2018.

11. Michael J. Nathanson, author interview, November 1, 2018.

12. Joel L. Fletcher, author interview, November 27, 2018.

13. Michael J. Nathanson, author interview, November 1, 2018.

14. Michael J. Nathanson, author interview, November 1, 2018.

15. Fletcher, Joel L. *Ken & Thelma: The Story of A Confederacy of Dunces*. Gretna, LA: Pelican Publishing Company, Inc., 2005. Page 148.

16. Fletcher, Joel L. *Ken & Thelma: The Story of A Confederacy of Dunces*. Gretna, LA: Pelican Publishing Company, Inc., 2005. Page 132.

17. Staff. (1981, June 27). "Orleans man is held in roommate's killing." *The Times-Picayune/The States-Item*.

18. Joel L. Fletcher, author interview, November 27, 2018.

19. MacLauchlin, Cory. *Butterfly in the Typewriter*. Boston: Da Capo Press, 2012. Page 215.

20. MacLauchlin, Cory. *Butterfly in the Typewriter*. Boston: Da Capo Press, 2012. Page 215.

21. MacLauchlin, Cory. *Butterfly in the Typewriter*. Boston: Da Capo Press, 2012. Page 58.

22. Michael J. Nathanson, author interview, November 1, 2018.

23. Michael J. Nathanson, author interview, November 1, 2018.

24. Michael J. Nathanson, author interview, November 1, 2018.

25. Joel L. Fletcher, author interview, November 27, 2018.

26. Michael J. Nathanson, author interview, November 1, 2018.

27. https://allkidscount.net/.

Chapter 3

1. Fletcher, Joel L. *Ken & Thelma: The Story of A Confederacy of Dunces*. Gretna, LA: Pelican Publishing Company, Inc., 2005. Page 167.

2. www.digitallibrary.tulane.edu/islandora/object/tulane%3A48596.

3. www.digitallibrary.tulane.edu/islandora/object/tulane%3A48671.

4. www.digitallibrary.tulane.edu/islandora/object/tulane%3A48719.

5. Toole, John Kennedy. *A Confederacy of Dunces*. London, UK: Penguin Books, 2011. Page 88f.

6. www.digitallibrary.tulane.edu/islandora/object/tulane%3A48586.

7. Frank Galati, author interview, September 26, 2018.

8. Frank Galati, author interview, September 26, 2018.

9. Frank Galati, author interview, September 26, 2018.

10. Corley, S. (1984, February 5). "Working With LSU's 'Dunces.'" *Sunday Advocate Magazine*.

11. Frank Galati, author interview, September 26, 2018.

12. www.digitallibrary.tulane.edu/islandora/object/tulane%3A71536.

13. www.digitallibrary.tulane.edu/islandora/object/tulane%3A71536.

14. Frank Galati, author interview, September 26, 2018.

15. www.digitallibrary.tulane.edu/islandora/object/tulane%3A48720.

16. www.digitallibrary.tulane.edu/islandora/object/tulane%3A48733.

17. AP. (1984, March 7). "Musical comedy gets good reviews." *Griffin News*.

18. AP. (1984, March 4). "*Confederacy of Dunces* Play May Wind Up On Broadway." *High Point Enterprise*.

19. Frank Galati, author interview, September 26, 2018.

20. Frank Galati, author interview, September 26, 2018.

Chapter 4

1. Pol Nevils, René; Hardy, Deborah George. *Ignatius Rising*. Baton Rouge: Louisiana State University Press, 2001. Page 215.

2. Marcia Nasatir, author interview, December 10, 2018.

3. Pol Nevils, René, and Deborah George Hardy. *Ignatius Rising*. Baton Rouge: Louisiana State University Press, 2001. Page 215.

4. Lippman, J. (1999, September 30). "'Dunces' Adaptation Remains Stuck In Mire of Rewrites and Handovers." *The Wall Street Journal.*

5. David Madden, author interview, February 8, 2019.

6. Boethius. *The Consolation of Philosophy.* Cambridge, MA: Harvard University Press 2008. Page 42f.

7. www.hollywoodreporter.com/news/jeff-berg-new-agency-icm-426189.

8. www.digitallibrary.tulane.edu/islandora/object/tulane%3A50019.

9. www.digitallibrary.tulane.edu/islandora/object/tulane%3A49980.

10. Fletcher, Joel L. *Ken & Thelma: The Story of* A Confederacy of Dunces. Gretna, LA: Pelican Publishing Company, Inc., 2005. Page 165.

11. www.digitallibrary.tulane.edu/islandora/object/tulane%3A49945.

12. www.digitallibrary.tulane.edu/islandora/object/tulane%3A49970.

13. /www.youtube.com/watch?v=dKsON W7UMsw.

14. www.digitallibrary.tulane.edu/islandora/object/tulane%3A48765.

15. David Madden, author interview, February 8, 2019.

16. Alan Ormsby, author interview, January 21, 2019.

17. Alan Ormsby, author interview, January 21, 2019.

18. Alan Ormsby, author interview, January 21, 2019.

19. Pol Nevils, René, and Deborah George Hardy. *Ignatius Rising.* Baton Rouge: Louisiana State University Press, 2001. Page 216.

20. www.medium.com/@johnschulte/thelma-louisiana-b2187ae73a46.

21. Pol Nevils, René, and Deborah George Hardy. *Ignatius Rising.* Baton Rouge: Louisiana State University Press, 2001. Page 218.

22. Pol Nevils, René, and Deborah George Hardy. *Ignatius Rising.* Baton Rouge: Louisiana State University Press, 2001. Page 217.

23. Pol Nevils, René, and Deborah George Hardy. *Ignatius Rising.* Baton Rouge: Louisiana State University Press, 2001. Page 220.

24. Martin, J. (1981, July 4). "Carson to make movie debut as movie mogul." *The Desert Sun.*

Chapter 5

1. www.telegraph.co.uk/films/2019/07/31/confederacy-dunces-stephen-fry-decades-long-struggle-adapt-unfilmable/.

2. Hall, M. (1981, April 12). "Thelma Toole blames book publishers for death of great writer—her son." *Clarion-Ledger.*

3. Marcia Nasatir, author interview, December 10, 2018.

4. Henry Bushkin, author interview, April 9, 2019.

5. Marcia Nasatir, author interview, December 10, 2018.

6. Henry Bushkin, author interview, April 9, 2019.

7. Henry Bushkin, author interview, April 9, 2019.

8. Alexander Ignon, author interview, February 17, 2019.

9. Alexander Ignon, author interview, February 17, 2019.

10. Alexander Ignon, author interview, February 17, 2019.

11. Alexander Ignon, author interview, February 17, 2019.

12. Alexander Ignon, author interview, February 17, 2019.

13. Toole, John Kennedy. *A Confederacy of Dunces.* London, UK: Penguin Books, 2011. Page 15.

14. Marcia Nasatir, author interview, December 10, 2018.

15. Alexander Ignon, author interview, February 17, 2019.

16. David Madden, author interview, February 8, 2019.

17. Alexander Ignon, author interview, February 17, 2019.

18. www.digitallibrary.tulane.edu/islandora/object/tulane%3A48498.

19. www.digitallibrary.tulane.edu/islandora/object/tulane%3A48503.

20. Henry Bushkin, author interview, April 9, 2019.

21. Pope, J. (1981, August 12). "Movie plans made for late author's work." *The Times-Picayune/ The States-Item.*

22. Pope, J. (1981, August 12). "Movie plans made for late author's work." *The Times-Picayune/ The States-Item.*

Chapter 6

1. Alan Ormsby, author interview, January 21, 2019.

2. Woodward, Bob. *Wired—The Short Life & Fast Times of John Belushi.* New York: Simon & Schuster, 1984. Page 221.

3. Woodward, Bob. *Wired—The Short Life & Fast Times of John Belushi.* New York, New York: Simon & Schuster, 1984. Page 366.

4. Judy Belushi Pisano, author interview, January 7, 2019.

5. Pol Nevils, René, and Deborah George Hardy. *Ignatius Rising.* Baton Rouge: Louisiana State University Press, 2001. Page 219.

6. Hall, M. (1981, April 12). "Thelma Toole blames book publishers for death of great writer—her son." *Clarion-Ledger.*

7. Pol Nevils, René, and Deborah George Hardy. *Ignatius Rising.* Baton Rouge: Louisiana State University Press, 2001. Page 219.

8. Judy Belushi Pisano, author interview, January 7, 2019.

9. Judy Belushi Pisano, author interview, January 7, 2019.

10. Hemeter, M. (1981, September 18). "Movies' unlikeliest new leading man." *The Times-Picayune/The States-Item.*

11. Hemeter, M. (1981, September 18). "Movies' unlikeliest new leading man." *The Times-Picayune/The States-Item.*

12. Statement from Michael Apted via Cort Kristensen, Michael Apted Film Company. 5/4/2019.

13. Lippman, J. (1999, September 30). "'Dunces' Adaptation Remains Stuck In Mire of Rewrites and Handovers." *The Wall Street Journal.*

14. Judy Belushi Pisano, author interview, January 7, 2019.

15. Woodward, Bob. *Wired—The Short Life & Fast Times of John Belushi.* New York: Simon & Schuster, 1984. Page 389.

16. Woodward, Bob. *Wired—The Short Life & Fast Times of John Belushi.* New York: Simon & Schuster, 1984. Page 417.

17. Lippman, J. (1999, September 30). "'Dunces' Adaptation Remains Stuck In Mire of Rewrites and Handovers." *The Wall Street Journal.*

18. Michael Arata, author interview, May 31, 2019.

19. Boethius. *The Consolation of Philosophy.* Cambridge, MA: Harvard University Press 2008. Page 28.

20. Ireland, D. (1982, July 31). "New Orleans seen as Burbank South." *The Times* (Shreveport, Louisiana).

21. David Ross McCarty, author interview, July 27, 2019.

22. David Ross McCarty, author interview, July 27, 2019.

23. Toole, John Kennedy. *A Confederacy of Dunces.* London, UK: Penguin Books, 2011. Page 32f.

24. David Ross McCarty, author interview, July 27, 2019.

25. UPI (1982, August 17). "Treen Expresses Sorrow at Official's Death." *Alexandria Daily Town Talk.*

26. David Ross McCarty, author interview, July 27, 2019.

27. David Ross McCarty, author interview, July 27, 2019.

28. David Ross McCarty, author interview, July 27, 2019.

29. www.digitallibrary.tulane.edu/islandora/object/tulane%3A48586.

30. Alexander Ignon, author interview, February 17, 2019.

31. Alexander Ignon, author interview, February 17, 2019.

32. Alexander Ignon, author interview, February 17, 2019.

33. Henry Bushkin, author interview, April 9, 2019.

34. Boethius. *The Consolation of Philosophy.* Cambridge, MA: Harvard University Press 2008. Page 24f.

Chapter 7

1. Staff. (1987, September 2). "Former judge, state legislator dies." *Hood County News.*

2. Staff. (1986, March 30). "GROPAX pleased with first year." *The Paris News.*

3. Susan O'Connell, author interview, September 17, 2018.

4. www.lonestarfilmfestival.com/copy-of-summer-film-camp.

5. Susan O'Connell, author interview, September 17, 2018.

6. Staff. (1970, July 19). "Happenings—Here, There and Everywhere." *The Sydney Morning Herald.*

7. Wallis, Keith. *And the World Listened: The Story of Captain Leonard Frank Plugge.* Devon, UK: Kelly Publications, 2008. Page 188.

8. Maidee Walker, author interview, September 4, 2018.

9. Maidee Walker, author interview, September 4, 2018.

10. Clay Langdon, author interview, February 11, 2019.

11. Anne Livet, author interview, August 29, 2020.

12. Anne Livet, author interview, August 29, 2020.

13. David Esbjornson, *Cast Breakdown for Confederacy of Dunces.* Internal document shared by the creator.

14. Toole, John Kennedy. *A Confederacy of Dunces.* London, UK: Penguin Books, 2011. Page 141.

15. Toole, John Kennedy. *A Confederacy of Dunces.* London, UK: Penguin Books, 2011. Page 105.

16. Toole, John Kennedy. *A Confederacy of Dunces.* London, UK: Penguin Books, 2011. Page 108.

17. Toole, John Kennedy. *A Confederacy of Dunces.* London, UK: Penguin Books, 2011. Page 196.

18. Toole, John Kennedy. *A Confederacy of Dunces.* London, UK: Penguin Books, 2011. Page 85.

19. Toole, John Kennedy. *A Confederacy of Dunces.* London, UK: Penguin Books, 2011. Page 85.

20. Lukianoff, Greg; Haidt, Jonathan. *The Coddling of the American Mind.* London, UK: Penguin 2019. Page 34.

21. Toole, John Kennedy. *A Confederacy of Dunces.* London, UK: Penguin Books, 2011. Page 52.

22. Toole, John Kennedy. *A Confederacy of Dunces.* London, UK: Penguin Books, 2011. Page 152.

23. Toole, John Kennedy. *A Confederacy of Dunces.* London, UK: Penguin Books, 2011. Page 184.

24. Toole, John Kennedy. *A Confederacy of Dunces.* London, UK: Penguin Books, 2011. Page 219.

25. Toole, John Kennedy. *A Confederacy of Dunces.* London, UK: Penguin Books, 2011. Page 182.

26. Toole, John Kennedy. *A Confederacy of Dunces.* London, UK: Penguin Books, 2011. Page 101f.

27. Toole, John Kennedy. *A Confederacy of Dunces.* London, UK: Penguin Books, 2011. Page 94.

28. Toole, John Kennedy. *A Confederacy of Dunces.* London, UK: Penguin Books, 2011. Page 87.

29. Toole, John Kennedy. *A Confederacy of Dunces.* London, UK: Penguin Books, 2011. Page 87.

30. Toole, John Kennedy. *A Confederacy of Dunces.* London, UK: Penguin Books, 2011. Page 85.

31. Toole, John Kennedy. *A Confederacy of Dunces.* London, UK: Penguin Books, 2011. Page 110.

32. Toole, John Kennedy. *A Confederacy of Dunces.* London, UK: Penguin Books, 2011. Page 109.

33. Toole, John Kennedy. *A Confederacy of Dunces.* London, UK: Penguin Books, 2011. Page 154.

34. Toole, John Kennedy. *A Confederacy of Dunces.* London, UK: Penguin Books, 2011. Page 182.

35. Toole, John Kennedy. *A Confederacy of Dunces.* London, UK: Penguin Books, 2011. Page 120.

36. Toole, John Kennedy. *A Confederacy of Dunces.* London, UK: Penguin Books, 2011. Page 251.

37. Toole, John Kennedy. *A Confederacy of Dunces.* London, UK: Penguin Books, 2011. Page 27.

38. Clay Langdon, author interview, February 11, 2019.

39. John Holt Smith, author interview, February 16, 2019.

40. Analisa Garcia, author interview, January 15, 2020.

41. Susan O'Connell, author interview, September 17, 2018.

42. John Holt Smith, author interview, February 16, 2019.

43. White, K. (1997, March 18). Psychologist kills self on Hwy. 154. *Santa Maria Times.*

44. www.digitallibrary.tulane.edu/islandora/object/tulane%3A51518.

45. David Madden, author interview, February 8, 2019.

46. Alexander Ignon, author interview, February 17, 2019.

47. Boethius. *The Consolation of Philosophy.* Cambridge, MA: Harvard University Press 2008. Page 29.

48. web.archive.org/web/20150810115840/http://bumbershootproductionsinc.com/projects/empire-man.html.

49. Roderick Taylor, author interview, April 27, 2019.

50. Roderick Taylor, author interview, April 27, 2019.

51. Roderick Taylor, author interview, April 27, 2019.

52. Roderick Taylor, author interview, April 27, 2019.

Chapter 8

1. Roderick Taylor, author interview, April 27, 2019.

2. Guillaud, B. (1982, June 20). "Film maker is looking for those who'll pay for a movie to play." *The Times-Picayune/The States-Item.*

3. Roderick Taylor, author interview, April 27, 2019.

4. Roderick Taylor, author interview, April 27, 2019.

5. www.digitallibrary.tulane.edu/islandora/object/tulane%3A51519.

6. www.digitallibrary.tulane.edu/islandora/object/tulane%3A51519.

7. Guillaud, B. (1982, June 20). Film maker is looking for those who'll pay for a movie to play. *The Times-Picayune/The States-Item.*

8. www.digitallibrary.tulane.edu/islandora/object/tulane:51522.

9. Lippman, J. (1999, September 30). "'Dunces' Adaptation Remains Stuck In Mire of Rewrites and Handovers." *The Wall Street Journal.*

10. Roderick Taylor, author interview, April 27, 2019.

11. Boethius. *The Consolation of Philosophy.* Cambridge, MA: Harvard University Press 2008. Page 32.

12. Stephen Geller, author interview, September 18, 2018.

13. John Holt Smith, author interview, February 16, 2019.

14. *ACOD Chronology Outline*, internal document from Bumbershoot Productions, shared by Carolyn Pfeiffer.

15. Roderick Taylor, author interview, April 27, 2019.

16. Roderick Taylor, author interview, April 27, 2019.

17. Roderick Taylor, author interview, April 27, 2019.

18. Roderick Taylor, author interview, April 27, 2019.

19. Roderick Taylor, author interview, April 27, 2019.

20. medium.com/@johnschulte/thelma-louisiana-b2187ae73a46.

21. MacLauchlin, Cory. *Butterfly in the Typewriter.* Boston: Da Capo Press, 2012. Page 244.

22. Boethius. *The Consolation of Philosophy.* Cambridge, MA: Harvard University Press 2008. Page 36.

23. Maidee Walker, author interview, September 4, 2018.

24. Maidee Walker, author interview, September 4, 2018.

25. Maidee Walker, author interview, September 4, 2018.

26. www.digitallibrary.tulane.edu/islandora/object/tulane%3A48250.

27. www.worldcollectorsnet.com/features/teenage-mutant-ninja-turtles/.

28. John Schulte, author interview, October 3, 2018.

Chapter 9

1. John Schulte, author interview, October 3, 2018.

2. medium.com/@johnschulte/thelma-louisiana-b2187ae73a46.

3. John Schulte, author interview, October 3, 2018.

4. John Holt Smith, author interview, February 16, 2019.

5. Roy Blount, Jr., author interview, March 13, 2019.

6. Maidee Walker, author interview, September 4, 2018.

7. Maidee Walker, author interview, September 4, 2018.

8. Susan O'Connell, author interview, September 17, 2018.

9. Toole, John Kennedy. *A Confederacy of Dunces.* London, UK: Penguin Books, 2011. Page 137.

10. Vachule, J. (1963, March, 25). "Fatal Trip of Deb Started Routinely." *Fort Worth Star-Telegram.*

11. de.findagrave.com/memorial/189796308/jane-langdon.

12. Clay Langdon, author interview, February 11, 2019.

13. Clay Langdon, author interview, February 11, 2019.

14. Toole, John Kennedy. *A Confederacy of Dunces.* London, UK: Penguin Books, 2011. Page 19.

15. Toole, John Kennedy. *A Confederacy of Dunces.* London, UK: Penguin Books, 2011. Page 78.

16. Toole, John Kennedy. *A Confederacy of Dunces.* London, UK: Penguin Books, 2011. Page 312.

17. Toole, John Kennedy. *A Confederacy of Dunces.* London, UK: Penguin Books, 2011. Page 258.

18. Toole, John Kennedy. *A Confederacy of Dunces.* London, UK: Penguin Books, 2011. Page 262.

19. Toole, John Kennedy. *A Confederacy of Dunces.* London, UK: Penguin Books, 2011. Page 264.

20. Toole, John Kennedy. *A Confederacy of Dunces.* London, UK: Penguin Books, 2011. Page 231.

21. Toole, John Kennedy. *A Confederacy of Dunces.* London, UK: Penguin Books, 2011. Page 83.

22. Toole, John Kennedy. *A Confederacy of Dunces.* London, UK: Penguin Books, 2011. Page 21.

23. Toole, John Kennedy. *A Confederacy of Dunces.* London, UK: Penguin Books, 2011. Page 210.

24. Toole, John Kennedy. *A Confederacy of Dunces.* London, UK: Penguin Books, 2011. Page 212.

25. Toole, John Kennedy. *A Confederacy of Dunces.* London, UK: Penguin Books, 2011. Page 114.

26. Toole, John Kennedy. *A Confederacy of Dunces.* London, UK: Penguin Books, 2011. Page 206.

27. Boethius. *The Consolation of Philosophy.* Cambridge, MA: Harvard University Press 2008. Page 94.

28. Toole, John Kennedy. *A Confederacy of Dunces.* London, UK: Penguin Books, 2011. Page 213.

29. Toole, John Kennedy. *A Confederacy of Dunces.* London, UK: Penguin Books, 2011. Page 162.

30. John Schulte, author interview, October 3, 2018.

31. Kendall Langdon Levy, author interview, February 10, 2019.

32. Walker, M. *A Confederacy of Dunces—First Draft.* Fort Worth, TX: Bumbershoot Productions, Inc., 1984. Cover page. Unpublished screenplay.

33. Fletcher, Joel L. *Ken & Thelma: The Story of A Confederacy of Dunces.* Gretna, Louisiana: Pelican Publishing Company, Inc., 2005. Page 178.

34. Toole, John Kennedy. *A Confederacy of Dunces.* London, UK: Penguin Books, 2011. Page 1.

35. Walker, M. *A Confederacy of Dunces—First Draft.* Fort Worth, TX: Bumbershoot Productions, Inc., 1984. Page 1. Unpublished screenplay.

Chapter 10

1. Toole, John Kennedy. *A Confederacy of Dunces.* London, UK: Penguin Books, 2011. Page 133.

2. Maidee Walker, author interview, September 4, 2018.

3. Susan O'Connell, author interview, September 17, 2018.

4. Schulte, J. (1986, February, 7). *Letter to Maidee Walker.* Personal archive of John Schulte, reprinted with the permission of the author.

5. Schulte, J. (1986, February, 7). *Letter to Maidee Walker.* Personal archive of John Schulte, reprinted with the permission of the author.

6. Schulte, J. (1986, February, 7). *Letter to Maidee Walker.* Personal archive of John Schulte, reprinted with the permission of the author.

7. Schulte, J. (1986, February, 7). *Letter to Maidee Walker.* Personal archive of John Schulte, reprinted with the permission of the author.

8. Schulte, J. (1986, February, 7). *Letter to Maidee Walker.* Personal archive of John Schulte, reprinted with the permission of the author.

9. Schulte, J. (1986, February, 7). *Letter to Maidee Walker.* Personal archive of John Schulte, reprinted with the permission of the author.

10. John Schulte, author interview, October 3, 2018.

11. John Schulte, author interview, October 3, 2018.

12. medium.com/@johnschulte/thelma-louisiana-b2187ae73a46.

13. Schulte, J. (1986, February, 7). *Letter to Maidee Walker.* Personal archive of John Schulte, reprinted with the permission of the author.

14. medium.com/@johnschulte/thelma-louisiana-b2187ae73a46.

Chapter 11

1. Kendall Langdon-Levy, author interview, February 10, 2019.

2. *ACOD Chronology Outline*, internal document from Bumbershoot Productions, shared by Carolyn Pfeiffer.

3. *ACOD Chronology Outline*, internal document from Bumbershoot Productions, shared by Carolyn Pfeiffer.

4. Maidee Walker, author interview, October 29, 2018.

5. Maidee Walker, author interview, September 4, 2018.

6. Maidee Walker, author interview, September 4, 2018.

7. Boethius. *The Consolation of Philosophy.* Cambridge, MA: Harvard University Press 2008. Page 91.

8. Maidee Walker, author interview, September 4, 2018.

9. John Schulte, author interview, October 3, 2018.

10. Maidee Walker, author interview, September 4, 2018.

11. Lippman, J. (1999, September 30). "'Dunces' Adaptation Remains Stuck In Mire of Rewrites and Handovers." *The Wall Street Journal.*

12. Josh Mostel, author interview, July 18, 2019.

13. *ACOD Chronology Outline*, internal document from Bumbershoot Productions, shared by Carolyn Pfeiffer.

14. *ACOD Chronology Outline*, internal

document from Bumbershoot Productions, shared by Carolyn Pfeiffer.

15. *ACOD Chronology Outline*, internal document from Bumbershoot Productions, shared by Carolyn Pfeiffer.

16. *ACOD Chronology Outline*, internal document from Bumbershoot Productions, shared by Carolyn Pfeiffer.

17. Maidee Walker, author interview, September 4, 2018.

18. www.tonyortega.org/2015/04/12/how-scientology-broke-up-tom-cruise-and-mimi-rogers-the-story-you-havent-heard/.

19. Maidee Walker, author interview, September 4, 2018.

20. Boethius. *The Consolation of Philosophy.* Cambridge, MA: Harvard University Press 2008. Page 64.

21. Maidee Walker, author interview, September 4, 2018.

22. Kendall Langdon-Levy, author interview, February 10, 2019.

23. Anne Livet, author interview, August 29, 2020.

24. John Schulte, author interview, October 3, 2018.

25. Maidee Walker, author interview, September 4, 2018.

26. John Schulte, author interview, October 3, 2018.

27. Chryssides, George D. *The A to Z of New Religious Movements.* Lanham, MD: Scarecrow Press, Inc. 2001. Page 191.

28. John Schulte, author interview, October 3, 2018.

29. Schulte, J. (1986, March, 31). *Letter to Shirley MacLaine.* Personal archive of John Schulte, reprinted with the permission of the author.

30. Schulte, J. (1986, March 25). *Letter to Warren Beatty.* Personal archive of John Schulte, reprinted with the permission of the author.

31. Schulte, J. (1986, March, 31). *Letter to Shirley MacLaine.* Personal archive of John Schulte, reprinted with the permission of the author.

32. Schulte, J. (1986, March, 31). *Letter to Shirley MacLaine.* Personal archive of John Schulte, reprinted with the permission of the author.

Chapter 12

1. Maidee Walker, author interview, September 4, 2018.

2. Maidee Walker, author interview, September 4, 2018.

3. Maidee Walker, author interview, September 4, 2018.

4. Maidee Walker, author interview, September 4, 2018.

5. Lippman, J. (1999, September 30). "'Dunces' Adaptation Remains Stuck In Mire of Rewrites and Handovers." *The Wall Street Journal.*

6. Mike Medavoy, author interview, December 17, 2018.

7. Mike Medavoy, author interview, December 17, 2018..

8. Mike Medavoy, author interview, December 17, 2018

9. Barbara Boyle, author interview, July 18, 2019.

10. Barbara Boyle, author interview, July 18, 2019.

11. Barbara Boyle, author interview, July 18, 2019.

12. Mike Medavoy, author interview, December 17, 2018.

13. Barbara Boyle, author interview, July 18, 2019.

14. Barbara Boyle, author interview, July 18, 2019.

15. *ACOD Chronology Outline*, internal document from Bumbershoot Productions, shared by Carolyn Pfeiffer.

16. *ACOD Chronology Outline*, internal document from Bumbershoot Productions, shared by Carolyn Pfeiffer.

17. *ACOD Chronology Outline*, internal document from Bumbershoot Productions, shared by Carolyn Pfeiffer.

18. *ACOD Chronology Outline*, internal document from Bumbershoot Productions, shared by Carolyn Pfeiffer.

19. *ACOD Chronology Outline*, internal document from Bumbershoot Productions, shared by Carolyn Pfeiffer.

20. *ACOD Chronology Outline*, internal document from Bumbershoot Productions, shared by Carolyn Pfeiffer.

21. Lippman, J. (1999, September 30). 'Dunces' Adaptation Remains Stuck In Mire of Rewrites and Handovers. *The Wall Street Journal*.

22. www.nytimes.com/2017/04/20/books/review/john-waters-by-the-book.html.

23. www.anothermanmag.com/life-culture/10538/50-questions-with-john-waters.

24. web.archive.org/web/20160304084216/http://www.bestofneworleans.com/gambit/john-waters-the-gambit-interview/Content?oid=1279111.

25. John Waters, author interview, December 7, 2018.

26. www.oneroomwithaview.com/2016/09/13/best-films-never-made-34-a-confederacy-of-dunces/.

27. www.youtube.com/watch?v=hDsjeHKs8xo.

28. Waters, John. *Crackpot—The Obsessions of John Waters*. New York: Scribner, 2003. Page 143.

29. Waters, John. *Role Models*. London, UK: Corsair, 2014. Page 46.

30. Waters, John. *Role Models*. London, UK: Corsair, 2014. Page 50.

31. Waters, John. *Crackpot—The Obsessions of John Waters*. New York: Scribner, 2003. Page 143.

32. Boethius. *The Consolation of Philosophy*.

Cambridge, MA: Harvard University Press 2008. Page 56f.

Chapter 13

1. www.youtube.com/watch?v=8Zh8ZQ3Yvj0.

2. Bernard Jay, author interview, December 7, 2018.

3. Jay, Bernard. *Not Simply Divine*. London, UK: Virgin Books 1993. Page 211.

4. *ACOD Chronology Outline*, internal document from Bumbershoot Productions, shared by Carolyn Pfeiffer.

5. Trevor Albert, author interview, March 8, 2019.

6. Trevor Albert, author interview, March 8, 2019.

7. Maidee Walker, author interview, September 4, 2018.

8. Maidee Walker, author interview, September 4, 2018.

9. Maidee Walker, author interview, September 4, 2018.

10. Maidee Walker, author interview, September 4, 2018.

11. Kendall Langdon-Levy, author interview, February 10, 2019.

12. Kendall Langdon-Levy, author interview, February 10, 2019.

13. Phil Dixon, author interview, October 10, 2018.

14. Susan O'Connell, author interview, September 17, 2018.

15. Maidee Walker, author interview, September 4, 2018.

16. Lippman, J. (1999, September 30). 'Dunces' Adaptation Remains Stuck In Mire of Rewrites and Handovers. *The Wall Street Journal*.

17. Carolyn Pfeiffer, author interview, February 6, 2019.

18. www.digitallibrary.tulane.edu/islandora/object/tulane%3A48193/datastream/PDF/view.

19. Trevor Albert, author interview, March 8, 2019.

20. Trevor Albert, author interview, March 8, 2019.

21. Stephen Geller, author interview, September 18, 2018.

22. Stephen Geller, author interview, September 18, 2018.

23. Stephen Geller, author interview, September 18, 2018.

24. Stephen Geller, author interview, September 18, 2018.

25. Stephen Geller, author interview, September 18, 2018.

Chapter 14

1. www.nytimes.com/1992/11/03/arts/joe-roth-leaving-fox-for-a-deal-with-disney.html.

2. Stephen Geller, author interview, September 18, 2018.

3. Toole, John Kennedy. *A Confederacy of Dunces*. London, UK: Penguin Books, 2011. Page 49.

4. Stephen Geller, author interview, September 18, 2018.

5. Toole, John Kennedy. *A Confederacy of Dunces*. London, UK: Penguin Books, 2011. Page 48.

6. Boethius. *The Consolation of Philosophy*. Cambridge, MA: Harvard University Press 2008. Page 74.

7. Stephen Geller, author interview, September 18, 2018.

8. Stephen Geller, author interview, September 18, 2018.

9. Stephen Geller, author interview, September 18, 2018.

10. Lippman, J. (1999, September 30). "'Dunces' Adaptation Remains Stuck In Mire of Rewrites and Handovers." *The Wall Street Journal*.

11. Susan O'Connell, author interview, September 17, 2018.

12. Susan O'Connell, author interview, September 17, 2018.

13. Trevor Albert, author interview, March 8, 2019.

14. Trevor Albert, author interview, March 8, 2019.

15. Toole, John Kennedy. *A Confederacy of Dunces*. London, UK: Penguin Books, 2011. Page 36.

16. Toole, John Kennedy. *A Confederacy of Dunces*. London, UK: Penguin Books, 2011. Page 103.

17. Toole, John Kennedy. *A Confederacy of Dunces*. London, UK: Penguin Books, 2011. Page 106.

18. Toole, John Kennedy. *A Confederacy of Dunces*. London, UK: Penguin Books, 2011. Page 249.

19. Toole, John Kennedy. *A Confederacy of Dunces*. London, UK: Penguin Books, 2011. Page 27f.

20. Toole, John Kennedy. *A Confederacy of Dunces*. London, UK: Penguin Books, 2011. Page 210.

21. Trevor Albert, author interview, March 8, 2019.

22. Stephen Geller, author interview, September 18, 2018.

Chapter 15

1. Stephen Geller, author interview, September 18, 2018.

2. Stephen Geller, author interview, September 18, 2018.

3. Stephen Geller, author interview, September 18, 2018.

4. Stephen Geller, author interview, September 18, 2018.

5. Trevor Albert, author interview, March 8, 2019.

6. Mann, R. (1984, November, 11). Jonathan Demme Starts Making Sense of His Career. *The Los Angeles Times*.

7. Plunka, Gene. *The Plays of Beth Henley: A Critical Study*. Jefferson, NC: McFarland, 2005. Page 23.

8. www.theatermania.com/new-york-city-theater/news/best-beth_484.html.

9. Trevor Albert, author interview, March 8, 2019.

10. Beth Henley, author interview, February 28, 2019.

11. Beth Henley, author interview, February 28, 2019.

12. Beth Henley, author interview, February 28, 2019.

13. Lippman, J. (1999, September 30). "'Dunces' Adaptation Remains Stuck In Mire of Rewrites and Handovers." *The Wall Street Journal*.

14. Beth Henley, author interview, February 28, 2019.

15. Beth Henley, author interview, February 28, 2019.

16. Beth Henley, author interview, February 28, 2019.

17. Trevor Albert, author interview, March 8, 2019.

18. Trevor Albert, author interview, March 8, 2019.

19. Beth Henley, author interview, February 28, 2019.

20. www.playbill.com/article/jonathan-demme-jumps-mediums-to-direct-a-beth-henley-yarn-com-191454.

Chapter 16

1. Beck, M., Jenel Smith, S. (1992, May 27). "Andrews gives 'Julie' tour a miss." *Victoria Advocate*.

2. Stone, J. (1980, January, 13). "End of a Riddle and the Beginning of a New Career." *The San Francisco Examiner*.

3. Stanley, J. (1989, June, 25). "Keeping the Faith In Movie Making." *The San Francisco Examiner*.

4. Stanley, J. (1989, June, 25). "Keeping the Faith In Movie Making." *The San Francisco Examiner*.

5. Susan O'Connell, author interview, September 17, 2018.

6. *ACOD Chronology Outline*, internal document from Bumbershoot Productions, shared by Carolyn Pfeiffer.

7. Susan O'Connell, author interview, September 17, 2018.

8. Susan O'Connell, author interview, April 2, 2019.

9. Susan O'Connell, author interview, September 17, 2018.

10. Susan O'Connell, author interview, September 17, 2018.

11. Susan O'Connell, author interview, September 17, 2018.

12. *ACOD Chronology Outline*, internal document from Bumbershoot Productions, shared by Carolyn Pfeiffer.

13. *ACOD Chronology Outline*, internal document from Bumbershoot Productions, shared by Carolyn Pfeiffer.

14. *ACOD Chronology Outline*, internal document from Bumbershoot Productions, shared by Carolyn Pfeiffer.

15. Woodward, Bob. *Wired. The Short Life and Fast Times of John Belushi.* New York: Simon & Schuster, 1984. Page 202.

16. *ACOD Chronology Outline*, internal document from Bumbershoot Productions, shared by Carolyn Pfeiffer.

17. *ACOD Chronology Outline*, internal document from Bumbershoot Productions, shared by Carolyn Pfeiffer.

18. Boethius. *The Consolation of Philosophy.* Cambridge, MA: Harvard University Press 2008. Page 109.

19. Susan O'Connell, author interview, September 17, 2018.

20. Penelope Spheeris, author interview, February 6, 2019.

21. Penelope Spheeris, author interview, February 6, 2019.

22. Penelope Spheeris, author interview, February 6, 2019.

23. Penelope Spheeris, author interview, February 6, 2019.

24. Penelope Spheeris, author interview, February 6, 2019.

25. Penelope Spheeris, author interview, February 6, 2019.

26. *ACOD Chronology Outline*, internal document from Bumbershoot Productions, shared by Carolyn Pfeiffer.

27. Susan O'Connell, author interview, September 17, 2018.

28. Lippman, J. (1999, September 30). "'Dunces' Adaptation Remains Stuck In Mire of Rewrites and Handovers." *The Wall Street Journal.*

29. Susan O'Connell, author interview, September 17, 2018.

Chapter 17

1. www.legacy.com/obituaries/postgazette/obituary.aspx?n=mary-ann-soderbergh-midge-bernard&pid=169629536&fhid=5643.

2. Joel L. Fletcher, author interview, November 27, 2018.

3. Frank Galati, author interview, September 26, 2018.

4. Lippman, J. (1999, September 30). "'Dunces' Adaptation Remains Stuck In Mire of Rewrites and Handovers." *The Wall Street Journal.*

5. Susan O'Connell, author interview, September 17, 2018.

6. Susan O'Connell, author interview, September 17, 2018.

7. Lippman, J. (1999, September 30). "'Dunces' Adaptation Remains Stuck In Mire of Rewrites and Handovers." *The Wall Street Journal.*

8. Susan O'Connell, author interview, September 17, 2018.

9. Lippman, J. (1999, September 30). "'Dunces' Adaptation Remains Stuck In Mire of Rewrites and Handovers." *The Wall Street Journal.*

10. www.variety.com/1993/film/news/par-rudin-soderbergh-put-on-dunces-caps-108627/.

11. Deborah Sue George, author interview, May 10, 2019.

12. Frank Galati, author interview, September 26, 2018.

13. Frank Galati, author interview, September 26, 2018.

14. Staff. (1988, October, 16). "Amnesty Establishes Memorial in Activist's Name." *The Los Angeles Times.*

15. www.variety.com/1993/film/news/par-rudin-soderbergh-put-on-dunces-caps-108627/.

16. www.vanityfair.com/news/2007/03/dollard200703.

17. www.theguardian.com/film/interview/interviewpages/0,,2276809,00.html.

18. Frank Galati, author interview, September 26, 2018.

19. Frank Galati, author interview, September 26, 2018.

20. Frank Galati, author interview, September 26, 2018.

21. Toole, John Kennedy. *A Confederacy of Dunces.* London, UK: Penguin Books, 2011. Page 25.

22. Toole, John Kennedy. *A Confederacy of Dunces.* London, UK: Penguin Books, 2011. Page 153.

23. Toole, John Kennedy. *A Confederacy of Dunces.* London, UK: Penguin Books, 2011. Page 51.

24. Toole, John Kennedy. *A Confederacy of Dunces.* London, UK: Penguin Books, 2011. Page 26.

25. Toole, John Kennedy. *A Confederacy of Dunces.* London, UK: Penguin Books, 2011. Page 82.

Chapter 18

1. Susan O'Connell, author interview, September 17, 2018.

2. Frank Galati, author interview, September 26, 2018.

3. Frank Galati, author interview, September 26, 2018.

4. Frank Galati, author interview, September 26, 2018.

5. Soderbergh, Steven. *Getting Away With It, Or: The Further Adventures of the Luckiest Bastard You Ever Saw.* London, UK: Faber and Faber, 1999. Page 167.

6. Frank Galati, author interview, September 26, 2018.

7. Frank Galati, author interview, September 26, 2018.

8. Frank Galati, author interview, September 26, 2018.

9. Galati, F. *A Confederacy of Dunces.* Los Angeles: Paramount Pictures. 1994. Cover page. Unpublished screenplay.

10. www.canoe.com/entertainment/celebrity/john-candy-smoked-a-pack-a-day-says-forensic-pathologist.

11. Roberts, Jem. *Soupy Twists—The Full, Official Story of the Sophisticated Silliness of Stephen Fry & Hugh Laurie.* London, UK: Unbound, 2018. Page I.

12. Fry, Stephen. (2008) *Stephen Fry in America—Episode 3: Mississippi.* UK: BBC Television.

13. www.youtube.com/watch?v=t-oTVR2wVog.

14. www.youtube.com/watch?v=t-oTVR2wVog.

15. Fry, Stephen. (2008) *Stephen Fry in America—Episode 3: Mississippi.* UK: BBC Television.

16. Susan O'Connell, author interview, September 17, 2018.

17. Susan O'Connell, author interview, September 17, 2018.

18. Fry, Stephen. *More Fool Me.* London, UK: Penguin Books 2014. Page 66.

19. Stephen Fry, author interview, October 30, 2018.

20. Susan O'Connell, author interview, September 17, 2018.

21. Stephen Fry, author interview, October 30, 2018.

22. Toole, John Kennedy. *A Confederacy of Dunces.* London, UK: Penguin Books, 2011. Page 103.

23. David Esbjornson. *Cast Breakdown for Confederacy of Dunces.* Internal document shared by the creator.

24. Toole, John Kennedy. *A Confederacy of Dunces.* London, UK: Penguin Books, 2011. Page 261.

25. Toole, John Kennedy. *A Confederacy of Dunces.* London, UK: Penguin Books, 2011. Page 157.

26. Toole, John Kennedy. *A Confederacy of Dunces.* London, UK: Penguin Books, 2011. Page 106.

27. Toole, John Kennedy. *A Confederacy of Dunces.* London, UK: Penguin Books, 2011. Page 183.

28. Toole, John Kennedy. *A Confederacy of Dunces.* London, UK: Penguin Books, 2011. Page 133.

29. Toole, John Kennedy. *A Confederacy of Dunces.* London, UK: Penguin Books, 2011. Page 335.

30. Toole, John Kennedy. *A Confederacy of Dunces.* London, UK: Penguin Books, 2011. Page 233.

31. Toole, John Kennedy. *A Confederacy of Dunces.* London, UK: Penguin Books, 2011. Page 218.

Chapter 19

1. Stephen Fry, author interview, October 30, 2018.

2. Daspin, E. (1995, February 2) Fry: Relentlessly Clever English Actor. *St. Louis Post-Dispatch.*

3. Susan O'Connell, author interview, September 17, 2008.

4. Inquirer Wire Services. (1995, February 26). "Missing British actor Stephen Fry sends a fax, says he fled play because of stage fright." *The Philadelphia Inquirer.*

5. Boethius. *The Consolation of Philosophy.* Cambridge, MA: Harvard University Press 2008. Page 20.

6. Barber, L. (1996, June 15). Who's Hugh? *The Age.*

7. Brooks, R. (1997, June 22) "I nearly gassed myself to death with exhaust fumes, says Fry." *The Observer.*

8. Younge, G. (1996, May 18). "Enter Fry, centre stage, for bravura performance on depression and suicide." *The Guardian.*

9. Ellison, M. (1995, February 24) "Fry flees the paper tigers." *The Guardian.*

10. Fry, Stephen. *More Fool Me.* London, UK: Penguin, 2014. Page 105.

11. Stephen Fry, author interview, October 30, 2018.

12. Soderbergh, Steven. *Getting Away With It, Or: The Further Adventures of the Luckiest Bastard You Ever Saw.* London, UK: Faber and Faber, 1999. Page 82.

13. Toole, John Kennedy. *A Confederacy of Dunces.* London, UK: Penguin Books, 2011. Page 250.

14. Stephen Fry, author interview, October 30, 2018.

15. Susan O'Connell, author interview, September 17, 2018.

16. Staff. (1997, February 16). Steven Soderbergh. *The Los Angeles Times.*

17. Soderbergh, Steven. *Getting Away With It, Or: The Further Adventures of the Luckiest Bastard You Ever Saw.* London, UK: Faber and Faber, 1999. Page 63.

18. Soderbergh, Steven. *Getting Away With It, Or: The Further Adventures of the Luckiest Bastard You Ever Saw.* London, UK: Faber and Faber, 1999. Page 60.

19. Soderbergh, Steven. *Getting Away With It,*

Or: The Further Adventures of the Luckiest Bastard You Ever Saw. London, UK: Faber and Faber, 1999. Page 62f.

20. Jeff Kleeman, author interview, December 10, 2019.

21. O'Donnell, Pierce, and Dennis McDougal. *Fatal Subtraction—How Hollywood Really Does Business.* New York: Doubleday, 1992.

22. Soderbergh, Steven. *Getting Away With It, Or: The Further Adventures of the Luckiest Bastard You Ever Saw.* London, UK: Faber and Faber, 1999. Page 72.

23. Soderbergh, Steven. *Getting Away With It, Or: The Further Adventures of the Luckiest Bastard You Ever Saw.* London, UK: Faber and Faber, 1999. Page 82.

24. Soderbergh, Steven. *Getting Away With It, Or: The Further Adventures of the Luckiest Bastard You Ever Saw.* London, UK: Faber and Faber, 1999. Page 134.

25. Deborah Sue George, author interview, May 10, 2019.

26. www.indiewire.com/2014/03/steven-soderbergh-throws-himself-under-the-bus-for-the-underneath-talks-criterion-king-of-the-hill-88388/.

27. www.indiewire.com/2014/03/steven-soderbergh-throws-himself-under-the-bus-for-the-underneath-talks-criterion-king-of-the-hill-88388/.

28. www.theplaylist.net/moneyball-backspin-continues-plus-look-20090706/.

Chapter 20

1. Soderbergh, Steven. *Getting Away With It, Or: The Further Adventures of the Luckiest Bastard You Ever Saw.* London, UK: Faber and Faber, 1999. Page 152f.

2. Soderbergh, Steven. *Getting Away With It, Or: The Further Adventures of the Luckiest Bastard You Ever Saw.* London, UK: Faber and Faber, 1999. Page 153.

3. Soderbergh, Steven. *Getting Away With It, Or: The Further Adventures of the Luckiest Bastard You Ever Saw.* London, UK: Faber and Faber, 1999. Page 155.

4. Boethius. *The Consolation of Philosophy.* Cambridge, MA: Harvard University Press 2008. Page 67.

5. www.esquire.com/entertainment/tv/a1191/esq0503-may-industry/.

6. Toole, John Kennedy. *A Confederacy of Dunces.* London, UK: Penguin Books, 2011. Page 278.

7. Soderbergh, Steven. *Getting Away With It, Or: The Further Adventures of the Luckiest Bastard You Ever Saw.* London, UK: Faber and Faber, 1999. Page 155.

8. Susan O'Connell, author interview, April 2, 2019.

9. Kallenberg, G. (1997, March 10). "Sobering peek into the fantasy factory." *Austin American-Statesman.*

10. Staff. (1997, February 16). "Steven Soderbergh." *The Los Angeles Times.*

11. Susan O'Connell, author interview, September 17, 2018.

12. Lippman, J. (1999, September 30). "'Dunces' Adaptation Remains Stuck In Mire of Rewrites and Handovers." *The Wall Street Journal.*

13. Lippman, J. (1999, September 30). "'Dunces' Adaptation Remains Stuck In Mire of Rewrites and Handovers." *The Wall Street Journal.*

14. www.vulture.com/2013/01/steven-soderbergh-in-conversation.html.

15. Susan O'Connell, author interview, April 2, 2019.

16. Lippman, J. (1999, September 30). "'Dunces' Adaptation Remains Stuck In Mire of Rewrites and Handovers." *The Wall Street Journal.*

17. Susan O'Connell, author interview, April 2, 2019.

18. Lippman, J. (1999, September 30). "'Dunces' Adaptation Remains Stuck In Mire of Rewrites and Handovers." *The Wall Street Journal.*

19. www.livingneworleans.com/?p=11496.

20. www.nola.com/rose/2009/09/the_60-second_interview_john_s.html.

21. Michael Arata, author interview, May 31, 2019.

22. Michael Arata, author interview, May 31, 2019.

23. Michael Arata, author interview, May 31, 2019.

24. Michael Arata, author interview, May 31, 2019.

Chapter 21

1. Michael Arata, author interview, May 31, 2019.

2. Michael Arata, author interview, May 31, 2019.

3. Michael Arata, author interview, May 31, 2019.

4. Michael Arata, author interview, May 31, 2019.

5. Michael Arata, author interview, May 31, 2019.

6. Michael Arata, author interview, May 31, 2019.

7. Michael Arata, author interview, May 31, 2019.

8. Michael Arata, author interview, May 31, 2019.

9. Michael Arata, author interview, May 31, 2019.

10. Michael Arata, author interview, May 31, 2019.

11. Michael Arata, author interview, May 31, 2019.

12. Michael Arata, author interview, May 31, 2019.

13. Boethius. *The Consolation of Philosophy.* Cambridge, MA: Harvard University Press 2008. Page 115f.

14. Michael Arata, author interview, May 31, 2019.

15. Toole, John Kennedy. *A Confederacy of Dunces.* London, UK: Penguin Books, 2011. Page 119.

16. Michael Arata, author interview, May 31, 2019.

17. Toole, John Kennedy. *A Confederacy of Dunces.* London, UK: Penguin Books, 2011. Page 2.

18. Michael Arata, author interview, May 31, 2019.

19. Michael Arata, author interview, May 31, 2019.

20. Michael Arata, author interview, May 31, 2019.

21. www.vanityfair.com/news/2007/03/dollard200703.

22. Michael Arata, author interview, May 31, 2019.

23. web.archive.org/web/20061209112233/http://www.maximonline.com/articles/index.aspx?a_id=7341.

24. Michael Arata, author interview, May 31, 2019.

25. www.ibtimes.com/pat-dollard-twitter-backlash-slaughter-muslims-tweet-called-hate-speech-or-was-it-joke-1567081.

Chapter 22

1. *ACOD Chronology Outline*, internal document from Bumbershoot Productions, shared by Carolyn Pfeiffer.

2. *ACOD Chronology Outline*, internal document from Bumbershoot Productions, shared by Carolyn Pfeiffer.

3. John Lesher, author interview, May 1, 2020.

4. Longino, B. (2005, August 21). "Director stays true to indie roots." *The Atlanta-Journal Constitution.*

5. *ACOD Chronology Outline*, internal document from Bumbershoot Productions, shared by Carolyn Pfeiffer.

6. Variety. (2001, May 18). Studio at odds over film rights to celebrated novel. *National Post.*

7. www.boxofficemojo.com/release/rl3027142145/weekend/.

8. www.telegraph.co.uk/films/0/harvey-scissorhands-6-films-ruined-harvey-weinstein/.

9. Strauss, B. (1993, December 12). Scott Rudin: portrait of a producer. *The Boston Globe.*

10. www.esquire.com/entertainment/tv/a1191/esq0503-may-industry/.

11. Boethius. *The Consolation of Philosophy.*

Cambridge, MA: Harvard University Press 2008. Page 50.

12. Variety. (2001, May 18). "Studio at odds over film rights to celebrated novel." *National Post.*

13. Variety. (2001, May 18). "Studio at odds over film rights to celebrated novel." *National Post.*

14. Biskind, Peter. *Down and Dirty Pictures.* London, UK: Bloomsbury 2005. Page 455.

15. Biskind, Peter. *Down and Dirty Pictures.* London, UK: Bloomsbury 2005. Page 455.

16. Beck, M. (2002, May, 30). "'Dunces' on film." *Kenosha News.*

17. www.nymag.com/nymetro/movies/columns/hollywood/n_7938/.

18. Deborah Sue George, author interview, May 10, 2019.

19. Jeffrey Hatcher, author interview, February 20, 2020.

20. Jonathan Gordon, author interview, April 11, 2019.

21. Mcfarlane, Ursula. (2019) *Untouchable.* UK: BBC Television.

22. Mark Gill, author interview, July 2, 2019.

23. Judah Engelmayer, author interview, April 24, 2019.

24. www.variety.com/2002/film/news/dunces-resurfaces-1117867898/.

25. Susan O'Connell, author interview, September 17, 2018.

26. Toole, John Kennedy. *A Confederacy of Dunces.* London, UK: Penguin Books, 2011. Page 338.

Chapter 23

1. www.variety.com/2002/film/markets-festivals/dunces-pic-caps-long-road-1117875718/.

2. www.mtv.com/news/1473766/drew-barrymore-mos-def-join-david-gordon-greens-dunces/.

3. Susan O'Connell, author interview, April 2, 2019.

4. Michael Arata, author interview, May 31, 2019.

5. *ACOD Chronology Outline*, internal document from Bumbershoot Productions, shared by Carolyn Pfeiffer.

6. www.mtv.com/news/1473766/drew-barrymore-mos-def-join-david-gordon-greens-dunces/.

7. Stein, R.; Meyer, C. (2003, August, 27). "Olympia Dukakis wants more character acting." *Santa Cruz Sentinel.*

8. Susan O'Connell, author interview, April 2, 2019.

9. *ACOD Chronology Outline*, internal document from Bumbershoot Productions, shared by Carolyn Pfeiffer.

10. www.variety.com/2002/film/news/dunces-resurfaces-1117867898/.

11. Toole, John Kennedy. *A Confederacy of Dunces*. London, UK: Penguin Books, 2011. Page 134.

12. www.variety.com/2002/film/news/dunces-resurfaces-1117867898/.

13. Boethius. *The Consolation of Philosophy*. Cambridge, MA: Harvard University Press 2008. Page 40.

14. Kehr, D. (2004, November 11). "Southern exposure." *South Florida Sun-Sentinel*.

15. Caro, M. (2003, March 9). "Regular guy makes ordinary love story." *Chicago Tribune*.

16. Alex Schott, author interview, July 25, 2019.

17. Alex Schott, author interview, July 25, 2019.

18. Mystelle Brabbee, author interview, April 5, 2019.

19. Mystelle Brabbee, author interview, April 5, 2019.

20. film.avclub.com/will-ferrell-1798213383.

21. uk.ign.com/articles/2003/06/25/photos-staged-reading-of-a-confederacy-of-dunces.

Chapter 24

1. Mystelle Brabbee, author interview, April 5, 2019.

2. Michael Arata, author interview, May 31, 2019.

3. Garret Savage, author interview, April 2, 2019.

4. uk.ign.com/articles/2003/06/25/photos-staged-reading-of-a-confederacy-of-dunces.

5. Mystelle Brabbee, author interview, April 5, 2019.

6. web.archive.org/web/20041215090001/http://www.mtv.com/movies/movie/257020/news/articles/1492900/story.jhtml.

7. www.indiewire.com/2011/04/david-gordon-green-talks-his-musical-dream-project-reveals-script-remake-of-ice-station-zebra-119368/.

8. www.theplaylist.net/the-lost-unmade-abandoned-projects-of-director-david-gordon-green-20140414/2/.

9. www.indiewire.com/2014/04/the-lost-unmade-abandoned-projects-of-director-david-gordon-green-87145/.

10. www.theplaylist.net/the-lost-unmade-abandoned-projects-of-director-david-gordon-green-20140414/2/.

11. www.indiewire.com/2011/04/david-gordon-green-talks-his-musical-dream-project-reveals-script-remake-of-ice-station-zebra-119368/.

12. www.indiewire.com/people/people_041025green.html.

13. film.avclub.com/will-ferrell-1798213383.

14. Ebert, R. (2006, May 29). "Director explains cancellation of 'Dunces.'" *The Dispatch*.

15. Mark Gill, author interview, July 2, 2019.

16. Mark Gill, author interview, July 2, 2019.

17. Mark Gill, author interview, July 2, 2019.

18. Mark Gill, author interview, July 2, 2019.

19. Mark Gill, author interview, July 2, 2019.

20. Mark Gill, author interview, July 2, 2019.

Chapter 25

1. Stephen Fry, author interview, October 30, 2018.

2. Jordan, R. (2002, May 17). "Almodóvar en la mirilla." *El Nuevo Herald*.

3. Stephen Fry, author interview, October 30, 2018.

4. www.thecritic.co.uk/a-confederacy-of-dunces-forty-years-on-a-book-that-can-change-your-life/.

5. www.deadline.com/2017/05/brad-grey-dead-cancer-age-59-1202093659/.

6. www.history.com/topics/natural-disasters-and-environment/hurricane-katrina.

7. www.nola.com/entertainment_life/movies_tv/article_6c81acc9-27c9-5701-88df-97543548fb3d.html.

8. Ebert, R. (2006, April 26). "'Confederacy of Dunces' is slowly coming." *The Dispatch*.

9. Ebert, R. (2006, May 29). "Director explains cancellation of 'Dunces.'" *The Dispatch*.

10. www.sfzc.org/teachers/zesho-susan-oconnell.

11. www.sickthingsuk.co.uk/09-people/p-carolynpfeifer.php.

12. Carolyn Pfeiffer, author interview, February 6, 2019.

13. Carolyn Pfeiffer, author interview, February 6, 2019.

14. Carolyn Pfeiffer, author interview, February 6, 2019.

15. Carolyn Pfeiffer, author interview, February 6, 2019.

16. Carolyn Pfeiffer, author interview, February 6, 2019.

17. *ACOD Chronology Outline*, internal document from Bumbershoot Productions, shared by Carolyn Pfeiffer.

18. Lisa Arent, author interview, January 9, 2020.

19. *ACOD Chronology Outline*, internal document from Bumbershoot Productions, shared by Carolyn Pfeiffer.

20. *ACOD Chronology Outline*, internal document from Bumbershoot Productions, shared by Carolyn Pfeiffer.

21. *ACOD Chronology Outline*, internal document from Bumbershoot Productions, shared by Carolyn Pfeiffer.

22. *ACOD Chronology Outline*, internal document from Bumbershoot Productions, shared by Carolyn Pfeiffer.

23. *ACOD Chronology Outline*, internal document from Bumbershoot Productions, shared by Carolyn Pfeiffer.

24. *ACOD Chronology Outline*, internal document from Bumbershoot Productions, shared by Carolyn Pfeiffer.

25. *ACOD Chronology Outline*, internal document from Bumbershoot Productions, shared by Carolyn Pfeiffer.

26. *ACOD Chronology Outline*, internal document from Bumbershoot Productions, shared by Carolyn Pfeiffer.

27. *ACOD Chronology Outline*, internal document from Bumbershoot Productions, shared by Carolyn Pfeiffer.

Part III

1. Foster Wallace, David. *Consider the Lobster and Other Essays.* London, UK: Abacus, 2007. Page 51.

Chapter 26

1. Robert Guza, author interview, March 7, 2020.
2. David Esbjornson, author interview, March 1, 2020.
3. Robert Guza, author interview, March 7, 2020.
4. Robert Guza, author interview, March 7, 2020.
5. David Esbjornson, author interview, March 1, 2020.
6. Jeffrey Hatcher, author interview, February 20, 2020.
7. Jeffrey Hatcher, author interview, February 20, 2020.
8. Robert Guza, author interview, March 7, 2020.
9. Robert Guza, author interview, March 7, 2020.
10. Jeffrey Hatcher, author interview, February 20, 2020.
11. David Esbjornson, author interview, March 1, 2020.
12. Robert Guza, author interview, March 7, 2020.
13. David Esbjornson. *Some thoughts about Confederacy of Dunces after the workshop in NOLA.* Internal document shared by the creator.
14. Robert Guza, author interview, March 7, 2020.
15. David Esbjornson, author interview, March 1, 2020.
16. David Esbjornson, author interview, March 1, 2020.
17. Jeffrey Hatcher, author interview, February 20, 2020.
18. Jeffrey Hatcher, author interview, February 20, 2020.
19. Jeffrey Hatcher, author interview, February 20, 2020.
20. Jeffrey Hatcher, author interview, February 20, 2020.
21. Robert Guza, author interview, March 7, 2020.
22. Jeffrey Hatcher, author interview, February 20, 2020.
23. David Esbjornson, author interview, March 1, 2020.
24. Robert Guza, author interview, March 7, 2020.
25. www.broadwayworld.com/boston/article/A-CONFEDERACY-OF-DUNCES-Breaks-Huntington-Theatre-Records-20151222.
26. www.huntingtontheatre.org/about/history/2015-2016/confederacy-of-dunces/.
27. David Esbjornson, author interview, March 1, 2020.
28. www.nytimes.com/2015/11/20/theater/review-nick-offerman-as-a-giant-of-new-orleans-resized.html.
29. www.variety.com/2015/legit/reviews/confederacy-of-dunces-review-nick-offerman-1201644861/.
30. David Esbjornson, author interview, March 1, 2020.
31. Jeffrey Hatcher, author interview, February 20, 2020.
32. Jeffrey Hatcher, author interview, February 20, 2020.
33. David Esbjornson, author interview, March 1, 2020.

Chapter 27

1. www.slashfilm.com/james-bobin-talks-zach-galifianakis-attached-a-confederacy-dunces/.
2. www.wgaeast.org/onwriting/phil-johnston-the-brothers-grimsby-zootopia/.
3. www.vulture.com/2012/05/exclusive-galifianakis-plays-ignatius-in-dunces.html.
4. www.youtube.com/watch?v=613ma_7dgCM.
5. Robert Guza, author interview, March 7, 2020.
6. lit.newcity.com/2012/05/01/nonfiction-review-butterfly-in-the-typewriter-by-cory-maclauchlin/.
7. www.deadline.com/2017/02/susan-sarandon-thomas-mann-diane-kruger-john-kennedy-toole-biopic-a-confederacy-of-dunces-1201905468/.
8. www.nola.com/entertainment_life/movies_tv/article_f08e1980-9370-5fb6-be3b-e224e6425f28.html.
9. www.trainwreckdsociety.com/2018/10/25/david-dubos-interview/.
10. www.deborahgeorge.net/screenplay.html.
11. Deborah Sue George, author interview, May 10, 2019.
12. www.tracking-board.com/a-confederacy-of-thelma-spec/.

13. www.history.com/this-day-in-history/gunfighter-clay-allison-killed.

14. web.archive.org/web/20150724005819/http://www.bumbershootproductionsinc.com/projects/clay-allison.html.

15. Lisa Arent, author interview, January 9, 2020.

16. Lisa Arent, author interview, January 9, 2020.

17. Analisa Garcia, author interview, January 15, 2020.

18. www.nytimes.com/2007/11/25/fashion/weddings/25Livet.html.

19. Lisa Arent, author interview, January 9, 2020.

20. Roderick Taylor, author interview, April 27, 2019.

21. Boethius. *The Consolation of Philosophy.* Cambridge, MA: Harvard University Press 2008. Page 43.

22. Analisa Garcia, author interview, January 15, 2020.

23. Analisa Garcia, author interview, January 15, 2020.

24. www.sfzc.org/teachers/zesho-susan-oconnell.

25. www.chicagotribune.com/entertainment/chi-harold-ramis-dead-20140224-story.html.

26. Stephen Geller, author interview, September 18, 2018.

27. Stephen Geller, author interview, September 18, 2018.

28. www.playbill.com/article/jonathan-demme-jumps-mediums-to-direct-a-beth-henley-yarn-com-191454.

29. www.theguardian.com/film/2017/oct/26/ashley-judd-bargained-escape-harvey-weinstein-room.

30. www.newyorker.com/news/news-desk/from-aggressive-overtures-to-sexual-assault-harvey-weinsteins-accusers-tell-their-stories.

31. www.theguardian.com/world/2020/mar/19/harvey-weinstein-new-york-state-prison-maximum-security.

Summary

1. Boethius. *The Consolation of Philosophy.* Cambridge, MA: Harvard University Press 2008. Page 47f.

2. Toole, John Kennedy. *A Confederacy of Dunces.* Introduction by Walker Percy. London, UK: Penguin Books, 2011. Page ix.

3. Frank Galati, author interview, September 26, 2018.

4. Stephen Geller, author interview, September 18, 2018.

5. www.youtube.com/watch?v=VwuN1EWqn14.

6. David Esbjornson. *Some thoughts about Confederacy of Dunces after the workshop in NOLA.* Internal document shared by the creator.

Bibliography

Biskind, Peter. *Down and Dirty Pictures*. London, UK: Bloomsbury, 2005.

Boethius. *The Consolation of Philosophy*. Cambridge, MA: Harvard University Press, 2008.

Fletcher, Joel L. *Ken & Thelma: The Story of* A *Confederacy of Dunces*. Gretna, LA: Pelican Publishing Company, Inc., 2005.

Fry, Stephen. *More Fool Me*. London, UK: Penguin, 2014.

Lippman, J. (1999, September 30). "'Dunces' Adaptation Remains Stuck In Mire of Rewrites and Handovers." *The Wall Street Journal*.

MacLauchlin, Cory. *Butterfly in the Typewriter*. Boston: Da Capo Press, 2012.

Plunka, Gene. *The Plays of Beth Henley: A Critical Study*. Jefferson, NC: McFarland, 2005.

Pol Nevils, René, and Deborah George Hardy. *Ignatius Rising*. Baton Rouge: Louisiana State University Press, 2001.

Soderbergh, Steven. *Getting Away With It, Or: The Further Adventures of the Luckiest Bastard You Ever Saw*. London, UK: Faber & Faber, 1999.

Toole, John Kennedy. *A Confederacy of Dunces*. London, UK: Penguin Books, 2011.

Waters, John. *Crackpot—The Obsessions of John Waters*. New York: Scribner's, 2003.

Waters, John. *Role Models*. London, UK: Corsair, 2014.

Woodward, Bob. *Wired. The Short Life and Fast Times of John Belushi*. New York: Simon & Schuster, 1984.

Interviews

Albert, Trevor. Via phone, March 8, 2019

Apted, Michael. Via email, April 5, 2019

Arata, Michael. Via phone, May 31, 2019

Arent, Lisa. Via phone, January 9, 2020

Belushi Pisano, Judy. Via phone, January 7, 2019

Berg, Jeff. Via email, December 17, 2018

Blount, Roy. Via email, March 13, 2019

Boyle, Barbara. Via phone, July 18, 2019

Brabbee, Mystelle. Via phone, April 5, 2019

Bushkin, Henry. Via phone, April 9, 2019

Dixon, Phil. Via phone, October 10, 2018

Engelmayer, Juda. Via email, April 24, 2019

Esbjornson, David. Via phone, March 1, 2020

Fletcher, Joel L. Via phone, November 27, 2018

Fry, Stephen. Via email, October 30, 2018

Galati, Frank. Via phone, September 26, 2018

Garcia, Analisa. Via phone, January 15, 2020

Geller, Stephen. Via phone, September 18, 2018

George, Deborah Sue. Via phone, May 10, 2019

Gill, Mark. Via phone, July 2, 2019

Gordon, Jonathan. Via email, April 11, 2019

Guza, Robert. Via phone, March 7, 2020

Harris, Lynn. Via email, January 14, 2020

Hatcher, Jeffrey. Via phone, February 20, 2020

Henley, Beth. Via phone, February 28, 2019.

Holt Smith, John. Via phone, February 16, 2019

Ignon, Alexander "Sandy." Via phone, February 17, 2019

Jay, Bernard. Via email, December 6, 2018

Kleeman, Jeff. Via email, December 10, 2019

Langdon, Clay. Via phone, February 11, 2019

Langdon-Levy, Kendall. Via phone, February 10, 2019

Lesher, John. Via email, May 1, 2020.

Livet, Anne. Via phone, August 29, 2020

Madden, David. Via phone, February 8, 2019

McCarty, David Ross. Via phone, July 27, 2019

McConnell, John. Via email, May 28, 2019

Medavoy, Mike. Via phone, December 17, 2018

Mostel, Josh. Via phone, July 18, 2019

Nasatir, Marcia, Via phone. December 10, 2018

Nathanson, Michael J. Via phone, November 1, 2018

O'Connell, Susan. Via phone, September 17, 2018; April 2, 2019

Ormsby, Alan. Via email, January 21, 2019

Pfeiffer, Carolyn. Via phone, February 6, 2019

Risher, Sara. Via email, December 8, 2019

Rodkin, Loree. Via email, December 4, 2019

Savage, Garret. Via email, April 2, 2019.

Schott, Alex. Via phone, July 25, 2019

Schulte, John. Via phone, October 3, 2018

Spheeris, Penelope. Via phone, February 6, 2019

Stelley, Christopher. Via phone, July 16, 2019

Taylor, Roderick. Via phone, April 27, 2019

Walker, Maidee. Via phone, September 4, 2018; October 29, 2018

Waters, John. Via email, December 7, 2018

213

Index